American Diversity

American Diversity

A Demographic Challenge for the Twenty-first Century

EDITED BY

Nancy A. Denton and Stewart E. Tolnay

State University of New York Press

Published by
State University of New York Press, Albany

For information, address State University of New York Press,
90 State Street, Suite 700, Albany, NY 12207.

Production by Diane Ganeles
Marketing by Patrick Durocher

Library of Congress Cataloging-in-Publication Data

American diversity : a demographic challenge for the twenty-first century / Nancy A. Denton and Stewart E. Tolnay, editors.
       p. cm.
    Papers presented at the 13th annual Albany Conference, "American Diversity: a democratic challenge for the twenty-first century."
    Includes bibliographical references (p.) and index.
    ISBN 0-7914-5397-9 (alk. paper) – ISBN 0-7914-5398-7 (pbk. : alk. paper)
       1. Pluralism (Social sciences)–Congresses. 2. United States–Population–Congresses.
    3. United States–Ethnic relations–Congresses. 4. United States–Race
    relations–Congresses. 5. Minorities–United States–Social conditions–Congresses. 6.
    Ethnicity–United States–Congresses. I. Denton, Nancy A. II. Tolnay, Stewart Emory.

    E184.A1 A6325 2002
    305.8'009373–dc21

                                                                                    2001049418

10 9 8 7 6 5 4 3 2 1

Contents

Part IV. Implications and Conclusions

Figures

Tables

Acknowledgments

The completion of this volume would not have been possible without the support of many people. First and foremost, we thank the contributors themselves. They not only generously gave their time and expertise to prepare and revise their chapters, but they also waited with superhuman patience as the editors slowly shepherded the book to completion.

Second, the conference that preceded this volume would not have been possible without financial support and help from the Department of Sociology. We are particularly grateful to Louise Tornatore for all she did to make the conference a success. We also gratefully acknowledge funding from the American Sociological Association's (ASA/NSF) Advancement of the Discipline and SUNY Albany's Vice President for Research.

Third, the Center for Social and Demographic Analysis, which is supported by grants from NICHD (P30HD32041) and NSF (SBR-9512290), supported the conference financially and provided technical support for the production of the manuscript.

Last, but hardly least, the manuscript would never have been delivered to SUNY Press without the help of Patricia DeForge, to whom we are most grateful. We also thank Patty Glynn for reproducing the figures and Wenquan Zhang for reproducing the maps.

Introduction: Multicultural Insights from the Study of Demography

Nancy A. Denton and Stewart E. Tolnay

Today, the United States, as a nation, is engaging in many discussions of its population diversity.[1] Nowhere is this trend more prominent than on college campuses, where discussions about what should be taught have resulted in what one observer has called "PC panic."(Gitlin, 1996:177). While these discussions do allow different opinions to be aired, and sometimes serve to bring together members of many different groups, the resulting dialogue about American diversity all too often sounds like a cacophony. Combining the voices of people not previously heard with much regularity, such as Blacks or women, with the new immigrants and native-born White Americans can often be contentious. For listeners as well as participants, it is often not clear how to make sense of the discussions or the underlying societal diversity that gives rise to them. Perhaps a common "starting line" for discussions of diversity and multiculturalism would lend some order to the currently dissonant and disorganized discussion. We argue that a better understanding of the racial and ethnic groups responsible for American diversity, and the demographic forces affecting those groups, is a reasonable point of departure for participants in the "diversity debates." It is toward that goal of better demographic understanding that the current volume is addressed.

The chapters in this volume reflect up-to-date demographic analyses of basic population processes in the contemporary U.S. population.[2] As such, they are not directed to the more politicized aspects of the national diversity debate per se. Yet, we argue in this introduction that they are relevant to the diversity debate because to understand the issues of diversity and political correctness, it is necessary to first understand the fundamental demographic processes that underlie them. This point it not necessarily obvious, so we will lay out our case here. In doing so, we will address such questions as: How can an analysis of demographic data provide any meaningful insights into the debate over American diversity? Given the stridency of the debate and the conflicts among people from the various groups, wouldn't law, history, economics, psychology, or any of a number of other disciplines have more to offer than demography, the study of numbers, births, and deaths? Isn't the demography of increasing numbers of different types of people obvious to all those commenting on the contemporary scene?

It is certainly true that nearly all discussions of U.S. population diversity talk about the numbers of different groups of people, and some even discuss the future implied by projecting these numbers forward in time. However, it is equally true that virtually no one contributing to the diversity debate has thoroughly examined the key demographic processes separately: fertility, mortality, and migration. Neither does the literature offer a reasonable discussion of the interrelationship among these demographic facts of life, or their association with the fundamental life processes of education, labor force participation, marriage, neighborhood context, and aging. But it is just such questions that are grist for the demographer's mill.

Demographers have long focused on documenting, describing, and explaining differences among groups of people with regard to many key aspects of life: the number of children women have, marriage rates, life expectancy, moving within a country or to a new one, educational attainment, labor force participation rates, neighborhood distributions, and aging. Furthermore, key elements in all social demographic analyses are race/ethnicity, gender, and social class. Thus, demographers are in a unique position to inform the debates about population diversity with more than just numbers. This is hardly to argue that demography is destiny, but rather that the momentum of demographic processes, well known to demographers, forms the underpinning of all the other aspects of people's lives in the modern world. In a very real sense, the social world we observe, including the substantial racial and ethnic diversity within it, is the product of those phenomena that occupy demographers.

We are arguing that some of the stridency and antagonism of the contemporary debates over racial and ethnic diversity results in part from either ignoring or fundamentally misunderstanding past, current, and future demographic changes in U.S. society. Understanding these demographic underpinnings challenges our assumption that we can completely control the increasing diversity, points out how some of the increasing diversity is internal to the United States and will continue regardless of what happens to immigration, and reveals that part of the "perceived" increasing diversity is the result of fundamental social changes (e.g., divorce, female labor force participation, childlessness, unmarried mothers) during the last 50 years that have affected all groups in U.S. society, and which, themselves, have generated controversy. Demography cannot magically "solve" the many contentious issues of the debate. However, if we are ever to make progress toward mutual acceptance, respect, and accommodation, we must not ignore the structural demographic underpinnings of contemporary changes in the U.S. population.

A focus on demography points us in two directions simultaneously: toward the *individual* and toward the *structural*. The basic population processes of birth, death, and migration are events that occur to individuals who make critical decisions that determine demographic outcomes. Clearly, a woman or a couple can choose whether or not to have a birth; adult individuals or families can choose whether or not to migrate; and exercise and not smoking can appreciably delay one's death. And, group differentials represent the sum of these individual events. Yet, from this basic truth, we are too often tempted to think that the demographic processes themselves are completely under individual level control. Social scientists continually provide macro-level evidence that indicates the operation of social forces that transcend the individual: the child poverty rate soars while the elderly poverty rate falls, even though the former group represents the future of the nation; women are denied access to abortion facilities because local sentiment and politics discourage the operation of convenient clinics; environmental pollutants increase morbidity and mortality, despite an individual's exercise regimen or diet; illegal immigrants continue to enter the country regardless, it seems, of what laws we pass or border controls we institute. Thus, despite the important role of individual-level decision making in determining behavioral outcomes, it is important to acknowledge the simultaneous operation of social structural forces that are far outside of any individual's control. The "demographic model" recognizes that all individual decisions are made, and individual behaviors are performed, within a structural context that has important consequences of its own.

This recognition that there are structural forces leading to increased population diversity that are outside the control of individuals, and to a lesser extent, outside the control of government, while not the focus of traditional demographic analysis, does flow naturally from it and provides a needed view in discussions about population diversity. Individualism is deeply rooted in and very important to the U.S. psyche, particularly for middle-class White Americans (Gans, 1988), so the effects of social structure are often very hard for Americans to understand (Mayhew, 1980, 1981). But the result of not understanding structural forces is that we do not understand fully our social problems and so are at risk of misdiagnosing them. Once a problem is misdiagnosed, no analysis, no matter how thoughtful, detailed, statistically rigorous, or well documented, will help alleviate the problem for the very simple reason that we have defined the problem incorrectly. A prime example of this point about incorrectly diagnosing problems is the role of law in immigration. In his chapter, Doug Massey argues that changes in immigration are better thought of as the result of macroeconomic forces than changes in law. While it is individuals and government that establish social structure, once established, social structures take on a life of their own and can be quite resistant to change. Demography, by focusing simultaneously on the individual and the structural, serves to emphasize this point.

In addition to recognizing the importance of structural opportunities and constraints as determinants of individual behavior, demographers have long had an interest in how different population groups (e.g., races or ethnicities) differ on the key population processes (e.g., mortality, marriage, or fertility). Having described intergroup differences, it is common for demographers to then ask, "How do different population groups adjust to one another?" When asked of immigrants, this question refers to the important process of "becoming American." Assimilation theory has had a lot of bad press—some would say it is deserved—but the underlying process to which assimilation refers, that of becoming more like the people in one's new country than like those left behind in one's country of origin, will continue (Alba, 1995). Witness African Americans—we focus all too often on how dissimilar they are from White Americans, but can we really argue that they are more similar to modern-day Africans? Perhaps in color and some relatively minor aspects of culture and heritage, but in terms of everyday life dreams, values, and behavior they are American, though there are signs of increasing disenchantment with the American Dream for middle-class African Americans (Hochschild, 1995:251).

Many of the newest Americans are people of color, and our historical treatment of African Americans in the United States means that the new immigrants face what Portes and Zhou (1993) argue is a process of segmented assimilation. For Hispanics in particular, involvement in an ethnic enclave, like that of the Cubans in Miami, may offer better roads to upward mobility than facing the discrimination and prejudice against Hispanics in the larger society. For Black immigrants, this problem is even more acute, as identification with American Blacks, given the history of discrimination and race relations in the United States, can be a downward route to membership in the underclass instead of a route to upward mobility, and a shot at entering the ranks of the "plunderclass."[3] Thus, by comparing adjustment to U.S. society across groups of different types, the demographic perspective simultaneously shows two things: first, that the magnitude of group differences may not be as large as stereotypes imply; and second, that some level of diversity and difference will remain. In other words, no matter what happens to immigration, newcomers will assimilate to *some* degree. The continued infusion of new members and their racial diversity may make the process not as fast or as complete as that of the White ethnics of the early part of this century, but in some way all will learn to be Americans and come to see themselves as Americans. To accept the truth of this statement requires only the demographic recognition that the newcomers themselves produce native-born children who grow up in the U.S. social structure. The emergence of the dramatic differences that separate first-generation immigrants from their second-generation offspring is one of the most profound, and predictable, processes known to social science.

Within the discipline of demography, this volume is unique because it provides the opportunity to read and reflect upon all the demographic processes at the same time. Most demographic research focuses exclusively on one or two of the basic demographic processes: fertility, mortality, migration, and the auxiliary processes of education, marriage, labor force participation, and aging. While the individual authors represented here do specialize in one of these, the volume's emphasis is on looking for the interactions and interrelationships across the demographic processes.

It is for this reason that we have included specialists from so many different areas—to make these interrelationships a key to this book. It is also important that we are *not* taking the more usual approach and having individual chapters about each of the groups that comprise the U.S. population. Such an approach, while in some cases offering more detail about individual groups' experiences in the United States, by its very nature focuses our attention away from the common social and economic structure in which we all reside. As Takaki has noted, "...regardless of who does the telling, much of what is presented as multicultural scholarship also tends to fragmentize American society by separately studying specific groups such as African Americans or Hispanics. Intergroup relationships become invisible, and the big picture is missing. This decontextualizing only reinforces the bewilderment already separating racially and ethnically diverse Americans from one another. We are left with shards of a shattered mirror of our diversity"(Takaki, 1994:299). All groups are subject to the same demographic processes, and by looking at the processes rather than the groups, we are able to see both *differences*, the topic of much concern today, as well as *similarities*, the patterns already present in society as well as those that may potentially emerge as we move into the future.

In the remainder of this introduction, our aim is to link the ten chapters of this volume together and show how each of the papers included in the volume helps to flesh out the argument of the importance of demography to the debate over U.S. population diversity. As we do so, we will try to explain exactly what the study of human demography is, how it involves more than just numbers as we demonstrate what demographic principles can offer to the current debates about U.S. diversity. We structure the volume in four parts: Part I looks at the initial numbers of people in each group, and takes up definitional issues regarding race and ethnicity, as well as the concept of population projections. Part II focuses on the three basic demographic processes, which together completely define national population change: migration, fertility, and mortality. Part III moves to a discussion of life course processes: geographical location, marriage, education and labor force, and aging. These processes are common across almost all people. Part IV provides a summary of the issues raised by the new diversity from the point of view of one of the nation's largest and oldest sources of population diversity, African Americans. In the end, we hope that the reader interested in how U.S. society is changing will be left with a firmer knowledge of the demographic underpinnings of contemporary U.S. population diversity and therefore a firmer base for his or her opinions on the issue of population diversity.

Part I. Population: The Initial Numbers

Fundamental to any understanding of our current concern with human diversity, then, is information on the relative numbers of people in each group. Counting people is first and foremost the business of demography. At the close of the twentieth century, the United States was home to roughly 281 million people. Of these, approximately 195 million are non-Hispanic Whites, the largest and culturally dominant group in the United States since the founding of the country, and the group with the strongest ties to European origins. Another 34 million people are non-Hispanic Blacks, mainly native-born descendants of the slaves who were first forced to come to the United States nearly 400 years ago.[4] About 13 million persons identify themselves as Asian, Native American, or Other, 4.6 million identify with two or more races, while 35 million are of Hispanic origin. In proportional terms, non-Hispanic Whites make up 69.4%, non-Hispanic Blacks 12.1%, with Hispanics and Asians/Native Americans at 12.5% and 4.6% respectively (U.S. Bureau of the Census, 2001a).

Each of these broad groups includes very heterogeneous subgroups as well. From the 2000 Census, we know that over 2 million people identified themselves as Native American, descendants of the persons originally here when Europeans arrived on this continent. This represented a huge increase from the 1980 Census as increasing numbers of people sought to claim their Native American roots. Persons of Asian origin are distributed across very different countries of origin: 23.7% are Chinese, 18.1% are Filipino, 16.4% are Indian, while about 10% are Vietnamese (11.0%), Korean (10.5%), or Japanese (7.8%) (U.S. Bureau of the Census, 2001b). Similarly, Hispanics are 58.5% Mexicans, 9.6% Puerto Ricans, 3.5% Cubans, with 28.4% from other countries in Central and South America. (U.S. Bureau of the Census, 2001b). In all, nearly 11% of the population is foreign born, with just over half (50.7%) born in Latin America, 27.5% in Asia and 15.6% in Europe. (U.S. Bureau of the Census, 2001c).

Even this simple summary of the numbers serves to establish a basic fact: compared to the beginning of the century, when the population was nearly

90% White Northern and Western European (Passell and Edmonston, 1994:43), contemporary U.S. society is very diverse, and much of the diverse population being discussed is already in residence here. While people understand that the population is more diverse, there is evidence that they overestimate the magnitude of the diversity (Gitlin, 1996:113). A recent study by the Kaiser Family Foundation reported that estimates of the percentage of the U.S. population that is White ranged from 45.5% to 54.8%, black from 20.5% to 25.9%, Hispanic from 14.6% to 20.7%, and Asian from 8.3% to 12.2%, depending on which group answered the question. Since the correct figures at the time of the study were 74% white, 11.8% Black, 9.5% Hispanic, and 3.1% Asian, it is clear that no group was even remotely close to an accurate estimate of its own or another group's relative size, and that estimates of the non-White populations were anywhere from 1.5 to 3 times the true value (Brodie, 1995). At the same time, there are substantial areas of the United States that are still mainly White: "In almost half the counties of the U.S., the Black population is less than 1 percent. California and Texas between them have more than half the Hispanics, while in the Midwest fewer than one person in 30 is Hispanic." (Gitlin, 1996:110–111). We cannot hope to deal with our diverse population unless we correctly understand the magnitude of the diversity.

We also sometimes feel as though the increasing diversity is "sudden," all the result of the recent immigrants when in reality, the change has been occurring for quite some time.

> "Simply put, the White percentage has been declining for decades, and the rate of decline accelerated after 1970 (though the rate of decline was frequently exaggerated in the press and popular lore). Between 1950 and 1970, the White percentage (including those Hispanics classified by the census as "White") declined by 2 percent, from 89.3 percent to 87.6 percent, while the Black percentage rose by 12 percent, from 9.9 percent to 11.1 percent. Between 1970 and 1990, the White percentage declined by more than 4 percent, twice the earlier rate, from 87.6 percent to 83.9 percent, while the Black percentage rose by a slightly smaller rate of 11 percent, from 11.1 percent to 12.3 percent. Still more striking changes were evident among Americans whose origins were in Latin America, Asia or the Pacific Islands. Between 1970 and 1990, the Hispanic population almost doubled, from 4.9 percent to 9.0 percent, while Asians and Pacific Islanders more than doubled, from 1.4 percent to 3.0 percent" (Gitlin, 1996:108).

Important as these initial numbers are to an accurate discussion of U.S. population diversity, they represent only the beginning of demography's contribution to the issue. In the next section we take up the task of seeing the future implications of these numbers for the diversity of the U.S. population.

Chapter One: Identity and Culture:
Understanding the Meaning of Race and Ethnicity

To project the population forward in time and come up with race/ethnic specific estimates, a demographer uses the numbers of persons in each race/ethnic group as a starting point. To the extent that the non-Hispanic White population is older than the rest of the population, then we know that their growth will be slower than that of people of color, *even if fertility were the same among all groups*. But this task of projection assumes that people will remain in their same race/ethnic group into the future, and more importantly, that children will be of the same race/ethnic groups of their parents.

As Mary Waters points out in the first chapter, "The Social Construction of Race and Ethnicity: Some Examples from Demography," knowing one's race/ethnic group is not a simple matter. The group that one personally identifies with may not be reflected in the Census categories, or one may think of oneself as a combination of the categories, but only one response had been allowed, until Census 2000. Hollinger points out that "the ethno-racial pentagon which divides the population into African American, Asian American, Euro-american, Indigenous and Latino segments, even as the labels for these five groups vary slightly" (Hollinger, 1995:8), reflects not race or communities of descent but "is a framework for politics and culture in the United States" (Hollinger, 1995:24). He continues, "they are not designed to recognize coherent cultures. They are designed, instead, to correct injustices committed by White people in the name of the American nation, most but not all of which can be traced back to racial classifications on the basis of morphological traits" (Hollinger, 1995:36).

Thus, the meaning of the racial ethnic categories is problematic to those seeking to define U.S. population diversity. To the extent that people change groups, to the extent that people identify with a different group than that into which outsiders classify them based on their physical characteristics, or to the extent that persons of different groups intermarry, then population projections will give false information about the future of the U.S. population. While we tend to think of race and ethnicity as something that is "fixed," the reality is that it is changeable and malleable (Winant, 1994). The difficulty of classifying the population by race/ethnicity serves as a strong reminder of the fact that even without further immigration, the diversity of the U.S. population is likely to change.

Chapter Two: Population Projections:
Future Numbers Implied by Initial Numbers

One of the contributions of demography is to take the initial numbers of people and project them forward in time to show what the population will look like in the future. Thus, to a demographer, the presence of the initial diversity outlined above has important intuitive implications for future diversity through the demographic processes of births and deaths. Population projections are the source of the often heard statement that by the middle of the twenty-first, century within the lifetimes of many current U.S. residents, non-Hispanic Whites will just barely be the majority of persons in this country (U.S. Bureau of the Census, 1992). While this statement is technically true, as Charles Hirschman points out in chapter 2, "Race and Ethnic Population Projections: A Critical Evaluation of their Content and Meaning," in order to make it one must make several assumptions, the truth of which are as yet unknown. These assumptions involve the meaning of the race/ethnic categories themselves, the number of future immigrants to the United States and race/ethnic differences in fertility as well as mortality patterns. Incorrect assumptions about *any* of these can lead to dramatically different future scenarios of the U.S. population size and the relative sizes of each group.

By focusing on these assumptions, we offer the nondemographer the opportunity to think about the meaning as opposed to the methodology of population projections. While there are different scenarios possible depending on what assumptions one makes, it is equally true that the parameters being assumed can only change within limited ranges, given how low mortality and fertility regimes currently are. It makes no sense to assume huge increases in the death rate nor the number of children per family. Thus, the current level of population diversity, combined with the current age structure, has some implications for increasing diversity over time: people of color are younger than non-Hispanic Whites on average, and since young people have children, even with fertility at near replacement levels, the implication is that their relative share of the population will increase over time. Put another way, the changes in the assumptions that would be required to make this NOT happen, namely that white family size increases but other family sizes do not, seem to be extremely unrealistic ones to make in the contemporary world.

Part II. Basic Demographic Processes and Diversity

The second part of this volume focuses directly on the three basic population processes of fertility, mortality, and migration. We begin with a discussion of migration not because it is the most important, but rather because it is the demographic process most often associated with the increasing diversity of the U.S. population. In the stridency of the diversity discussions, one is sometimes left with the impression that if we could simply end immigration, the issues relating to population diversity would vanish.

Chapter Three: New Arrivals: Current and Future Numbers of Immigrants

New immigrants arrive daily, and in 1998 they numbered about 660,477, a decrease from the 915,900 who arrived in 1996 and the 798,378 who arrived in 1997. The immigrants overwhelmingly come from Asia (32.2%) and North America (38.3%). Europe accounts for another 14.1%, South America 6.8%, Africa 5.7%, and Oceania 0.7%. Within the North American group, 19.8% are from Mexico, about 11.0% are from the Caribbean and another 5.4% are from Central America (U.S. Immigration and Naturalization Service, 1998). Refugees and illegal immigrants are not included in these figures, so the number of newcomers can approach a million in some years. It is this immigration that is always thought of first when one considers the diversity of the U.S. population. Efforts to control the flow of immigrants receive wide discussion in the media and by politicians, and in fact, immigration is the population process most often assumed to be under the control of law. Much of our current debate on American Diversity actually centers on immigration law. Are the laws we have adequate? Should we change them? Are they being adequately enforced? These issues have involved us for much of the past century, from the quota laws of the 1920s, which sought to limit immigration and structure the origin of immigrants to match the Northern and Western European orientation of the resident population, through the 1986 Immigration Reform and Control Act (IRCA) and the Immigration Law of 1990.

Yet as we learn from Doug Massey's paper in chapter 3, "The New Immigration and Ethnicity in the United States,"[5] the effectiveness of previous attempts to control immigration was perhaps more influenced by world economic conditions and world events than by law. Furthermore, if one works through the legislative process of actually trying to change the law, as Bach (1993) does, then it becomes clear that other than reducing the absolute number of immigrants allowed, substantial changes in the categories are going to be very politically difficult, no matter how good they seem in "sound bites." Substantial numbers of the new arrivals come because they are related to someone here, and politicians are not likely to win re-election by voting to keep out their constituents' relatives. Others come to fill needed jobs, and going against business interests does not help in re-election either. We are essentially now in a worldwide system of immigration, and what the demographic studies of migrants tell us (and what lawmakers all too often ignore) is that immigration is fundamentally a social process. Stopping it is not simply a matter of changing the law. Immigration is a part of our national culture, and a part of both our own and many sending countries' social structure. As such, it is neither completely within the power of the individual nor the legal system to control.

Chapter Four: Fertility Differentials

While many would allow an important role for immigration as a source of demographic diversity, the role of past immigration makes another contribution to U.S. diversity in the form of births to former immigrants. Many students of introductory demography are surprised to learn that the primary source of population growth over the course of U.S. history was not immigration, but what demographers call natural increase, the excess of births over deaths (Weeks, 1996:57). Today, immigration accounts for only about one-third of the population growth in the United States, with the remaining two-thirds being attributable to natural increase. This fact alone is sufficient to point to the fallacy of focusing solely on immigration in current debates about multiculturalism and diversity. Another way to think about this point is that even if we were somehow able to ban all future immigration to the United States from any source, the diversification of the U.S. population would remain and would continue to grow, albeit more slowly than it will with continued immigration.

Gray Swicegood and Phil Morgan in chapter 4, "Racial and Ethnic Fertility Differentials in the United States," take up the issue of fertility differentials in the contemporary United States. In the context of U.S. fertility being historically low, it is easy to ignore the relatively small differences in family size observed for various subgroups of the population. Swicegood and Morgan point out, however, that these small differences do have implications for the relative future sizes of groups. They also caution us that the assumption of a fertility convergence as people assimilate to life in the United States is by no means certain, given how small families tend to be now. Again, fertility is individual, but the diversity implied by even small intergroup differences has social structural implications.

Chapter Five: Mortality Differentials

The relative sizes of various subgroups in the population are also affected by how long each group lives, or at birth, how long each group is expected to live. To the extent that newcomers to the United States, particularly from less developed countries, benefit from the better health care and nutrition available here, and certainly their children derive this benefit in many cases, then their life expectancy rises when compared to their country of origin. In chapter 5, "Mortality Differentials in a Diverse Society," Richard Rogers provides us with information on both the methodology of studying differences in mortality (including the concomitant difficulties of getting consistent definitions of individuals at birth and death), as well as the importance of specifying the conditions under which mortality differences arise. He challenges us to think in terms of what the mortality differentials he documents would look like if the underlying social and economic conditions of the diverse groups were the same, at the same time as he informs us of the magnitude of the differentials that currently exist. His chapter also points to the importance of biological differences in studying the impact of disease on populations, while at the same time cautions us that skin color or the racial pentagon (White, Black, Hispanic, Asian, and Native American) so often used in U.S. statistics does NOT correspond to true biology.

Once one begins to think through the process of diversity from a demographic perspective then, the error of focusing only on immigration as the source of diversity becomes apparent. A recent study by Edmonston and Passell shows that in 1990, 33.7% of Asians and 59.1% of Hispanics are native born (1994:341–342), and thus increase population diversity by giving birth to native-born U.S. citizens.

Part III. Life Cycle and Diversity

While chapters 3, 4, and 5 have focused on the primary demographic processes of fertility, mortality, and migration, it is well known to demographers that these fundamental processes are influenced by other life-cycle events of the population. As people go through life, their regional and neighborhood locations, educational attainment, occupations, and choice of marriage partners can lead to differences in their fertility, mortality, and migration behaviors, which in turn affect the diversity of the population. It is to these life-cycle components that we turn our attention in Part III.

Chapter Six: Neighborhood Diversity and Housing Policy

Part of the difficulty underlying many of our national discussions of population diversity is the fact that the diversity is not evenly spread across all areas of the Unites States. The work of William Frey and others shows that racial and ethnic diversity is greatest in the coastal states and much less pronounced inland (Frey 1995). Regionally, the West is the most diverse, with nearly one fifth-(18.8%) of its population Hispanic, combining with 7.7% Asians and 5.1% Blacks, but in the other three regions, Blacks are the largest minority group (Harrison and Bennett, 1995:150). These large-scale disparities imply the possibility of an interstate debate, with California, New York, and Florida pitted against the remainder of the nation. This has not occurred for two reasons. First, the diversity is not evenly spread across the cities and counties of the states that have most of it. Second, patterns of White separation from people of color are present in all the largest cities and suburbs, regardless of the diversity of the region or state.

It is thus fitting that Michael White and Eileen Shy's chapter, "Housing Segregation: Policy Issues for an Increasingly Diverse Society," does not focus on large-scale regional differences but on more local, neighborhood-based differences which help to fuel the national debates. Their chapter delves into the causes of this separation, causes that are tied to our nation's history of prejudice and discrimination against "foreigners"—against those who are not part of "us." At the same time, this chapter emphasizes the fact that one of the groups defined as "not us," namely African Americans, have always been singled out and remain so today. Continued high levels of racial residential segregation are an important component of the national discussion about diversity, even if they are seldom acknowledged as such.

Chapter Seven: Adapting to the American Economy

Everyone, be they immigrant or native born, knows and finds that their individual fate in U.S. society is a function of two important individual variables: education and labor force participation. These two characteristics interact to determine individuals' relative success or failure, as well as that of their children. Increasingly, success is determined not just by quantity (how many years of schooling, how many weeks or hours worked) but also by quality (how good the school, how well paying and what promotion potential the job has). As wage rates fell during the 1980s, only those who had a college degree experienced a stable wage rate (Mare, 1995), thus emphasizing the important link between education and labor force rewards.

The paper by Joseph Hotz and Marta Tienda, "Education and Employment in a Diverse Society: Generating Inequality through the School-to-Work Transition," looks at these issues across all the major groups of the U.S. population. Particularly noteworthy is their finding that early work experience, obtained prior to finishing school, is a substantial advantage in later life. To the extent that young Whites are more likely to have access to these early jobs, then attaining the same level of education does not mean as large a reward for Blacks as it does for Whites. In exploring the complexities of this important transition for women as well as men, and for Hispanics as well as for Blacks and Whites, this paper embodies the essence of the demographic perspective: namely, that all groups are subject to the same fundamental processes, and hence it allows us to notice both our diversity *and* our differences.

Chapter Eight: Patterns of Intermarriage

In addition to locating somewhere in a neighborhood, completing education and earning a living, large numbers of people in the contemporary United States spend their adult lives in marriages, and an even larger number of them raise children. The increasing population diversity that is the subject of this volume has two direct implications for the institution of marriage: first, a greater variety of people translates into more diverse choices of marriage partners, and second, as noted in the Hirschman and Waters chapters above, the children of racially or ethnically mixed marriages pose challenges to the system of racial and ethnic identity. In fact, current writing on the issue of racial categorization frequently singles out persons of mixed race as the source of what may ultimately lead to a dismantling of the racial/ethnic categories themselves in statistical, if not behavioral, terms (Zack, 1993:142–144; Hollinger, 1995:43–44; Cf. Zack, 1995; Root, 1992).

Gillian Stevens and Michael Tyler begin their chapter, "Ethnic and Racial Intermarriage in the United States: Old and New Regimes" by noting that in traditional assimilation theory, intermarriage has been and remains a "litmus test" of full assimilation. While same-race marriages still predominate in about 98% of all the marriages for White men, White women and Black women, 6% of Black men have a non-Black spouse in 1990. Asians, Hispanics, and those who report their race as "Other" marry within their own group roughly 80% of the time, though Asian women report a non-Asian spouse twice as often as Asian men. Marital homogamy within the Native American population has declined dramatically in recent decades, most likely as a result of the increasing numbers of people who are now "claiming" their Native American heritage (Hollinger, 1995:46). In their discussion, Stevens and Tyler point to a number of cautions regarding predicting future changes in intermarriage, especially the changing nature of the institution of marriage itself, which both lessens the potential for intermarriage and lessens the time spent in any union, including interracial ones.

Chapter Nine: Population Aging

The last contribution that demography makes to the discussion of population diversity comes from the fundamental importance of the basic demographic variable of age. Since the United States was formerly more numerically dominated by Whites than is true presently or will be true in the future, the racial composition of the population is very different for the old as opposed to the young. This difference is illustrated by Cynthia Taeuber in chapter 9, "Sixty-five Plus in the USA." She begins by reviewing the overall trend toward an older population as the baby boom ages, and becomes the grandparent generation, noting that the size of the elderly population varies by state and that there are important implications for providing for the care of the elderly that we must face.

Several implications follow from these facts. First, the needs of the young for schooling and other training are not as salient to the older population when the young don't look like them and are not related to them (Preston, 1984; Thurow, 1996). Support for taxes to pay for schools, playgrounds, health care, and all the other things that children need is thus jeopardized by the diverging colors of different age groups of the population. Second, as the baby boom (those born 1945–1964) becomes elderly, the people available to take care of them are increasingly people of color. Yet the elderly have had less intimate experience with people of color than the younger population, so the potential for social conflict is enhanced. Third, by virtue of being concentrated in younger ages, the newest members of U.S. society will be engaged in the support of the elderly, but they will not necessarily be well represented among them. Nor, with the temporariness of immigration in many migrant's minds, will they necessarily plan to be here for their own golden years. Thus, they will not have both of Preston's (1984) motives of working to support their elderly parents, whom they would otherwise have to support, as well as working to support themselves since they will hopefully one day become old. All of these implications flow from the basic fact that the changing age structure of the population, to an increasingly older one, will be experienced at different paces by the different race/ethnic groups. As a result, the general dislocations suggested by the aging of the population may lead to greater social conflict than the mere aging of the population itself would imply.

Part IV. Implications and Conclusions

These demographic points relevant to contemporary population diversity serve to provide a context for discussions of contemporary U.S. population change and increasing diversity. In so doing, they raise issues that require more thought and attention on all of our parts. The first of these, and the subject of the final chapter in the book, is: Does the increasing population diversity have specific implications for African Americans, and what are they? Since African Americans are the nation's longest-resident (and until recently, largest) minority group, given the decimation of the Native American population, it only seems fair to single them out for special discussion.

Chapter Ten: Implications of Increasing Diversity for African Americans

It is possible to argue that the increasing diversity of the U.S. population, brought on at least in part because of changes in immigration, would be less troublesome had the United States solved what Myrdal (1944) referred to as the "American Dilemma." Likewise, one can also say that increasing diversity increases the urgency for Whites to try to solve the many problems associated with race now. Had we developed a more mutually satisfactory and equitable relationship with Blacks, we might be better able to deal with the diversity the immigrants provide. Certainly we would not have to face the second and third paths of segmented assimilation outlined by Portes and Zhou, whereby Hispanic Americans, particularly Cubans, find themselves remaining within their ethnic enclave, and immigrants of Black race are faced with possible assimilation into the Black underclass (Portes and Zhou, 1993).

In chapter 10, Hayward Horton raises some of these issues in the context of the treatment of race in the field of demography. His chapter, "Rethinking American Diversity: Conceptual and Theoretical Challenges for Racial and Ethnic Demography," traces how, despite the importance of the concept of race to many different demographic analyses, demographers as a group have tended to ignore the role of racism. He argues strongly for its incorporation into the main areas of the discipline and presents a theoretical model showing how its use can provide different answers and different ways of thinking about the relative status of Blacks in U.S. society.

↩

In addition to focusing on one specific group, we can also gain from contemplating both the past and the future in our attempts to understand current population diversity. How different are these issues from those we have faced in the past? What does the nature of this diversity imply for our definition of ourselves as a nation? While the demographic focus of this volume offers little direct evidence on either of these questions, the discussion of the demographic diversity in each of these chapters serves to bring these issues into sharp relief. We will summarize some recent perspectives on them here, not as the last word, but to encourage wider discussion and broader reading.

The arrival of immigrants and the concomitant changing of the complexion of the U.S. population is certainly not a new phenomena, nor is this the first time that it has aroused concern. In one sense, our concerns as the new century begins bear a striking similarity to those we had at the beginning of the 20th century. We are still living with what Hollinger describes as "...*non*ethnic ideology of the nation" (Hollinger, 1995:19), despite the fact that we have a predominately *ethnic* history and present. Then, as now, there are concerns that the new immigrants are taking away our country.

At the beginning of both the 20th and 21st centuries, we are concerned with our identity and our unity as a country. As Fuchs has noted, "Even if that movement (immigration restriction) is partly successful, immigration is likely to continue at high levels, and it is important to pay attention to the public policies that will help unify immigrants and their children as Americans" (Fuchs, 1993:171). In 1910 roughly one-third of the U.S. population was foreign-born or of foreign stock, compared to about one-fifth today (Passel and Edmonston, 1994:39). As Watkins points out, with each new wave "commentators debated the differences between the newcomers and the 'Americans,' who were often, of course, the descendants of earlier newcomers. ...was it possible that...[they] would ever be 'like us'? "(Watkins, 1994:2).

From the vantage point of today, it is clear that the concern over the immigrants in 1910 was out of proportion to what happened to U.S. society. In many ways we thrived as a nation and our place in the world is more prominent now than then. But this does not relieve us from the responsibility to think about the sort of future we envision for the country. As Fuchs has argued, "... diversity is an American strength, but unless we protect the central principles of individual rights that makes diversity possible, we will drift toward racial and ethnic separatism" (1993:186). Fragmentation into warring factions is hardly a goal toward which to strive, though Rose (1993) has pointed out that many of the same tactics to gain integration in use today were previously used by the Southern, Central, and Eastern European immigrants. That those immigrants were eventually accepted should give us pause as we argue that today's new immigrants and their demands will lead to the fragmentation of U.S. society. Yet as the situation of African Americans so vividly reminds us, to some extent the old way of assimilating was and is reserved for those of the White race. Then what of the people of color who comprise the new immigrants?

Fear of the answer to questions like these flourishes best in ignorance. Despite evidence that Americans do not know the correct demographic dimensions of the current diversity (Brodie, 1995; Gitlin, 1996:113), we have no choice but to move forward together. Hollinger (1995) presents us with a carefully thought-out vision of what he calls a "post-ethnic" society. He argues for building upon the racial and ethnic affiliations so prominent today, stressing the voluntary nature of these affiliations while at the same time recognizing the power of the "ethno-racial pentagon" to identify people likely to be discriminated against, and stresses a cosmopolitan definition of ourselves as "citizens of the world." In his view, "Being an American amid a multiplicity of affiliations need not be dangerously threatening to diversity. Nor need it be too shallow to constitute an important solidarity of its own." (Hollinger, 1995:163). That there are problems ahead is certain, but as we think about them, we might do well to remember the words of Paul Spickard: "Almost no White American extended family exists today without at least one member who has married across what two generations ago would have been thought an unbridgeable gap." (quoted in Gitlin, 1996:113) While we have no illusions that this volume of essays will transform the current diversity debate from cacophony to symphony, we do believe that the authors have helped us take a significant step toward a much fuller understanding of the demographic underpinnings of the debate. One hopes that future discussions of American diversity will build on their important contributions, and move us even further ahead.

Notes

1. Even an incomplete list of book titles on this topic is long: Benjamin DeMott, *The Trouble with Friendship: Why Americans Can't Think Straight About Race;* Lawrence Fuchs, *The American Kaleidoscope: Race, Ethnicity and the Civic Culture*: Todd Gitlin, *The Twilight of Common Dreams: Why America is Wracked by Culture Wars*; Kofi Buenor Hadjor, *Another America: The Politics of Race and Blame*: Jennifer Hochschild, *Facing Facing Up to the American Dream*; David Hollinger, *Postethnic America: Beyond Multiculturalism*; Ronald Takaki, *A Different Mirror: A History of Multicultural America*; Howard Winant: *Racial Conditions: Politics, Theory, Comparisons*. In addition, the many books specifically about African Americans are also relevant: Stephen Carter, *Confessions of an Affirmative Action Baby;* Shelby Steele, *The Content of Our Character,* etc.

2. Because only limited data are currently available from the 2000 census, the chapters in this volume rely primarily on data for 1990. In a few chapters information from the 2000 "short form" is included. Data from the 2000 "long form" have not yet been released. Go to www.census.gov for the latest information available.

3. The term "plunderclass" was coined by Tolnay (1999) in *The Bottom Rung: African American Family Life on Southern Farms*. In the current context, we use it to offer some balance to social scientists' preoccupation with the social problems

plaguing the underclass. The plunderclass would include those members of the upper and upper-middle classes who have benefitted disproportionately from such trends as the increasingly regressive nature of taxation in the U.S., and corporations' exportation of jobs to low-wage developing nations. In a very real sense, the same social and economic forces that have improved the fortunes of the plunderclass have had negative consequences for the underclass, and working poor, in America.

4. The legal slave trade to the United States ended in 1808, though illegal slave smuggling continued well after. Thus, the vast majority of African Americans have ancestries in the U.S. that are several generations long – far longer than most living Americans with European roots.

5. This chapter can also be found in *Population and Development Review*, vol. 21, no. 3 (Sept.1995), pp. 631-652.

References

Alba, Richard. 1995. "Assimilation's Quiet Tide." *Public Interest* 119:3–18.

Bach, Robert L. 1993. "Recrafting the Common Good: Immigration and Community." *Annals, AAPS* 530:155–70.

Brodie, Mollyann. 1995. "The Four Americas: Government and Social Policy Through the Eyes of America's Multi-racial and Multi-ethnic Society." A Report of *The Washington Post*/Kaiser Family Foundation/Harvard Survey Project.

Edmonston, Barry and Jeffrey S. Passel. 1994. "The Future Immigrant Population of the United States." Pp. 317–353 in *Immigration and Ethnicity: The Integration of America's Newest Arrivals*, Barry Edmonston and Jeffrey S. Passel, editors. Washington, D.C.: Urban Institute Press.

Frey, William H. 1995. "The New Geography of Population Shifts." Pp. 271–336 in *State of the Union: America in the 1990's, Volume Two: Social Trends*, Reynolds Farley, editor. New York: Russell Sage Foundation.

Fuchs, Lawrence H. 1993. "An Agenda for Tomorrow: Immigration Policy and Ethnic Policies." *Annals, AAPS* 530:171–186.

Gans, Herbert J. 1988. *Middle American Individualism: The Future of Liberal Democracy.* New York: The Free Press.

Gitlin, Todd. 1996. *The Twilight of Common Dreams: Why America is Wracked by Culture Wars?* New York: Metropolitan Books.

Harrison, Roderick and Claudette Bennett. 1995. "Racial and Ethnic Diversity." Pp. 141–210 in *State of the Union: America in the 1990's, Volume Two: Social Trends*, Reynolds Farley, editor. New York: Russell Sage Foundation.

Hochschild, Jennifer L. 1995. *Facing Up to the American Dream: Race, Class, and the Soul of the Nation*. Princeton: Princeton University Press.

Hollinger, David A. 1995. *Postethnic America: Beyond Multiculturalism*. New York: Basic Books.

Mare, Robert D. 1995. "Changes in Educational Attainment and School Enrollment." Pp. 155–213 in *State of the Union: America in the 1990's, Volume One: Economic Trends*, Reynolds Farley, editor. New York: Russell Sage Foundation.

Mayhew, Bruce H. 1980. "Structuralism Versus Individualism: Part I, Shadowboxing in the Dark." *Social Forces* 59:335-375.

Mayhew, Bruce H. 1981. "Structuralism Versus Individualism: Part II, Ideological and Other Obfuscations." *Social Forces* 59:627–648.

Myrdal, Gunnar. 1944 [1962]. *An American Dilemma: the Negro Problem and Modern Democracy*. New York: Harper & Row.

Passel, Jeffrey S. and Barry Edmonston, 1994. "Immigration and Race: Recent Trends in Immigration to the United States." Pp. 31–72 in *Immigration and Ethnicity: The Integration of America's Newest Arrivals*, Barry Edmonston and Jeffrey S. Passel, editors. Washington, D.C.: Urban Institute Press.

Portes, Alejandro and Min Zhou. 1993. "The New Second Generation: Segmented Assimilation and Its Variants." *Annals, AAPS* 530:74–96.

Preston, Samuel H. 1984. "Children and the Elderly: Divergent Paths for America's Dependents." *Demography* 21:435–57.

Root, Maria P. 1992. *Racially Mixed People in America*. Newbury Park: Sage.

Rose, Peter I. 1993. "Of Every Hue and Caste": Race, Immigration, and Perceptions of Pluralism." *Annals, AAPS* 530:187–202.

Takaki, Ronald. 1994. "At the End of the Century: The "Culture Wars" in the U.S. Pp. 296–299 in *From Different Shores: Perspective on Race and Ethnicity in America*, Ronald Takaki, editor, 2nd edition. New York: Oxford University Press.

Thurow, Lester C. 1996. "The Birth of a Revolutionary Class." *The New York Times Magazine*, May 19, Pp. 46–7.

Tolnay, Stewart E. 1999. *The Bottom Rung: African American Family Life on Southern Farms*. Urbana: University of Illinois Press.

U.S. Bureau of the Census. 1992. *Current Population Repirts, P25-1092, Population Projections of the United States by Age, Sex, Race, and Hispanic Origin: 1992–2050*. Washington, D.C.: U.S. Government Printing Office.

U.S. Bureau of the Census. 2001a. Overview of Race and Hispanic Origin. Census 2000 Brief. C2KBR/01-1. Issued March 2001.

————.2001b. Profiles of General Demographic Characteristics. 2000 Census of Population and Housing: United States. Issued May 2001.

————. 2001c. Census 2000 Supplementary Survey Profile for United States. http://www.census.gov.c2ss/www/Products/Profiles/200/Tabular/C@SSTTabl e2/01000US.htm. Accessed 9/20/01.

U.S. Immigration and Naturalization Service. 1998. *Statistical Yearbook of the Immigration and Naturalization Service*. U.S. Government Printing Office: Washington, D.C., 2000.

Watkins, Susan Cotts, ed. 1994. *After Ellis Island: Newcomers and Natives in the 1910 Census*. New York: Russell Sage Foundation.

Weeks, John R. 1996. *Population: An Introduction to Concepts and Issues*. Sixth Edition. Belmont: Wadsworth.

Winant, Howard. 1994. *Racial Conditions: Politics, Theory, Comparisons*. Minneapolis: University of Minnesota Press.

Zack, Naomi. 1993. *Race and Mixed Race*. Philadelphia: Temple.

Zack, Naomi, editor. 1995. *American Mixed Race: The Culture of Microdiversity*. Lanham, MD: Rowman and Littlefield.

Part I

Population: The Initial Numbers

Chapter 1

The Social Construction of Race and Ethnicity: Some Examples from Demography

Mary C. Waters

The social construction of race and ethnicity is a taken-for-granted premise of much of current thinking and research about ethnicity. However, the fact that ethnicity and race are socially constructed is often not factored into demographic and other quantitative research, and is often at odds with the ways in which ethnicity is conceptualized in everyday life. In this chapter I explore some of the contradictions between our theoretical assumptions that race and ethnicity are socially constructed and our everyday practices in demography and social life in general that assume a fixed and lasting permanence to ethnic and racial identities.

I understand social construction to mean that racial and ethnic groups are not biological categories but social ones. This means that these categories vary across time and place, that new categories come into existence over time, and other ones cease to have meaning to people. This also means that the construction of race and ethnic categories reflects shared social meanings in society, and that those shared social meanings also reflect differences in power relations. Finally, the social construction of race and ethnicity means that rather than being an immutable fixed characteristic, racial and ethnic identities at the individual level are subject to a great deal of flux and change—both intergenerationally, over the life course, and situationally.

I take this definition of race and ethnicity as a given in my work, and it is one of the central facts I try to convince my students of in introductory race and ethnic relations courses. Yet, this approach has its limits. An incident that occurred in a large lecture class I taught recently on race and ethnicity shows both the strengths and weaknesses of this approach.

After class one day, a young freshman woman came to see me and asked if I could help her to determine her identity. She is from a small town in the rural South, and her mother told her that she is an American Indian, but that they were not real American Indians because they were mixed in with Blacks. In addition, she knew she was part Irish and Scottish. She applied to many universities and she checked various boxes on the applications, depending on the instructions. She preferred to check all boxes that applied to her identity.

25

After she arrived at Harvard, she began getting mail from the Black Students Association, and she was getting pressure from other Black students about not hanging around with Blacks. So, she assumed that Harvard had assigned her to be Black. However, she is not at the university alone. She has an identical twin sister who is also at Harvard, and who checked the same boxes as she did. However, her sister is receiving mail from the Native American Students Association and is being lobbied to attend their meetings on campus.

My student wanted two things from me. One, she wanted my aid in navigating the University's bureaucracy to find out what identity the University thought she was, and how they decided that. Two, she wanted to know what sociological principle could justify what she perceived as an absurd situation—she and her identical twin sister having different racial identities. She also wanted to know whether either she or her sister would be allowed by the University to change their identity.

If there was any story that fit with my analysis of ethnicity and race as social constructions, this one did. Here were two genetically identical twins, attending the same university, and yet assigned to different races, and already feeling some social consequences (in the form of peer pressure and political lobbying by student organizations) because of that classification. However, the story also shows some of the limits to a social constructionist approach—this situation was deeply disturbing to this young woman and her sister; it caused some consternation in the University administration when I investigated it; and it is understood by most people who hear about the story as an aberration. It is seen as an absurd problem to be rectified, not a reflection of the reality that multiple ancestries exist among a large proportion of the population in the United States, and that people often choose or are forced into one category for purposes of administrative classification or counting schemes. The story is a confirmation of the socially constructed nature of race, at the same time as it warrants its telling because it is an exception to a world in which we can and do assume that race and ethnicity are fixed characteristics, that individuals have only one socially meaningful identity, and that if we know a person's ancestry or genetic makeup, we can determine their race and ethnicity from that genealogical information.

In this chapter, I address this contradiction in the way we accept the constructed nature of ethnicity and race, and the ways in which we assume all the time that ethnicity and race are stable and real. In the specific realm of demographic measurement, I examine the fact that ethnicity is both an independent and a dependent variable, and I explore this by examining population projections by race and ethnicity. First, I describe the current measurement of race and ethnicity, and suggest some of the ways in which our measurement and use of the data assumes that ethnicity and race is more fixed and concrete than it really is. Next, I describe the choices intermarried parents make about race and ethnic identity in conditions in which they are forced to choose a race for their children, and finally, I explore some of the political and social forces likely to shape and constrain individuals as they determine their ethnic and racial identities in the future.

How We Measure Race and Ethnicity

While race and ethnicity can be measured many different ways, and is measured in very different ways on different surveys, in the United States at least the vast bulk of our demographic data comes from the decennial census and from government administrative records. The federal government attempted to standardize its data collection on race and ethnicity in 1978 when the Office of Management and Budget (OMB) issued a federal directive (Number 15) designating the standards for reporting race and ethnic data. This directive established five federal reporting categories, which are American Indian or Alaska Native, Asian or Pacific Islander, Black, Hispanic, and White. Federal administrative agencies that collect data on race and ethnic identity can collect the data with more detail, but the data must be able to aggregate to these standard categories. In 1997 the OMB revised this directive. The revisions included separating the Asian and Pacific Islander category into two categories—one called "Asian" and one called "Native Hawaiian or Other Pacific Islander." The OMB also changed the labels of two categories—"Hispanic" is now Hispanic or Latino and "Black" is now Black or African American. Perhaps the most controversial decision the OMB made in 1997, however, is to begin to allow people to identify with more than one of the racial categories but not to add a separate "multiracial" category. (Federal Register, 1997:58784).

The decennial Census collects data in considerably more detail. There are currently three questions on the census that collect the bulk of the demographic data on race and ethnicity in the United States. These questions are the race question, the Spanish Origin question, and the ancestry question. Images of each question are included in Figure 1.1. The race question was a closed-ended question that provided a list of possible responses, which included the categories White; Black, African Am., or Negro; American Indian or Alaska Native (with a space for the person to fill in the name of their tribe); Asian Indian, Chinese, Filipino, Japanese, Korean, Vietnamese, Other Asian; Native Hawaiian, Guamanian or Chamorro, Samoan, Other Pacific Islander (with the last of both of these groups sharing the same space to fill in the name of their race); and Some other race (also with a blank space). The question was labeled Race in 2000, 1990 and 1970; in 1980, it just provided the categories without a title for the question. Until the 2000 census the race question specifically told respondents that they were not to give two answers,

Figure 1.1
2000 Census Questions on Hispanic Origin, Race and Ancestry

NOTE: Please answer BOTH Questions 5 and 6.

5 **Is this person Spanish/Hispanic/Latino?** *Mark* ⊠ *the **"No"** box if **not** Spanish/Hispanic/Latino.*

☐ **No,** not Spanish/Hispanic/Latino
☐ Yes, Mexican, Mexican Am., Chicano
☐ Yes, Puerto Rican
☐ Yes, Cuban
☐ Yes, other Spanish/Hispanic/Latino — *Print group.*

6 **What is this person's race?** *Mark* ⊠ *one or more races to indicate what this person considers himself/herself to be.*

☐ White
☐ Black, African Am., or Negro
☐ American Indian or Alaska Native — *Print name of enrolled or principal tribe.*

☐ Asian Indian
☐ Chinese
☐ Filipino
☐ Japanese
☐ Korean
☐ Vietnamese
☐ Other Asian — *Print race.*

☐ Native Hawaiian
☐ Guamanian or Chamorro
☐ Samoan
☐ Other Pacific Islander — *Print race.*

☐ Some other race — *Print race.*

10 **What is this person's ancestry or ethnic origin?**

(For example: Italian, Jamaican, African Am., Cambodian, Cape Verdean, Norwegian, Dominican, French Canadian, Haitian, Korean, Lebanese, Polish, Nigerian, Mexican, Taiwanese, Ukrainian, and so on.)

but to only choose one response. In 2000 the race question instructed people to "mark one or more races" and 2.4% of the population chose two or more races.

Table 1.1
Assignment of Multiracial Responses in the 1990 Census

Response	Assigned	Total Number
Black and White	Black	47,835
Mixed	Other	32,505
Mulatto	Other	31,708
White and Black	White	27,926
Eurasian	Asian	19,190
Amerasian	Asian	18,545
Biracial/Interracial	Other	17,202
White Japanese	White	9,329
White Filipino	White	7,081
Creole	Other	6,244

Source: U.S. Bureau of the Census. Census of 1990.

In Census 2000 the Hispanic origin question was moved ahead of the Race question and also presented the respondents with fixed response categories. The choices given to respondents included No (not Spanish, Hispanic), Yes, Mexican, Yes, Puerto Rican, Yes, Cuban, and Yes Other Spanish/ Hispanic with a space to write in the specific response. Finally, the ancestry question was a fill-in-the-blank question, which asked "What is this person's ancestry or ethnic origin?" Under the blank line a number of possible responses were given as examples. The ancestry question allowed people to give more than one group. The instructions said, "Persons who have more than one origin and cannot identify with a single group may report two ancestry groups."

Analyses of these data from both the 1980 and 1990 Censuses show enormous change, flux, and inconsistency, a pattern likely to be repeated in detailed analyses of Census 2000 once ancestry data become available. For instance, analyzing the ancestry data from the 1980 Census, Lieberson and Waters (1986; 1988; 1993) found evidence of change in the ancestries reported across the life course of individuals, and intergenerationally. For instance, parents who were intermarried tended to simplify the ancestry information they reported for their children. Farley (1991) also found evidence that the numbers of people reporting particular ancestries in the Census did not match those reported in sample surveys conducted by the Current Population Survey.

Some spectacular changes were reported, especially comparing data from two or more censuses. For instance, the American Indian population grew from 552,000 to 1,959,000 between 1960 and 1990 at a rate of 255%. This rate of growth is impossible demographically and definitely resulted from people changing their identities from Non-Indian to Indian on the race question. Eschbach (1993) found not only that the growth in the numbers of Indians was in large part due to "new Indians"—people identifying as Indian who had not before, but also that the regional location of these "new" Indians was sufficiently different than the location of consistently identified Indians as to appear to show large migration flows. By Census 2000, 2,475,956 persons identified American Indian or Alaska Native as their only race, with an additional 1,643,345 listing this group in combination with another race.

The "Other" race category also grew during this period, from 6.8 million in 1980 to 9.8 million in 1990, a growth rate of 45%. This probably reflects a growing number of Hispanic Origin people who wish to report their Hispanic origin on the race question, and for whom it is speculated the race question categories seem inappropriate (McKenney and Cresce, 1993:207). By Census 2000, the "Other" race category had grown to 18.5 million, with 15,359,073 listing it as their only race and the remainder listing it in combination with other races. Just over 90% of those who listed this as their only race were of Hispanic origin, as were 58.8% of those who listed "Other" in combination with one or more other races.

The ancestry question also showed considerable changes between 1980 and 1990, which are most likely due to individuals changing their responses. For instance in 1980, English was the biggest ancestry group in the country with 49.6 million people reporting it. In 1990 that number fell to 32.7 million. In 1990 the largest ancestry group in the nation was German, which increased from 49.2 million to 58.0 million. One possible explanation for this is that German was listed as the first possible example on the ancestry question in 1990 but was the fourth listed in 1980. (McKenney and Cresce, 1993:188). There was other evidence of a strong "example effect" on reporting in the ancestry question. "Cajun" was listed as an example in 1990 but not in 1980, and the number of Cajuns grew dramatically from about 30,000 in 1980 to about 600,000 in 1990. French, which was an example in 1980 but not in 1990, declined from about 13 million to 10 million. (McKenney and Cresce, 1993:189). Since ancestry data have not yet been released from Census 2000, exact comparisons are not possible. However, it is of interest to note that German, Cajun and French were not listed as examples on the 2000 form, so if the pattern observed in the past holds, we can expect to record declines in the populations reporting these groups as their ancestry.

The slippery nature of ethnicity confounds census takers in the United States, as well as in countries around the globe (Statistics Canada and U.S. Bureau of the Census, 1993). There are also other pieces of evidence that show flux and inconsistency in ethnic identification. For instance, birth and death certificates contain information on the race and ethnicity of the individual, which are determined in various ways. Before 1989 the race of an infant in published natality statistics was determined through a complex algorithm. "If both parents were White, the baby was White, if one parent was Hawaiian, the baby was Hawaiian; if only one parent was White, the child was assigned the race of its other than white parent. If both parents were other than white, the child was assigned its father's race." In 1989 this was changed; and for all infants they were assigned the same race as the mother. As Hahn and Stroup (1994) explain, if this rule of the mother's race was applied retrospectively to all births in 1987, the new procedure would "increase White births by 1.7%, while decreasing Black births by 4.7%, American Indian births by 19.2%, and Hawaiian births by 29.7% (Hahn and Stroup, 1994:9). Mortality statistics have been even more variable, since the recording of race and ethnicity on death certificates is generally done by funeral directors. Hahn et al. (1992) have found a great deal of inconsistency in the reporting of race on the death certificate when it is matched to the birth certificate for infants who died in the first year of life. They found that Whites received different racial classifications on their birth and death certificates only 1.2% of the time. Blacks were inconsistently identified 4.3 % of the time, and other races were inconsistently identified a full 43.2% of the time. (Hahn et al., 1992).

All of these pieces of data show enormous flux and inconsistency in the data that try to "objectively" measure race and ethnicity (see also Hirschman, page 56). The reality is that while the major race and ethnic groups in the United States stay relatively stable in the short run, there is enormous movement and fuzziness when you look closely at the boundaries of the groups, and when you look for consistency and stability at the individual level. This is due to a variety of causes—both substantive in terms of the socially constructed and volatile nature of ethnicity itself, and technical in terms of the measurement error that is present in any attempt to measure social phenomena (Lieberson and Waters, 1993). Thus, these changes in aggregate counts and inconsistencies in individual reports can be traced to factors affected by these two causes—genuine flux in identity over the course of an individual's life; differences in measurement because self-identification and other identification do not match; and differences in perception of the overlapping or conceptual definition of categories (for instance, many people choose "Other" race because they want to tell the Census Bureau that they are Hispanic in terms of their race, as well as in terms of their Spanish origin.)

Ethnicity and Race as Variables in Demographic Studies

One consequence for demographers of the fact that ethnicity is socially determined and in flux is that ethnicity can both influence demographic and social factors we are interested in, but in addition, and this is less commonly acknowledged, it can be determined by these factors. Take for example the case of migration. Often, a demographer will pose a question about differential migration of different ethnic groups. This research question poses ethnicity as an independent variable and asks whether a person's ethnic identity affects their propensity to migrate and the destination chosen. This type of question assumes ethnicity as a given and unproblematic trait, and uses either survey or census data to assign an individual to a particular group and then looks at their migration behavior. However, it is quite possible that the causal arrows could work in the opposite direction—past migration decisions can affect reported race or ethnic identity.

For instance, Spickard and Fong (1995) note that Pacific Islanders in Hawaii often report multiethnic backgrounds and identify with two or three of those identities in the multiethnic milieu of the Hawaiian islands. However, when such a person with White, Hawaiian, Asian Indian, and Samoan backgrounds moves to Los Angeles, the pressure to "choose one" identity could lead this person to "see herself and is treated only as a Samoan, without the multiethnic consciousness." Indeed, Spickard and Fong identify a key feature of Pacific Islander ethnicity as being situational—with people identifying in different ways in different social milieus. So too, Eschbach (1993:644–645) finds that a simple study of migration of American Indians in the United States is impossible without also taking into account changing identifications. He finds that "Almost all of the apparent redistribution of the Indian population between prior censuses and the 1980 Census is attributed to changes in identification rather than to migration."

The changing nature of people claiming an identity also has implications for socioeconomic measures of Indian well-being. Snipp (1989) has found that those claiming an Indian race are much poorer than those claiming an Indian ancestry. Any study of changing income patterns among American Indians must be careful about which questions are used to identify the population, but also must be mindful of the fact that any changes in socioeconomic status could be due to new, more affluent people identifying as Indian.

In my own recent work on Black West Indian immigrants in New York City I find a related phenomena (Waters, 1994). An analysis of the pattern of racial and ethnic identity among the children of immigrants—the second generation—in my sample of adolescents shows two very different approaches to adopting an American identity. Some of the teenagers distance themselves from American Blacks, and are very involved in their parents' ethnic communities and identify strongly as Jamaican American or Trinidadian American. Other teens do not see their parents' national origins as important to their own sense of identity; they identify as American Black and will only mention their parents' ethnic origins if asked specifically about their parents' birthplace.

These different patterns of choices are highly related both to parents' socioeconomic status and to the relative school success of the youngsters. Teens who are doing well in school tend to be "ethnic," and those who are not doing well tend to be "American." If this pattern holds in larger samples, then the effect on socioeconomic studies of the second generation could be influenced strongly by differential reporting of West Indian backgrounds in the second generation. If successful young adults identify as West Indian, and unsuccessful young adults say they are African American, then estimates of the differential success of West Indians in the United States will overestimate the success of the second generation relative to native Blacks. This estimate is important for a number of political debates about the nature of racism in American society (Farley and Allen, 1987; Sowell, 1978; Model, 1991).

A third example of the ways in which ethnicity should be seen as both an effect as well as a cause is in studies of intermarriage. Lieberson and Waters (1988; 1993) have found evidence that married couples tend to simplify their ancestries to "match up" with those of their spouse. They suggest that standard demographic studies of intermarriage, which ask whether ethnicity affects choice of marriage partner, might not also be measuring the opposite question—whether choice of marriage partner affects ethnic identity choice. They suggest that religious intermarriage studies might provide a model for dealing with this problem. It has long been recognized that religious conversion at the time of marriage would bias estimates of religious intermarriage downward if the only data one worked with were current religion of both spouses. As a result, religious intermarriage studies use two variables—religion at age 16, and current religion to measure intermarriage. Perhaps a measure such as current ethnicity and ethnicity at age 16 will be necessary to measure ethnic intermarriage in a time of mixed ethnicities and changing identifications.

The Challenge of Multiracial People

Perhaps the greatest challenge to measurement of ethnicity and to the long-run stability and integrity of the groups themselves, however, lies in the long-run results of intermarriage—the children of intermarried couples. Intermarriage creates offspring who share both parents' race and ethnicities. Ultimately, intermarriage can produce changes in the size and composition of groups, and can produce new groups through a process of hybridization. The existence of people who straddle the categories we set up to count them shows the dynamic nature of race and ethnicity as individuals cross boundaries, as some categories possibly empty out, and as new hybrid categories are born. In addition, the fact that intermarriage occurs at all illustrates a central point—that the social construction of race and ethnicity creates a dynamic and changing environment for demographers trying to analyze race and ethnicity—and that the patterns of choices and patterns of change in the population both reflect underlying demographic trends and directly contribute to those trends.

One of the most important factors affecting the social classification system of race and ethnicity in a society is the system of rules governing the identities of people of mixed ethnic and racial backgrounds. Historically, in the United States, the offspring of Black–White unions have been forced to identify as Black through the "one drop rule." The offspring of other races married to Whites, such as Native Americans and Asians, have generally been classified as non-White, but with far less vigilance and certitude. The offspring of mixed ethnicities—German and English for example—have had no formal societal pressures to identify one way or another (Davis, 1991; Dominguez, 1986, Spickard, 1989).

As long as minority groups in the United States were legally excluded from immigrating and kept separate by law and by custom, and as long as the status of those children who did result from an intermarriage was rigidly defined, the definition of the categories that define the groups and the assignment of people to the groups were relatively straightforward. Consequently, the long-run existence of the groups could be assumed and easily assured. However, since the 1960s there have been some major changes in American society that are changing the nature of the definition of minority groups. The removal of laws enforcing segregation as a result of the Civil Rights movement, most notably the Civil Rights Act of 1964 and the Voting Rights Act of 1965, and the removal of racist restrictions on who could immigrate to the United States through the Immigration Act of 1965, has led to a different milieu in which racial and Hispanic groups interact in the United States. Increasing interactions among individuals of different groups and growing social and geographic mobility have characterized the situation of minorities in the United States in the last 30 years. At the same time, the requirement of the legislation passed to remedy past and current discrimination was to count these groups in a straightforward way into mutually exclusive categories.

The requirement to count our minorities in the United States means that there must be rules about how to deal with people whose identity straddles the categories. The Census Bureau and most other statistical agencies of the government rely on self-identification. However, for purposes of reporting race and Hispanic origin, until 2000 the Census Bureau did not allow people to self-identify simultaneously with two different groups. The Office of Management and the Budget issued Directive 15 in 1978 advising that in the case of people who are of mixed origins, "The category which most closely reflects the individual's recognition in his community should be used for purposes of reporting"(Federal Register, 1978). However, since the Census Bureau did not have information on how individuals are recognized in their communities, they designed a procedure to assign a single race to an interracial child if the parents had disobeyed the instructions and checked two separate boxes or had written in something like multiracial as a response. If an unacceptable response was given to the race question, the Census Bureau assigned the child to the mother's race, if the mother was in the household. In other cases, when the mother's race was unknown, multiracial individuals were assigned the first race that they reported (i.e., the first box checked on the form). This represents a change in policy, because in 1970 when persons with parents of different races were in doubt as to their classification, the race of the father was used.

This attention to classifying mixed-*race* individuals is different than the way mixed-*ethnic* individuals were recorded in the Census. Because of the need for unambiguous data for legislative reasons, mixed-race people, and mixed Spanish-origin people must be put into only one mutually exclusive category. Mixed-ancestry people are permitted to report multiple origins. In 1990 among those reporting at least one specific ancestry, 28% reported at least a second ancestry as well.

The decision about how to classify people with more than one ancestry or identity has important, and often unrecognized, implications for population growth and decline (see Hirschman, page 63). If one had begun in the year 1900 and estimated the numbers of people in White ethnic groups a century later, without taking into account intermarriage and identification choices, one would have under- or overestimated the size of groups (Hout and Goldstein, 1994).

As intermarriage has risen among all Americans, the assumption of mutually exclusive categories has begun to break down. Intermarriage among racial and Hispanic groups has been growing. Using a classification of only five racial groups, which understates the levels of intermarriage that one could obtain with finer distinctions, the number of interracial couples rose by 535% from 1960 to 1980, to nearly 2% of all married couples. Analysis of the 1990 census shows that the number of racially intermarried couples has risen to 2.7%. However, unlike the children of mixed ethnic couples, until very recently the Census Bureau has been forcing mixed racial couples to report only one race for their children. Mixed race children now make up 3.2% of all annual births in the nation, up from 0.7% in 1968. This represents an increase in absolute numbers from 22,100 in 1968 to 110,500 in 1989. (Usdansky, 1992).

Census Data on Mixed Race People

Relying on self identification, the Census Bureau until 2000 required mixed-race people to choose an identity and required the parents of a mixed-race child to choose for him or her. A growing number of people refused to choose, checked two or more boxes, or wrote in a mixed-race identity in the line called Other. The Census Bureau did not allow this choice to stand and reassigned these individuals whenever possible into a racial category. In fact, when people specifically wrote in a multiracial response on the Census form, the Census Bureau reclassified them. The top ten written-in multiracial responses and the race they were assigned to by the Census Bureau is provided in Table 1.1. The main rule the Census Bureau followed was to put the person into the first race listed. The Census Bureau reports that they received many phone calls during the 1990 Census from mixed-race people requesting aid in answering the race question. (McKenney and Cresce, 1993). There is now a nationwide organization of parents of interracial children who have been lobbying the federal government for a new category on all official statistics for multiracial people. (Njeri, 1993; Spickard and Fong, 1995).

Given the 1997 decision of the OMB to allow identification with more than one race, the year 2000 Census was the first census to allow people to identify with more than one race. The Census Bureau conducted tests of a multiracial question in sample surveys in preparation for Census 2000. These included the May 1995 Current Population Survey, the 1996 National Content Survey, and the 1996 Race and Ethnic Targeted Test. These tests all found that the number of people choosing more than one race was statistically small—between 1% and 2%. In the 2000 Census 2.4% chose more than one race, representing 6,826,228 people. Yet, rising intermarriage means that the number of potential multiracials is quite sizeable, especially among American Indians, Hispanics, and Asians—groups with high intermarriage rates. (Qian, 1997).

While it is impossible to tell from the 1980 and 1990 Censuses what percentage of adults are themselves of multiple racial origins (and data on couples are not yet available for 2000), it is possible to look at intermarried couples and the decisions they are forced to make about their children's identities because of the design of the census. The ethnic or racial identities reported in the Census by parents in the household and the identities reported for their children show various patterns. In a recent paper William Alonso and I explored the choices parents make for children in answering the 1980 Census, and we developed a method for simulating future population change, which takes the pattern of these identity choices as well as levels of intermarriage into account (Alonso and Waters, 1993). The results of such a simulation show that the flux in race and ethnicity stemming from such changes could have significant effects on the future composition of the U. S. population—effects that a straight population projection would miss.

To examine the patterns of these choices, we drew a sample of the Public Use Microdata Sample (PUMS) 5% 1980 individual level census data, restricting the sample to married-couple parents, both spouses in their first marriage, with no more children present in the household than the mother reported giving birth to.[1] This was done to control as much as possible for blended families, stepchildren, and adoptions.

Table 1.2
Race of Children of Interracially Married Parents with White Mother by Race of Father: United States, 1980

RACE OF CHILDREN

Father's Race	Percent "White"	Percent Father's Race	Percent "Other"[1] Race	Percent "All Other Races"[2]	Total
Black	21.92	69.10	8.51	0.47	55,020
Native Am.	50.99	48.21	0.65	0.15	85,620
Japanese	42.58	43.93	11.56	1.93	10,380
Chinese	34.96	48.73	15.25	1.06	9,440
Filipino	54.25	39.23	4.64	1.88	18,100
Korean	57.89	31.58	10.53	0	2,280
Asian					
Indian	74.13	20.22	3.48	2.17	9,200
Vietnamese	45.71	48.57	2.86	2.86	700
Hawaiian	42.89	53.95	2.89	0.27	7,600
Other Asia	55.46	36.24	6.11	2.19	4,580

Source: Calculated from the 1980 United States Census Public Use Data Sample A, 5% sample.

[1] Includes children whose parents selected "Other Race" from among the options given to them by the Census Bureau.

[2] This is a residual category including all children whose parents chose a specific race that was not the same as the father's race, the mother's race, or the category "Other Race." These children were given one of the other specific races recognized by the Census Bureau.

Tables 1.2 and 1.3 provide basic information on the choices of identity for children in these intermarried households. In the situation in which the mother is White and the father is some other race (Table 1.2), compared to all the other groups, Blacks have a much higher retention of being Black—69.1% of the children are Black. Another 8% are reported "Other," and 22% are reported as White. In contrast, 50% of the offspring of White mothers and Native American fathers are reported to be White, 43% of Japanese-White children are reported as White, 35% of Chinese-White children are reported as White, and 58% of Korean-White children are reported by their parents to be White. In sharp contrast, when the father is Asian Indian and the mother is White only, 20% of the children stay Asian Indian. A much lower percentage of children of Japanese, Chinese, and Filipino fathers married to White mothers remain identified with their father's Asian origins. While these Asian groups do show a large proportion of the children as "Other" race (11.56% for children of Japanese fathers, 15.25% for children of Chinese fathers, and 10.53% for children of Korean fathers), even if one ignores those high percentages, there are still far more children identifying with their mother's White race.

Table 1.3
Race of Children of Interracially Married Parents with White Father by Race of Mother: United States, 1980

RACE OF CHILDREN

Mother's Race	Percent "White"	Percent Mother's Race	Percent "Other" Race[1]	Percent "All Other Races"[2]	Total
Black	21.89	70.82	6.04	1.25	15,900
Native American	51.27	47.48	0.73	0.52	88,000
Japanese	67.19	24.87	6.68	1.26	38,040
Chinese	61.53	26.43	9.54	2.5	13,620
Filipino	63.04	32.62	2.73	1.61	37,340
Korean	73.64	21.33	4.45	0.58	24,280
Asian Indian	93.31	5.20	0.74	0.75	5,380
Vietnamese	64.44	29.78	5.33	0.45	9,000
Hawaiian	56.06	42.86	1.08	0	9,240
Other Asia	63.92	32.66	3.42	0	12,860

Source: Calculated from the 1980 United States Census Public Use Data Sample A, 5% sample.

[1] Includes children whose parents selected "Other Race" from among the options given to them by the Census Bureau.

[2] This is a residual category including all children whose parents chose a specific race that was not the same as the father's race, the mother's race, or the category "Other Race." These children were given one of the other specific races recognized by the Census Bureau.

Table 1.3 shows the intergenerational transfer rates for situations in which the father is White and the mother is non-White. The differences here for the Asian groups are even more striking. For instance, in families where the father is White and the mother is Asian Indian, 93% of their children are labeled White. In households where the mother is Japanese, only 25% of the children are labeled Japanese. In households where the mother is Chinese, only 26% of the children are Chinese.[2]

Thus, these tables of parents' identities by children's identities show that there is no one rule governing the choices made by parents about mixed-race children's identities. There is some evidence that some parents try to choose neither parents' identities by checking Other. Parents do not choose completely based on the maternal or paternal identity, and some parents choose "majority White" identities, and some choose "minority non-White identities."

Population Simulation

Alonso and Waters (1993) take the results of the patterns of these choices of parents for their children's identities and combine them with levels of inter-marriage to simulate the change in the composition of the population over five generations. The simulation does not take into account immigration, which is of course the largest element affecting the future size and composition of America's minority population. It also does not take into account differential fertility, or the reproductive behavior or choices of people who are not married, or not in their first marriage. Thus, the exercise is not a projection, but a sim-ulation designed to show the effects intermarriage can have on ethnic change, and the pitfalls of population projections that assume no intermarriage.

Standard population projections have been predicting the future decline of the White non-Hispanic population for a while now. For instance, in 1990 *Time Magazine* ran a cover story with the provocative title, "What Will the United States be like when Whites Are No Longer a Majority?" (*Time Magazine*, 1990). However, as Hirschman (page 57) points out, all of these standard population projections of racial and ethnic groups do not take inter-marriage and multiracial and multiethnic children into account.

Alonso and Waters (1993) used 1980 Census data on race and Hispanic origin for each member of the household to examine the effect of intermarriage and ethnic identity choices on the future population. We constructed a table giving the number of married couples by racial or ethnic groups of husband and wife, and observed the frequencies of children by group for each type of couple. This yields a matrix of 32 by 32 separate categories of race/Hispanic origin combinations of mother's by father's by children's identity. We then determine the underlying propensity of each group to intermarry.[3] Each couple is assigned two children, and the children are given group identities according to the observed frequencies of identities for that type of couple. The children are then "grown up" and married off, maintaining the underlying intermarriage rates and identity choices of the original marriage table. The process is repeat-ed for five generations, or roughly a period of 125 years. Changes in the rela-tive sizes of the various groups from the first to the final generation are then examined. Since the simulation models a stationary population (one without growth due to fertility or immigration), the simulated changes are entirely due to patterns of intermarriage and heritability of group identities.

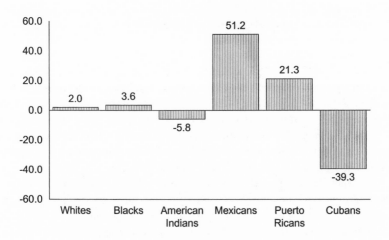

Figure 1.2
Projected Change in Size of Race and Hispanic Groups
over Next Five Generations

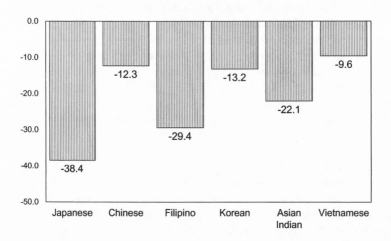

Figure 1.3
Projected Change in Size of Asian Groups
over Next Five Generations

The pattern of changes in groups is quite variable. Key findings are presented in Figures 1.2 and 1.3. Overall, Whites increase by only 2%, and Blacks grow very slightly at 3.6%. American Indians decline at 5.8%. Mexicans and Puerto Ricans grow quite a bit, at 51.2% and 21.3%, respectively. Cubans decline overall by 39.3% due to a relatively high degree of outmarriage and a propensity for those outmarried couples to state that the child is White non-Hispanic. Overall, Hispanics as a whole grow by more than 25% while Asian groups all decline in the simulation. This is due to relatively high levels of intermarriage and to a substantial number of intermarried couples of different Asian groups who state that their children are not Asian, and to intermarried Hispanic parents absorbing their multiethnic children as Hispanic. While immigration of Asians into the United States will no doubt dwarf this underlying trend in aggregate statistics, nevertheless there is already, and will be in the future, considerable movement by individuals across the Asian/white boundary. For a group such as the Japanese who currently have very small numbers of immigrants coming into the United States, this overall trend in intermarriage and heritability could lead to a real decline in the relative size of the group.[4]

The number of simplifying assumptions in this simulation means that this is not what will happen to the future population of the United States. However, this exercise does demonstrate that standard demographic population projection methods can seriously overestimate the stability of socially constructed categories of race and ethnicity. Population projections are an extreme example of demographers assuming fixed identities and categories. This is especially egregious because it is projecting into the future all of the errors in past measurement. The design of the census is backwards-looking in the first place; it is responding to political pressures and problems with the wording of the last census. So, for instance, just as the numbers of immigrants coming to the United States grew in the 1970s and the beginnings of a vast wave of second-generation children were born, the Census Bureau replaced the birthplace of parents question with the ancestry question, reacting to the fact that European immigrants who were vastly reduced in the 1920s had aged generationally to the point that the birthplace of parents' data no longer were capturing many second-generation people. Thus, the Census adopted the ancestry question and dropped the birthplace of parents question. We can now see with hindsight that if the furious debate over immigration at the turn of the Twentieth century had been accompanied by population projections, such projections would have seriously erred because of the social changes in the meanings of ethnic and racial boundaries that have occurred in the Twentieth Century. As Paul Spickard and Rowena Fong (1995: 1367) note, "Almost no White American extended family exists today without at least one member who has married across what two generations ago would have been thought an unbridgeable gap." This has changed both the nature of the categories we use for classifying the population, as well as the raw counts of people within each category.

While the federal government collected and tabulated data on people who identify with more than one race, these results will not be used for apportionment. The recommendation to allow people to choose more than one race effectively decouples response from reporting. Allowing more than one response means that there needs to be consistent rules on how those who choose more than one race will be tabulated. These rules will be necessary in order to have comparable data across agencies and to meet requirements of the law to have mutually exclusive and exhaustive data. The report of the Race and Ethnic Targeted Test (RAETT), conducted by the Census Bureau (U.S. Bureau of The Census, 1997) in 1996 outlined several possible tabulation methods for dealing with multiracial people:

> 1. Single race approach. This approach would count all people who marked more than one race in a "multiple race" category, similar to the "Other" race category that the Census uses now. The information then that a person identified as Asian and White, for example, would be lost. The benefit of this approach is that there is no ambiguity in counting and no chance of double counting.

> 2. All inclusive approach. This approach would count a person in each race that they marked. This would involve double or triple counting. If a person said they were Asian and White they would be counted in both of those categories. This would mean that the counts would add to more than 100% and you would end up with a count of races, not of people.

> 3. Historical series approach. This approach would reclassify those who chose more than one race back into a single race in a set of mutually exclusive categories that add up to 100%. This approach, it was stressed in the report (page 37), produced counts that were statistically the same as those produced by the status quo race question, for all groups except for the Alaska Native targeted sample.

My impression from reading the interagency report is that the method described as the "historical series approach" is the most likely approach because it affords the greatest continuity with previous data. As I understand it, the historical series approach assigns a person who reports their race to be both White and any one of the other OMB categories, (Black, Hispanic, Asian, or American Indian) to be in the latter category, not White. Since the majority of current intermarriage does involve a White spouse, this method would classify a large number of multiple-race people into a single race. In effect, however, the "historical series approach" uses the "one drop rule." Those people who are part White are classified as the non-White race. This may be the current "best guess" about how these people are "socially identified" in their communities, but it does recreate the classification dilemma that the self-identified multiracial community is trying to move beyond. The political debate about this issue has tended to concentrate on the counts and identities of African Americans. This is very understandable given the history of race relations in this country. All of the statistical and demographic research, however, points to this change having the biggest effect on American Indians, Alaskan Natives, and Asian and Pacific Islanders. The actual data from Census 2000 shows that adding the people who chose a particular race in a multiple race combination to those who chose it as a single race would increase the size of the Native American and Alaska Native group by 66.4% and the Native Hawaiian and Other Pacific Islander population by 119.2%. In contrast, Other Races would increase by 20.6% and Asians would increase by 16.2%, compared to 5.1% for the category Black or Aftrican American and 2.5% for whites. It is clear that this new method of counting and how these results are tabulated will have severe implications for the size of smaller groups with relatively high intermarriage rates.

Some Future Scenarios

Social demographers need to combine demographic measurement and simulations and projections with the realization that social and political forces in society shape these trends as much as fertility and mortality and migration statistics. Recognizing these forces, I conclude by suggesting some of the ways in which demographic changes combined with political and social forces might influence some of the ethnic and racial developments that will occur in the country in the years to come. Major factors that will affect the social meaning of ethnic and racial categories in the United States include the overall progress we make in reducing discrimination and racial inequality, as well as the degree of success we achieve in incorporating the children and grandchildren of the current waves of non-European immigrants to the United States into the economy and polity (Waters and Eschbach, 1995). Without continued efforts to reduce discrimination and segregation between Whites and Blacks, the overall level of intermixing, as well as intermarriage, will remain lower than the levels of other non-White groups and Whites. If the children and grandchildren of non-European immigrants to the United States do not achieve the same degree of economic mobility as the descendants of European immigrants did during our nation's history, this could be reflected in sharper patterns of boundary maintenance between white and non-White groups. (See Gans, 1990 for his theory of second-generation decline as a pessimistic scenario on this topic.) So too the type of incorporation or assimilation that immigrants adapt could shape the degree of intermarriage and the rules shaping decisions of multiethnic individuals about reaffiliation. (Portes and Zhou, 1993).

Let me suggest three possible scenarios in the future that might have very differential effects on both intermarriage and the identities available for mixed-race and ethnic people. The first possible scenario is the continued salience and meaningfulness of the categories we have now. In fact, we could see a process by which these categories are reinforced and shape future identities. This is because we now have a very widespread governmental system for classifying the population that has real material rewards and punishments for rising or declining numbers. Since the Civil Rights movement in the 1960s the government has become increasingly involved in counting the population by race and ethnicity in order to monitor enforcement of antidiscrimination laws. Such enforcement involves classifying the population into mutually exclusive categories. The paradox, of course, is that the more successful the society is in reducing barriers between groups, the more likely it is that relationships will form across these racial and ethnic boundaries, and thus make it more difficult to continue counting the population.

This is a political paradox that we have not faced directly. In fact, in the current political climate it is likely to be conservatives who advocate eradicating governmental classification of race and ethnicity and a race neutral approach to social problems. Often it is minority group members and organizations as well as liberal political forces who argue most strongly for continued monitoring, which means continued classification by rigid rules into race and Hispanic origin categories. The rhetoric of race-neutral language, which was the province of integrationists such as Martin Luther King, has been appropriated by conservatives who argue that race-conscious policies are at odds with a race-neutral state. Those who care about the future of America's minority populations are so busy fighting for continued vigilance in enforcement, the very rhetoric of a race neutral society has been lost to them.

The second possible scenario is that there could be a polarization among the groups to Black and White, with the other races either whitening or darkening based on their intermarriage patterns with Whites and Blacks. In his study of Chinese immigrants in the segregated Mississippi delta, James Loewen (1988) found that Chinese, who were considered non-White legally and socially in the mid Nineteenth Century, slowly changed their status so that by the 1960s they were accepted as equivalent to Whites in the area. The price they paid for such social movement was the ostracism of families of Chinese who had married Blacks, and continued social distance between Blacks and Chinese on every level. (Loewen's book opens with the following quote from a White Baptist minister in the delta: "You're either a white man or a nigger here. Now, that's the whole story. When I first came to the Delta, the Chinese were classed as nigras. [And now they are called whites?] "That's right" (Loewen, 1988). In effect, the Chinese accepted the color line in Mississippi as a price for stepping over it.

Could it be that the non-White, non-Black immigrants and their children in the United States could be offered the same nightmarish bargain? Several authors have suggested that the success of new non-White immigrants comes at the expense of Black Americans (Miles, 1992). While high rates of inter-marriage between Whites and Asians and Hispanics are not matched by similarly high rates of intermarriage between Whites and Blacks, there has been a large increase in the number of Black–White marriages. However, the one drop rule of racial classification of Black–White people in the United States still operates; in fact, it is nowhere more vigorously defended than among Black Americans themselves (Njeri, 1993; Waters, 1991; Davis, 1991). Patterns of residential segregation described by Denton and Massey (1989) point to differential patterns of segregation for Black Hispanics as opposed to White Hispanics, with Black Hispanics experiencing levels of segregation much closer to that of Black Americans in general. Alonso and Waters (1993) also show that Black and White Hispanics tend to marry within their racial categories more so than within their ethnic categories—thus Black Cubans are more likely to choose a Black non-Cuban spouse than a Cuban non-Black spouse.

Finally a third, and to my taste more desirable, scenario for the future could be a blurring of the lines of distinction across all of these ethnic and racial categories—in effect a melting pot model that included all Americans regardless of color. If this scenario develops, the boundaries separating race and Hispanic origin groups from White ethnic groups could fade in importance and social relevance, even as they continue to exist despite increased flows across them. Such a scenario would lead to changes in the salience of group boundaries as well as to the creation of new categories and the probable emptying of other categories. The growth in the population of people claiming an identity as multiracial and requesting governmental recognition is an example of this type of flux. I believe that for such a scenario to come about we need to somehow come to terms politically with our short-run need to count and classify and label the population and our long-run need to achieve a race-blind society in which people are free to claim an identity that includes any, all, or none of their ancestries.

To return to the example of my student who is both Black, American Indian, and Scottish and Irish, one can see some of all of these influences operating on her identity. The one drop rule of racial classification for Blacks in the United States is definitely undergoing change and challenges currently. My student did not automatically place herself in the Black category. The pressure she feels from the Black student association to "reaffiliate" and the administrative rules that require the University to place her in one category are currently at odds with her and her sister's desire to identify with all of their backgrounds. Her uneasiness with the University's decision to assign her and her sister to separate races shows the enormous emotional importance people assign to their identities and to what has come to be perceived as a right of self-identification. The paradox is that I believe the strong pressure on the University to classify and report on their minority student enrollment is very much responsible for her being at the University in the first place and at the same time that pressure is "racializing" the student body in a way that does not allow what could be a natural evolution towards multiethnicity and blurred boundaries to proceed smoothly. As demographers plot the increasing hetero-geneity of the American population, we should be cognizant of the fact that we are classifying and counting by a variable that should be allowed to evolve, grow, and perhaps even cease to matter in the future.

Notes

1. This analysis is part of a larger collaborative research project with William Alonso on the implications of mixed-race children's identities for the future ethnic and racial composition of the United States. See, "The Future Composition of the American Population: An Illustrative Projection" by William Alonso and Mary C. Waters, Paper presented at the 1993 Winter Meetings of the American Statistical Association, Fort Lauderdale, Florida.

2. Of course, at this level of aggregation, it is not possible to determine whether some of these parents are of mixed Asian heritage, or whether mixed Asian parents are themselves more or less likely to report their children as being Asian. In other words, we do not know whether parents reporting themselves as Japanese or Chinese are themselves the offspring of an intermarriage.

3. This is done by decomposing the matrix into a saturated log-linear model. The terms of the interaction matrix, in logs, may be interpreted if positive as the strength of the affinity of men of one group and women of another or the same group, and as the level of avoidance if negative.

4. The groups vary greatly in size so that these relative increases and decreases translate into quite different sizes of absolute change. Altogether the share of Whites in the total population increases by 0.097%; Blacks share increases by 0.140%.

References

Alonso, William and Mary C. Waters. 1993. "The Future Composition of the American Population: An Illustrative Projection." Paper presented at the 1993 Winter Meetings of the American Statistical Association, Fort Lauderdale, Florida.

Davis, F. James. 1991. *Who is Black?: One Nation's Definition.* University Park, PA: Pennsylvania State University Press.

Denton, Nancy and Douglas Massey. 1989. "Racial Identity among Caribbean Hispanics: The Effect of Double Minority Status on Residential Segregation." *American Sociological Review* 54: 790–809.

Dominguez, Virginia R. 1986. *White by Definition: Social Classification in Creole Louisiana.* New Brunswick, N. J.: Rutgers University Press.

Eschbach, Karl. 1993. "Changing Identification among American Indians and Alaska Natives." *Demography,* vol. 30, no. 4, November, pp. 635–652.

Farley, Reynolds. 1991. "The New Census Question About Ancestry: What Did It Tell Us?" *Demography* vol. 28, no. 3, August, pp. 411–430.

Farley, Reynolds and Walter R. Allen. 1987. *The Color Line and the Quality of Life in America.* New York: Russell Sage Foundation.

Gans, Herbert. 1990. "Second Generation Decline: Scenarios for the Economic and Ethnic Futures of the Post 1965 American Immigrants." *Ethnic and Racial Studies,* 15(2), April, pp. 173–192.

Hahn Robert A., Joseph Mulinare and Steven M. Teutsch. 1992. "Inconsistencies in Coding of Race and Ethnicity Between Birth and Death in United States Infants: A New Look at Infant Mortality 1983 through 1985." *Journal of the American Medical Association,* January 8, 1992, v. 267 n. 2, pp. 259–264.

Hahn, Robert and D. Stroup. 1994. Race and ethnicity in public health surveillance: criteria for scientific use of social categorics. *Public Health Reports* 109:7-15.

Hout, Michael and Joshua Goldstein. 1994. "How 4.5 Million Irish Immigrants Became 40 Million Irish Americans: Demographic and Subjective Aspects of the Ethnic Composition of White Americans." *American Sociological Review,* 59:64–82.

Lieberson, Stanley and Mary C. Waters. 1988. *From Many Strands: Ethnic and Racial Groups in Contemporary America.* New York: Russell Sage Foundation.

———1986. "Ethnic Groups in Flux: The Changing Ethnic Responses of American Whites." *Annals of the American Academy of Political and Social Science,* vol. 487 (September), pp. 79–91.

————1993. "The Ethnic Responses of Whites: What Causes Their Instability, Simplification and Inconsistency?" *Social Forces,* vol. 72, no. 2, December, pp. 421–451.

Loewen, James. 1988. *The Mississippi Chinese: Between Black and White.* Prospect Heights, IL: Waveland Press.

McKenney, Nampeo R. and Arthur R. Cresce. 1993. "Measurement of ethnicity in the United States: experiences of the U.S. Census Bureau." Pp. 173-221 in Statistics Canada Bureau of the Census, *Challenges of Measuring an Ethnic World: Science, Politics and Reality.* Washington, DC: U.S. Government Printing Office.

Miles, Jack. 1992. "Blacks vs. Browns." *The Atlantic,* vol. 270, no. 4, October, pp. 41–60.

Model, Suzanne. 1991. "Caribbean Immigrants: a Black Success Story?" *International Migration Review,* vol. 25, no. 2, pp. 248–277.

New York Times. 1992. "Death Rates for Minority Infants were Underestimated, Study Says." Pp. A14 Wednesday, January 8, 1992.

Njeri, Itabari. 1993. "Sushi and Grits: Ethnic Identity and Conflict in a Newly Multicultural America." In Gerald Early, ed., *Lure and Loathing: Essays on Race, Identity, and the Ambivalence of Assimilation,* pp. 13–40. New York: Penguin Press.

Portes, Alejandro and Min Zhou. 1993. "The New Second Generation: Segmented Assimilation and Its Variants." *Annals of the American Academy of Political and Social Science,* vol. 530, November, pp. 74–96.

Qian, Zhennchao. 1997. "Breaking the Racial Barriers: Variations in Interracial Marriage Between 1980 and 1990." *Demography,* vol. 34, no. 2, May pp. 263–276.

Snipp, Matthew. 1989. *American Indians: The First of this Land.* New York: Russell Sage Foundation.

Sowell, Thomas. 1978. *American Ethnic Groups.* Washington DC.: Urban Institute.

Spickard, Paul R. 1989. *Mixed Blood.* Madison: University of Wisconsin Press.

Spickard, Paul and Rowena Fong. 1995. "Pacific Islander Americans and Multiethnicity: A vision of America's Future." *Social Forces,* vol. 73, no. 4, June, pp. 1365–1383.

Statistics Canada and U.S. Bureau of the Census. 1993. *Challenges of Measuring an Ethnic World: Science, Politics and Reality.* Washington DC.: U.S. Government Printing Office.

Time Magazine. 1990. "What Will the United States Be Like When Whites Are No Longer a Majority?", vol. 135, no. 15, April 1990, pp. 28–31.

United States Office of Management and Budget. 1978. Statistical Directive No. 15: "Race and Ethnic Standards for Federal Agencies and Administrative Reporting." *Federal Register* 43:19269–19270, May 4.

————1997. "Revisions to the Standards for the Classification of Federal Data on Race and Ethnicity: Notices." *Federal Register* 62:58782–58790, October 30.

U.S. Bureau of the Census 1997. "Results of the 1996 Race and Ethnic Targeted Test." Population Division Working Paper No. 18, May 1997.

Usdansky, Margaret L. 1992. "For interracial kids, growth spurt." *USA Today*, Friday, December 11, 1992, pp. 07.A.

Waters, Mary C. 1991. "The Role of Lineage in Identity Formation Among Black Americans." *Qualitative Sociology*, vol. 14, no. 1, Spring, pp. 57–76.

————1994. "Ethnic and Racial Identities of Second-Generation Black Immigrants in New York City." *International Migration Review,* 28(4), Winter pp. 795–820.

Waters, Mary C. and Karl Eschbach. 1995. "Immigration and Ethnic and Racial Inequality in the United States." *Annual Review of Sociology,* vol. 21:419–446.

Chapter 2

Race and Ethnic Population Projections: A Critical Evaluation of Their Content and Meaning

Charles Hirschman

Introduction

In recent years, the U.S. Census Bureau has added racial and Hispanic-origin populations as part of the standard projections of the American population to the middle of the Twenty-first century. Some of the numbers in these ethnic population projections have stimulated considerable popular interest—in particular, the projected decline in the proportion of the White non-Hispanic population to about one-half (or less) of the total U.S. population. Fears about the future ethnic composition of the American population are frequently noted with alarm by anti-immigration lobbies, some journalists, and a few politicians. Although public rhetoric has not reached the level of the hysteria that was part of the response to the immigration from Eastern and Southern Europe during the first two decades of the Twentieth century, there are ominous parallels.

Population projections are usually considered an esoteric topic in applied demography. Although there is occasional general interest stimulated by concerns of too rapid (or too slow) population growth, the field is largely left to technical demographers, applied statisticians, and urban planners. Within this realm of professional users, there is a healthy skepticism about the limits of population projections beyond the short-term of 10 to 20 years. Beyond this time frame, unforeseen changes in fertility, mortality, and migration frequently lead to population trends that diverge from prior projections. Long-term population projections of the American population have rarely anticipated actual demographic changes (Preston, 1993).

In this chapter, I raise fundamental questions about the technical bases and the standard interpretation of the long-term projections of the U.S. population by race and ethnicity. In addition to the unknowns of the standard demographic components of growth (especially net international migration), race and ethnic population projections are flawed by the lack of information about future trends in intermarriage and changes in ethnic identity among the descendants of intermarried couples. Even if past (and future) trends in international migration and intermarriage were known with complete certainty, ethnic identities in the future are very likely to depend on events that cannot be extrapolated from the past. The discussion about race and ethnic population projections tells us more about the current state of ethnic relations in American society than future population trends.

The Content of Race and Ethnic Population Projections

Population projection is one of the most valuable tools in applied demography. Although there are many technical details for the specialist to master, the basic ideas are simple to grasp. Beginning with a base population (arrayed by sex and age), mortality, fertility, and net-migration rates are used to project the base population forward into the future. The standard cohort-component framework uses the first projected population (one or five years into the future) as the base population for the next step of the projection, and so on (Shryock and Siegel, 1971:377). While current levels of fertility, mortality, and migration can be used for the first step of the projection, successive steps must rely on assumptions about future changes in the components of population growth. Uncertainty about future trends in fertility, mortality, and migration is what makes long-term projections such a hazardous enterprise.

The practical demand for population projections is greatest for subnational areas, especially for cities and metropolitan planning units concerned with future needs for schools, transportation, housing, and other facilities. The problem is that migration, which may not be an important component of national-level projections, typically looms as the most important element of population change for local areas. All population projections must assume that future changes reflect some continuity with the past, but this assumption is much weaker for migration than for fertility and mortality. The biological bases of fertility and mortality provide a modicum of inertia that mitigates against rapid change. In contrast, the volatility of migration in response to economic conditions means that the useful time horizon for local-area population projections is much less than for national projections. Long-term race and ethnic population projections are problematic for the same reason as local-area population projections: both are heavily dependent on future trends in migration (international migration in the case of race and ethnic population projections). This is, however, only one of the many problems that make it difficult, if not impossible, to construct meaningful race and ethnic population projections.

At first glance, population projections by race and ethnicity seem to be a reasonable idea. In the standard grouping of population attributes, ethnicity is considered to be an ascriptive characteristic—one that is fixed at birth and remains the same over a person's lifetime (Schnore 1961). If this assumption is met, then ethnic population projections can be constructed if the requisite fertility, mortality, and migration data are available. Ethnic fertility and mortality patterns are known for the present, and convergence is often a reasonable assumption for the future. As noted above, there is great uncertainty about future trends in international migration. For some ethnic groups (Asians and Hispanics), assumptions about future immigration are the most important elements of future population projections. In this chapter, I review the components of several recent population projections by race and ethnicity and then evaluate the demographic assumptions underpinning these projections. I also raise the question of whether race and ethnicity are likely to remain ascribed characteristics in American society.

The Census Bureau and others have published U.S. population projections by race and ethnicity to the middle of the next century (Day, 1996; Bouvier, 1992; Edmonston and Passel, 1992; 1994; Smith and Edmonston, 1997, chapter 3). Even with differing assumptions, the projected race and ethnic composition of the future U.S. population is fairly similar in these alternative projections. According to the Census Bureau "middle series" projections for 2050, the American population will be 53% non-Hispanic White, 14% non-Hispanic Black, 1% American Indian, 9% Asian, and 22% Hispanic (Day, 1996:13).[1] The race and ethnic composition in Edmonston and Passel's projections for 2050 are broadly similar: 57% non-Hispanic White, 12% non-Hispanic Black, 1% American Indian, 11% Asian, and 20% Hispanic (Edmonston and Passel, 1994:334). The National Research Council (NRC) race/ethnic projections with mutually exclusive ethnic assignment led to very similar projections in 2050: 51% non-Hispanic White, 14% Black, 8% Asian, and 26% Hispanic (Smith and Edmonston, 1997:121). These modest differences are well within the range of highest and lowest series published by the Bureau of the Census.

The primary differences between the present and the projected ethnic composition in 2050 are the relative decline of the White non-Hispanic population (declining from about three-quarters to approximately one-half of the population) and the relative increases in the shares of the Asian origin (from 3% to 8%–11%) and Hispanic origin (from 9% to 20%–26%) populations. The relative size of the Black and American Indian populations will also increase but not as rapidly as the Asian and Hispanic populations. Although future immigration is a major component of the projected changes, the projected ethnic balance would shift in the same direction (relative decline in the proportion of non-Hispanic Whites) even without further immigration. If there were to be zero net immigration after 1994, the Census Bureau projections show that the White non-Hispanic population would decline to 61% of the total population in 2050 (a decline of 13 percentage points from 1995, instead of the 21 percentage-point decline projected with immigration) (Day, 1996:13, 23).

The Assumptions Driving the Projections

There are modest differences in the assumptions about the future course of fertility and mortality in the various population projections that may account for some of variations in the expected ethnic composition of the population in 2050. The Bureau of the Census assumes that overall life expectancy will improve from about 75.9 in 1995 to 82.0 in 2050 with the current Black–White differential of about 7 years widening to 9 years (Black life expectancy is projected to increase from 69.4 to 74.2 years and for Whites from 76.8 to 83.6 years (see Day, 1996:2). The Census Bureau also assumes that fertility remains constant for current high fertility populations (i.e., Hispanic TFR of 3.0 and Black TFR of 2.4), and that White fertility will rise from a current TFR of 2.0 to 2.2. Edmonston and Passel posit differential fertility levels by generation (their projections incorporate generations for each ethnic population), converging towards replacement-level fertility over time and across all populations. The NRC projections accepted most of the Bureau of the Census assumptions for current fertility, but used a generational model (with current data on fertility by generation) to project future fertility (Smith and Edmonston 1997:86). The most important difference is that lower second- and third-generation Hispanic fertility is projected to result in a lower overall Hispanic TFR of 2.6 in 2050 in the NAS series compared to the Census Bureau's assumption of a constant Hispanic TFR of 3.0 for the entire period (see also Swicegood and Morgan, page 99).

Although the variations in assumptions in fertility and mortality matter, especially for the absolute size of the future population, the most important demographic component determining the future ethnic composition of the population is international migration. Immigration has a disproportionate impact on future estimates of the Asian and Hispanic populations. Similar to the problem of local area projections, for which internal migration is the great unknown, estimates of future levels of international migration are dependent on unforeseeable economic forces and the very unpredictable political context that shapes immigration law.

In spite of the great uncertainty about the future course of immigration to the United States, the assumptions about international migration are very similar in the Bureau of the Census, NAS, and Edmonston/ Passel projections. The Census Bureau (middle series) and NAS middle assumption is of 820,000 net annual immigrants for the indefinite future (Day, 1996:2; Smith and Edmonston, 1997:88–89). Edmonston and Passel assume a current level of 900,000 net annual immigrants rising to 950,000 in the year 2005 (Edmonston and Passel, 1994). The similarity of these extrapolations is because all of them draw upon the recent patterns of international migration.

The "middle" net-immigration assumption of 820,000 migrants per year in the Census Bureau's projections is actually the composite of a series of specific flows, including 685,000 legal immigrants, 115,000 refugees, 225,000 undocumented immigrants, 5,000 migrants from Puerto Rico, 10,000 civilian citizen arrivals, and 220,000 emigrants (Day, 1996:28). Edmonston and Passel project annual levels of 855,000 legal immigrants, 200,000 net undocumented immigrants, 70,000 Puerto Rican and other civilian arrivals, and 175,000 annual emigrants (Edmonston and Passel, 1994). The assumption of continued high immigration from Latin American and Asia is reflected in the predicted ethnic composition of immigration: 42% Hispanic and 28% Asian of annual net immigration in the Census Bureau series, and 42% Hispanic and 32% Asian in the Edmonston and Passel series (Day, 1996:2; Edmonston and Passel, 1994).

The similarities in these two series should not, in my opinion, be the basis of confidence in the projected levels of future international migration. The estimates of future net immigration are simply the latest data projected forward. For the short run, 5 years or so, this is likely to be close to the mark. Beyond that, however, there is no way to predict how immigration laws will be changed and what impact they will have. There have been several major overhauls in immigration and refugee policy since the landmark reforms in 1965. At any point in the last 35 years, the absolute levels of immigration and the projections based on those levels would have been radically different than those contained in the recent projections. For example, the Census Bureau's latest projections assume future net annual immigration to be 820,000, an increase of 76% over the assumption of 500,000 per year made only a few years earlier.

History as a Testing Ground for Ethnic Population Projections

For ethnic population projections to be useful, two essential attributes have to be met: first, there must be good data on the components of future growth; and second, the assumption of ethnic categories as ascriptively defined populations must be valid. One possibility to evaluate the latter assumption is to look at history, where the logic of the population-balancing equation can control the former. If the initial and final populations are available from Census data and the components of population growth can be measured from independent sources, then we can compare discrepancies between the expected and enumerated populations based on the logic of the population-balancing equation identity—the population at time two equals population at time one plus births, minus deaths, plus net migrants.

A fundamental problem is, however, the inconsistent measurement of ethnicity in different censuses. For example, the definition and measurement of the Hispanic and Asian populations have varied considerably across censuses. Nor are data on the components of population growth available by ethnic groups except for the most recent period. There are two recent studies, however, that are worthy of close examination. In one study, the components of population growth for racial groups and the Hispanic population are estimated, but without the possibility of ethnic change (except by natural increase and immigration). The other study estimates ethnic change from any source (not limited to natural increase and immigration), but only for White ethnic groups.

Based on heroic efforts to piece together partial data and iterative estimation methods, Passel and Edmonston (1994) have estimated the relative contributions of immigration and natural increase for the five major race/ethnic populations (non-Hispanic White, Black, Hispanic, Asian, and American Indian), by generational status, from 1900 to 1990. Although their methodology precludes any residual of population change that might question the assumption that race/ethnic categories are fully ascriptive populations (thereby closed to intermarriage and changes in ethnic identity), the results are very instructive.

Passel and Edmonston estimate the contribution of immigration to the growth of the American population over the Twentieth century and to changes in the contemporary ethnic balance (1994). The U.S. population is 30% larger in 1990 than it would have been without immigration (including immigrants and the descendants of immigrants) from 1900 to 1990. Over this period (1900 to 1990), 60% of the increase attributable to immigration has consisted of additions to the non-Hispanic White population. Only in the years from 1970 to 1990 has immigration from Latin America and Asia led to increases in the proportions of Asians and Hispanics and a modest decrease in the relative proportion of the White population. In sum, international migration has, until very recently, had a significant impact on the ethnic balance in the United States.[2] The population fraction of non-Hispanic Whites was 75% in 1990—only slightly below what it would have been had all immigration ceased after 1900 (81%) or after 1970 (80%) (Passel and Edmonston, 1994).

In their study, Passel and Edmonston assumed fixed ethnic boundaries. A paper by Hout and Goldstein (1994) provides a strong challenge to this assumption, at least for the case of White ethnic groups. Hout and

Goldstein compared the "expected" 1980 population of four White ethnic populations (English, Irish, German, and Italian) to the number of persons who identified with that ancestry group in the 1980 Census. The expected 1980 populations were created as a function of initial size, immigration, length of time since arrival, and net reproduction rates. The expected numbers were further adjusted for differential fertility and weighted so that the total expected population agreed with the enumerated Census population. Differences between expected and Census ethnic populations can be interpreted as primarily due to selective ethnic identification among those who are the descendants of mixed (intermarried) ancestry.

The single largest difference in Hout and Goldstein's analysis is that twice as many persons (40 million) claim Irish ancestry in the 1980 Census as would be expected (21 million) on the basis of demographic analysis under the assumption of endogamous marriage. This discrepancy is most likely due, according to the authors, to the high rate of intermarriage among the Irish and a very high likelihood of subjective identification with Irish heritage among those with partial Irish ancestry (Hout and Goldstein, 1994:79).

Although the trends among White Americans of European ancestry cannot be glibly generalized to racial/ethnic groups with differing phenotypic characteristics, the implications are potentially significant. The present-day definition of "races" was cast much wider only a few decades ago. Assumptions about the differing biological capacities and temperaments between the races of Europe (especially for those from Eastern and Southern Europe) were widely accepted by many, if not most, educated persons for the first half of the Twentieth century. If these ethnic divisions proved to be porous, in spite of the stigma of "crossing," then perhaps contemporary race barriers may appear to be so in the future.

Patterns of Ethnic Intermarriage

The first crack in the assumption of closed ethnic populations is intermarriage. While intermarriage does not necessarily directly change ethnic identity (although it may), the classification of children of interethnic marriages is uncertain. Although small departures from the assumption of a closed population (closed to intermarriage) might not invalidate future projections, high levels of intermarriage would undermine the logic of mutually exclusive population categories.

Almost all population projections assume "one sex reproduction," that is, future births are a function of assumed fertility rates multiplied times the number of women in the reproductive years. Although this method ignores men, there is not an inevitable bias in the estimation of future births. With a significant degree of intermarriage, however, the numbers of intermarried persons, their fertility, and the assignment of ethnicity of their progeny are new factors to be considered in the accounting methods of population projections. An historical perspective provides some basis to evaluate this question (Kalmijin, 1998; Shinagawa and Pang, 1996).

A relevant case for our present discussion is the change in intermarriage patterns among white ethnics in the United States over the Twentieth century. Based on data from the 1910 U.S. Population Census and a sample of New York City marriage license records for 1908–1912, Pagnini and Morgan (1990) analyzed the incidence of ethnic intermarriage among immigrants and other populations at the turn of the century. They reported almost complete endogamy within nationality and generation categories. This finding coincided with the conventional wisdom of the era, namely, that the "new" immigrant groups from Eastern and Southern Europe were unlikely to assimilate fully into American society. Population projections of European ethnic groups would have seemed like an entirely reasonable activity.

Two to three generations later, it is difficult to find any evidence of ethnic endogamy among White ethnics in the United States. The research of Lieberson and Waters (1988) based on the 1980 Census and of Alba and his colleagues (Alba and Golden, 1986; Alba, 1990) based on survey data show widespread ethnic intermarriage among White Americans with most respondents reporting multiethnic ancestry. The results of Hout and Goldstein (1994) show that demographic methods of forward estimation (when the components of growth can be directly measured) of White ethnic populations led to major inconsistencies with contemporary counts. The problem is, of course, that high levels of ethnic intermarriage have made ethnic identity an option for Whites rather than an ascribed status (Waters, 1990).

The historical experiences of White ethnic groups do not necessarily predict that the same patterns will hold for racial groups and Hispanics. Recent research, however, does show significant levels and rising trends of intermarriage patterns for Asian Americans (Kitano, Yeung, Chai, and Hatanaka, 1984; Sung, 1990; Wong, 1989), Mexican Americans (Murguia and Frisbie, 1977; Cazares, Murguia, and Frisbie, 1984), and American Indians (Sandefur, 1986; Eschbach, 1995).

According to the 1990 Census, 31% of Hispanic-origin couples (classified by the race/ethnicity of the female spouse or partner) are intermarried (Harrison and Bennett, 1995:166). Intermarriage is at about the same level for Asian Americans, and even higher for American Indians (Harrison and Bennett 1995:166). Although the number of Black–White marriages has historically been much lower, there has been an upward trend over the last 30 years. The percentage of Black intermarried couples rose from 3.8% in 1980 to 6.3% in 1990 (Harrison and Bennett 1995:166, see also Kalmijin, 1993; Stevens and Tyler, page 221).

These figures call into question the assumption of universal ethnic homogamy in the conventional race and ethnic population projections prepared by the Bureau of the Census. Indeed, the recent population projections prepared by the National Research Council (NRC) include explicit assumptions of intermarriage by generation in order to project race and ethnic populations. The NRC estimates of exogamy (based on census and birth statistics data) are shown in Table 2.1.

Table 2.1
Estimates of Exogamy Rates by Ethnic Group and Immigrant Generation, 1995-2050 by the National Research Council Panel on the Demographic and Economic Impacts of Immigration

	IMMIGRANT GENERATION			
Race/Ethnicity	*First*	*Second*	*Third*	*Fourth or More*
White	0.10	0.09	0.08	0.08
Asian	0.13	0.34	0.54	0.54
Black	0.14	0.12	0.10	0.10
Hispanic	0.08	0.32	0.57	0.57

Source: Smith and Edmonston 1997: 132.

These projected levels of intermarriage create a wide band of uncertainty around any future population projections by race and ethnic groups. If the history of interethnic marriage among Whites is any guide, current levels of interracial marriage will rise even further in the future. In addition to increasingly liberal attitudes toward intermarriage, the significant pool of persons with mixed ethnic ancestry changes the social environment for intermarriage. Not only does the decrease in the proportion of the population with "pure" ethic ancestry create fewer options for marriage solely within their ethnic community, but it also exposes the myth of universal endogamy. For some groups (e.g., American Indians and Hawaiians) the majority of persons in the community are of mixed ancestry, and there is no stigma attached to intermarriage.

The Uncertainty of Ethnic Identity

The race and ethnic classifications used in the Census and the federal statistical system are socially constructed composites that have arisen from a variety of historical and contemporary influences (Waters, page 25; Snipp, 1989, chapter II). Although the central variable of "race" has been included since the first U.S. Census in 1790, the categories used in the Census racial classification have changed over the years, as have the methods of measurement (from interviewer assignment to respondent's choice). In the 1980 Census, several Asian nationality groups were added as race categories, and in 1990, a new format and instructions were used for the Census race question (U.S. Bureau of the Census 1990; for a summary of changes in the measurement of race in earlier censuses, see U.S. Bureau of the Census 1975:3–4). In the year 2000, the census allowed multiple responses on the race question (Office of Management and Budget, 1997a; 1997b) and 2.4% of the population chose more than one race (U.S. Bureau of the Census, 2001).

The conventional practice by most users of census data is to accept the race categories as given, and then to assign ethnicity within (or in addition to) race groups with other variables such as birthplace, parental birthplace, and mother tongue (or current language). Because these other variables were only indirect signals of ethnic attachments and because there was thought to be an important public need to know the "true" numbers (and characteristics) of the population by race and ethnicity, there has been pressure from ethnic groups to add direct questions on ethnicity in the Census. In 1970, a new Census question on Hispanic origin was added, and in 1980, a new question on ancestry was added. The latter question was added, however, with the deletion of the long-standing Census question on birthplace of the respondent's father and mother. This wealth of new data has stimulated considerable research and new thinking about the measurement and meaning of race and ethnicity in the United States (Lieberson and Waters, 1988; Lott, 1998). One of the unanticipated findings from the first wave of research with multiple measures of race and ethnicity was the inconsistency of responses and the difficulty of assuming that one dimension can be inferred from another (Farley, 1991; Hirschman, 1983; Lieberson and Santi, 1985; Levin and Farley, 1982).

Theoretical ambiguity may be the normal state of scholarship, but it is much more difficult to allow inconsistency in the measurement of official statistical data. Census data (and other statistical sources) are used to allocate federal funds and to inform public policy. To try to minimize some of the uncertainty and confusion about race and ethnic categories, the Office of Federal Statistics Policy and Standards in the Office of Management and Budget (OMB) issued Statistical Directive 15 on "Race and Ethnic Standards for Federal Statistics and Administrative Reporting" in 1978 (see Waters, page 27 and Office of Management and Budget, 1995).

Statistical Directive 15 recognized two race/ethnic dimensions for data collection and reporting by government agencies: Race (defined as four groups: American Indian/Alaska Native, Asian/Pacific Islander, Black, and

White) and Hispanic/non-Hispanic origin. The rules for data collection (and presentation) allow for either independent or overlapping measurement of these two dimensions. For example, government data could have two questions (or tables), one for race (with the four populations mentioned above or more detailed categories that can be collapsed into these four) and another for Hispanic-origin (this item may also be measured with more detailed categories, e.g., Mexican, Puerto Rican, Cuban, Other Hispanic/Latino). The decennial Census includes both a race question and a Hispanic-origin question. The other acceptable format under OMB Statistical Directive 15 combines these two dimensions into five mutually exclusive categories with a Hispanic-origin category that includes persons of all racial groups, and the non-Hispanic population subdivided by the four race categories.

In spite of a valiant effort to standardize data collection on race and ethnicity, the implementation of OMB's Statistical Directive 15 has faced continual problems. Even if there were no conceptual problems or political considerations, it is not an easy task to explain the logic and nuanced reasoning that lies behind the seemingly arbitrary definitions in the OMB race and ethnic classifications and the appropriate methods for data collection and presentation. The root problems are, however, much deeper. Ethnic identities are in flux in contemporary America, and it is difficult, if not impossible, to make assumptions about fixed identities and stable boundaries that are the bases of statistical measurement. There are a growing number of loose threads that threaten to unravel the conceptualization and measurement of both "race" and the combined race/ethnic categories in the OMB scheme (Perlmann, 1997).

The growing uneasiness with the current methods of measuring race and ethnicity was reflected in two conferences. In April 1992, the Census Bureau and Statistics Canada convened a conference to re-examine the measurement of race and ethnicity in censuses (Statistics Canada and U.S. Bureau of the Census, 1993). In February 1994, the Committee on National Statistics of the National Research Council, at the request of the OMB, held a workshop to evaluate the race and ethnic classifications in Statistical Directive 15 (Edmonston et al., 1996). The papers and discussions at these conferences have clarified the statistical problems, the social dilemmas, and the political concerns that affect the measurement of race and ethnic categories. Many of these issues are also addressed in the report of the Interagency Committee for the Review of the Racial and Ethnic Standards to the Office of Management and Budget (Office of Management and Budget, 1997a, Appendix 2)

The statistical problems of measurement are evident in nonresponse to some questions and the reliability of responses. In the 1990 Census, the allocations for nonresponse were 2.7% for the race question (up from 1.5% in 1980) and 10% for the Hispanic-origin item (up from 3.5% in 1980) (McKenney and Cresce, 1993:208–210).[3] About 5.5% checked the "other race" category in the

2000 Census (up from 3.0% in 1980 and 3.9% in 1990). Most of the "other race" responses are persons of Hispanic origin. Rodriguez (1992) argues that Latinos do not misunderstand the Census race categories, but that the Census categories do not reflect Latin American conceptualization of race and ethnicity. The U.S. system of mutually exclusive White or Black categories (with nothing in-between) does not provide meaningful options for many Latinos (for a historical discussion of the development of the concept of race, see Harris, 1968).

For most White Americans, the ties to ethnic identity are fairly tenuous. About 15%–16% of the population responds with "American" or leaves the line blank when asked about their ancestry in the 1980 and 1990 Censuses. The number of persons reporting English ancestry declined from 50 to 33 million, and the number reporting German rose from 49 to 58 million from 1980 to 1990—most likely in response to the examples listed on the census form (McKenney and Cresce 1993:213). In a study of the meaning of ethnicity based upon in-depth interviews among a sample of Catholic Americans, Waters (1990) reported that many respondents seem to select an ethnic identity for idiosyncratic reasons from among the several choices offered by the national origins of their ancestors. Although the volitional nature of ethnic identity of Whites cannot be generalized to the experiences of minorities for whom "racial" identity is imposed by others, there is a significant number of persons of Hispanic descent and of other mixed ancestry for whom neither appearance nor cultural behavior provides recognizable cues for ethnic recognition.

There are other challenges to the legitimacy of the current Census and OMB classifications. The most basic problem is the internal logic in the construction of ethnic categories. The American Indian/Native American category is thought to represent descendants of indigenous peoples of the United States, but until 2000 native Hawaiians and indigenous peoples of American territories in the Pacific were grouped with Asians and Pacific Islanders. It is not clear where descendants of indigenous peoples of Central and South America (who do not speak Spanish) should be classified since they are not natives of North America and are not of Hispanic origin.

One of the most perplexing questions is how to handle persons of mixed ancestry. The traditional convention of including all persons of any African ancestry (the "one drop rule") in the Black/African American population reflects the legacy of racism. There are a significant number of persons who are both Black and Hispanic (a smaller number of persons of Asian and American Indian origin who also have a Hispanic identity). Individual self-identity and perception/treatment by others are not always the same for persons of mixed ancestry.

In the 1980s, a social movement emerged that attempted to create a new statistical category of "multiracial" for use in the census and in all government forms that collect race and ethnicity data. Concerned parents of children with a mixed racial heritage feel that the current system of mutually exclusive race categories lowers the self-esteem of their children who do not fit into any of the existing categories (Office of Management and Budget, 1997a: 36880; Edmonston et al., 1996). Some school districts have created a multiracial category for local statistical records, and several state legislatures also approved adding a multiracial category to all statistical forms that ask for race and ethnic data. The number of children in interracial families has increased from less than 500,000 in 1970 to more than 2 million in 1990 (U. S. Bureau of the Census, 1997:2-1).

Another element in the current negotiation over race and ethnic measurement is the political interests of the groups themselves (Peterson, 1997). In the political arithmetic of our multicultural society, greater numbers mean greater visibility and weight in both informal and formal politics. The addition of a sample question on Hispanic origin in the 1970 Census and its movement to a 100% question in the 1980 Census reflect the political awareness of the Hispanic community (Choldin, 1986). The politics of modifying census practices to enlarge the numbers of some ethnic groups is not at all new; Dudley Kirk reports that many European censuses in the 1920s and 1930s were adjusted with this aim in mind (Kirk, 1946, cited in Lieberson, 1993).

The interests of stakeholders were clearly apparent in the planning of the race and ethnic questions in the 1990 Census (U.S. Bureau of the Census, 1990). In the mid-1980s, there were discussions about whether and how the Census Bureau should modify the race, Hispanic origin, and ancestry questions for the 1990 Census. Plans and pretesting of alternative questions were undertaken with advice from Interagency Working Groups, Open Public Hearings, and a large number of Census Advisory Committees (including advisory committees representing the concerns of the American Indian and Alaska Native, Asian and Pacific Islander, Black, and Hispanic communities). Although there was a proposal to combine the race and ethnic questions, the final recommendation was to keep separate race and Hispanic-origin questions because it "could result in the undercount of certain racial groups and the Hispanic origin population" (among other reasons) (U.S. Bureau of the Census, 1990:5).

In spite of the extensive review process and testing of a variety of alternatives, the final race question in the 1990 Census was revised at almost the last minute (late 1988) to add specific Asian and Pacific Islander populations as categories that could be checked-off (instead of listing a global API category and asking respondents to write in specific populations) (U.S. Bureau of the Census, 1990:15). The objective of the representatives of the Asian American community and their congressional representatives was to insure that the count of Asians was not diminished by the omission of the list of specific Asian groups on the Census form. Historical precedent was on the side of the Asian American community; Japanese and Chinese have been included as categories in the Census race question for over 100 years. In other contexts, however, the political effort to include nine Asian and Pacific Islander "nationality" groups (Chinese, Filipino, Hawaiian, Korean, Vietnamese, Japanese, Asian Indian, Samoan, Guamanian, and others) as "races" would have seemed absurd, if not offensive. For many persons, there is no clear or "correct" response to the Census race question (e.g., a Vietnamese immigrant of Chinese heritage). The subjective nature of responses to the Census means that individuals can choose whatever categories they want, but the ambiguity of ethnic identity and measurement is causing increasing concern for those who collect and interpret the nation's statistics.

The one community with less interest in maximizing numbers is the American Indian community. Entitlement programs operated by the Bureau of Indian Affairs require tribal affiliation for eligibility. If the substantial number of persons who claim American Indian ancestry were to become eligible for these entitlements, there may well be fewer resources for the members of currently recognized tribes. In the 1990 Census, 1.96 million persons identified themselves as American Indians, Eskimo, or Aleut in the race question, but 8.7 million persons considered themselves to have American Indian ancestry. In the final recommendations for the revision of Statistical Directive No. 15, OMB decided leave "American Indian or Alaska Native," as one major category and to create a new major category for "Native Hawaiian or Other Pacific Islander" (Office of Management and Budget, 1997b).

Early results from the 2000 Census also bear out the argument of complexity and fluidity in choosing race. The number of people who chose only "American Indian and Alaska Native" rose to 2.5 million and almost 400,000 identified only with the new "Native Hawaiian or Other Pacific Islander" category. Of the 2.4% of the total population who chose more than one race, 93% chose two and another 6% chose three, so almost no multiracial people identify with more than three races. Almost one third (32.3%) of the population who chose more than one race chose the category "White and Some other race," a group that is 58.8% Hispanic. The only other combinations of races that accounted for more than 10% are "White and American Indian/Alaska Native" (15.9%), "White and Asian" (12.7%) and "White and Black or African American" (11.5%), with the combination "Black and Some other race" (6.1%) the only combination chosen by more than 5%. (U.S. Bureau of the Census, 2001). Analyses comparing answers to the race question to the ancestry question, as well as comparisons of different family members racial choices cannot be done until more data are released.

It is difficult to contend that the populations defined by race and ethnicity in the Census or in OMB's Statistical Directive 15 (original or revised) can be considered as ascriptively defined. The statistical problems that confound measurement and the political processes that surround definition and data collection of race and ethnic groups reflect the underlying problems of porous boundaries and indeterminateness of ethnic identity for a growing number of Americans.

Race and Ethnic Projections with Uncertainty

With an awareness of many of these issues, the National Research Council Panel on the Demographic and Economic Impacts of Immigration produced population projections by race and ethnicity to the year 2050 that incorporated current levels of intermarriage, variations in ethnic attribution, and variations in international migration (Smith and Edmonston 1997, Chapter 3). Ethnic attribution is the likelihood that children from interracial marriages will choose to identify with one group or another. Based on the race/ethnicity of the children in mixed marriages (presumably assigned by a parent) from the 1990 Census, ethnic attribution ranged from a low of 0.39 of Asian race/ethnicity for children with one Asian parent to a high of 0.64 attribution of Hispanic origin for children with one Hispanic parent (Smith and Edmonston, 1997:133).

Simply allowing for variations in ethnic attribution (holding international migration and intermarriage to current levels), the potential number of Whites in 2050 ranged from 175 to 220 million, the number of Blacks from 43 to 59 million, the number of Asians from 23 to 43 million, and the number of Hispanics from 64 to 114 million (Smith and Edmonston, 1997:133). This is just one of several potential sources of uncertainty in population projections by race and ethnicity. Significant variations in intermarriage and international migration could also have major effects that would rival those of ethnic attribution (as could fertility and mortality differentials).

Perhaps the greatest uncertainty arises from the assumption that persons will consider themselves (and be considered by others) to be one (and only one) of our current race and ethnic categories. With a growing number of persons with complex race ancestries, this seems most unlikely. Just as many Whites claim to multiple ethnic ancestries at the present time (or just to be an "American" without any ethnic identity), the progeny of interracial marriages may not wish to be fit into a single category. The official recognition that persons can check more than one race in the 2000 Census is likely to accelerate this process.

Discussion and Conclusions

Two decades ago, there was widespread concern that excessive population growth was the major demographic problem confronting the United

States. As fertility rates have declined, the issue of population growth has moved to the back burner of national concerns. Other population issues, including the aging of the population, changes in family structure and adolescent fertility, and the continuing exodus of the middle class from the cities, are topics that have kept demographic research on the front pages of national attention and policy concerns. None of these topics, however, has rivaled the interest and controversy generated by another demographic process—immigration (Chiswick and Sullivan, 1995). The new immigration flows of the 1970s and 1980s have fed into the political debates of the 1990s. Even with frequent platitudes that the United States is a nation of immigrants, the political reality is that taking a hard stand against immigrants can be very popular with some segments of the American population.

What contribution can demographic scholarship make to the policy concerns and political debates over immigration? One small step is to evaluate the demographic implications of future immigration with population projections. These exercises can be very useful. Population projection models show that moderate levels of immigration in the coming years will postpone the arrival of negative population growth, will lead to a somewhat higher eventual population size, and will mitigate the inevitable trend to a much higher ratio of the elderly-dependent population to the working-age population. Although the precise levels of future immigration cannot be known, it is clearly useful to know the directions of change in these important demographic dimensions.

One seemingly logical extension of the population projection exercise is to estimate the future population by race and ethnic groups. Ethnic divisions are clearly one of the most salient dimensions of American society. Moreover, it is clear that contemporary immigration from Latin America and Asia will increase ethnic diversity in the coming years. There are two serious problems, however, with this logical exercise. First, the critical assumption of race and ethnic groups as ascriptively-defined populations with fixed boundaries is a very tenuous one and is likely to become an even more tenuous assumption for the future. The second issue is that race and ethnic population projections are being used, without careful thought or reflection, as firm demographic evidence to show that American society and culture are being threatened by continued immigration. These claims rest on very dubious assumptions.

With intermarriage rates of Hispanics, American Indians, and Asians with others (primarily Whites) running from 25% to 50%, it seems clear that the future of American ethnicity will not be one of separate communities with differing languages, cultures, and rivalries. Although at much lower levels for other groups, the apparent doubling of the Black–White intermarriage rate from 1980 to 1990 may be a harbinger that even the widest racial fault line in America is not immutable. It these trends continue, the growing density of interethnic familial ties and the increasing number of children of mixed ancestry will surely weaken traditional racial and ethnic divisions in the United States.

The growing problems of defining and measuring race and ethnicity in recent censuses, and the intense political efforts to change (or maintain) ethnic categories reveal the profound flux in ethnic identities that has been created by recent trends in intermarriage. If the experiences of Southern and Eastern European groups in the first half of the Twentieth century are any guide, then the coming decades will see an exponential increase in ethnic intermarriage and shifts in ethnic identity. Population projections that rely on the conventional criteria of race and ethnic measurement will be increasingly anachronistic.

The use of race and ethnic population projections in the political debate over immigration can be best illustrated with an examination of Leon Bouvier's book entitled, *Peaceful Invasions: Immigration and Changing America* (1992). Although Bouvier uses demographic projections of the population by race and ethnicity to argue the threat of continued immigration, he is careful to reject the racist fears and metaphors that are sometimes used by others in the anti-immigration camp. Precisely because Bouvier's book is so reasonably written and relies on demographic logic and methods, it is certain to be seen as a scholarly and detached statement that will be widely used in the political debates over immigration policy and the implications for American society.

Although the future ethnic composition projected by Bouvier is fairly similar to that projected by the Census Bureau, the underlying assumptions are almost invariably selected to show more rapid growth of minorities, especially the Hispanic population. On the volatile issue of net illegal immigration, Bouvier says (without any citation), "While guesses range from 100,000 to 1 million per year, more reasonable estimates lie in the vicinity of 300,000 to 500,000 per year" (p. 19). Both the Census Bureau and the Edmonston and Passel projections use figures of 200,000 to 225,000 per year—which are much closer to the estimates conducted by the most careful demographic research on the topic (Warren and Passel, 1987; Woodrow, 1992). On the possibility of intermarriage among persons from Latin America and Asia, he reports an increasing trend, but that "they remain a relatively rare occurrence" (p. 115) even though this statement is footnoted to a reference that notes more than one-third of the marriages of third-generation Japanese Americans are with Whites.

Beyond the technical limitations of his projections and the assumption of continued ethnic endogamy, Bouvier's discussion is colored by his frequent expressions of the potential problems created by too many of "them." Consider the following statements:

> "Immigrants today are mostly young Latinos and Asians who settle in major cities, especially in California, New York, and Texas. If current demographic trends continue, within 25 years Anglos would no longer be the majority

population in these states and by 2060 the Anglo population would become
a minority in the United States. The United States would then be the only
industrial nation with no ethnic majority (p. 5),"

and

"If the United States truly were a color-blind society, changes in ethnic composition would be of little consequence. Unfortunately that is not the case.
Minorities and most of the newest immigrants are disproportionately represented in the nation's lower class (p. 40)."

Bouvier is not alone in his thinking that continued immigration and the growing diversity of the U. S. population is one of the major demographic problems
confronting the country. I suspect that many White Americans share these sentiments and that some political leaders will exploit their fears in the coming
years. This would not be an entirely new political phenomenon. The anti-
immigrant movements that led to the Chinese Exclusion Act of 1882 and the
immigration legislation of the 1920s that established national-origin quotas
were based on similar fears. The potential for such a similar backlash against
contemporary immigrants is a serious political problem for American society.
There is, however, very little reliable evidence that would support strong
claims about future changes in the ethnic composition of the American population. If the experience of the Twentieth century suggests anything, it is that
future generations of Americans are likely to have quite different notions of
race and ethnicity than those at present.

Notes

1. The projections are produced by race (White, Black, American Indian,
and Asian) and also for the Hispanic (who may be of any race) and the non-Hispanic
(subdivided by race) populations.

2. Immigration from Europe in the Nineteenth century led to an increase in
the relative proportion of Whites and a diminution of the relative numbers of African
Americans and American Indians.

3. The allocation for the sample questionnaire was less. There was a cutback
in funding for the 1990 Census that limited field follow-up for the short-form questionnaires (McKenney and Cresce, 1993:185).

References

Alba, Richard D. 1990. *Ethnic Identity: The Transformation of White America.* New Haven: Yale University Press.

Alba, Richard D. and R.M. Golden. 1986. "Patterns of Ethnic Marriage in the United States." *Social Forces,* 65:202–223.

Bouvier, Leon F. 1992. *Peaceful Invasions: Immigration and Changing America.* Lanham: University Press of America.

Cazares, Ralph B., Edward Murguia, and W. Parker Frisbie. 1984. "Mexican American Intermarriage in a Nonmetropolitan Context." *Social Science Quarterly,* 65:626–634.

Chiswick, Barry and Teresa Sullivan. 1995. "The New Immigrants." In Reynolds Farley, ed., *State of the Union: America in the 1990s,* vol. 2:211–270. New York: Russell Sage.

Choldin, Harvey M. 1986. "Statistics and Politics: The 'Hispanic Issue' in the 1980 Census." *Demography,* 23:403–418.

Day, Jennifer Cheeseman. 1996. *Population Projections of the United States, by Age, Sex, Race, and Hispanic Origin: 1995 to 2050, Current Population Reports, Series P25-1130.* Washington, DC: U.S. Government Printing Office.

Edmonston, Barry and Jeffrey S. Passel. 1992. "Immigration and Immigrant Generations in Population Projections." *International Journal of Forecasting,* 8:459–476.

Edmonston, Barry and Jeffrey S. Passel. 1994. "The Future Immigrant Population of the United States." In Barry Edmonston and Jeffrey S. Passel, eds., *Immigration and Ethnicity: The Integration of America's Newest Arrivals,* pp. 317–353. Washington, DC: The Urban Institute Press.

Edmonston, Barry, Joshua Goldstein, and Juanita T. Lott, eds. 1996. *Spotlight on Heterogeneity: The Federal Standards for Racial and Ethnic Classification Summary of a Workshop.* Washington, DC: National Academy Press.

Eschbach, Karl. 1995. "The Enduring and Vanishing American Indian." *Ethnic and Racial Studies,* 18:89–108.

Farley, Reynolds. 1991. "The New Census Question About Ancestry: What Did it Tell Us?" *Demography,* 28:411–430.

Harris, Marvin. 1968. "Race." In David L. Sills, ed., *International Encyclopedia of the Social Sciences,* vol. 13, New York: The Macmillan Company and the Free Press, pp. 263–268.

Harrison, Roderick and Claudette Bennett. 1995. "Racial and Ethnic Diversity" In Reynolds Farley, ed., *State of the Union: America in the 1990's Volume Two: Social Trends*. New York: Russell Sage Foundation, pp. 141–210.

Hirschman, Charles. 1983. "The Melting Pot Reconsidered." *Annual Review of Sociology*, 9:397–423.

Hout, Michael and Joshua R. Goldstein. 1994. "How 4.5 Million Irish Immigrants Became 40 Million Irish Americans: Demographic and Subjective Aspects of the Ethnic Composition of White Americans." *American Sociological Review*, 59:64–82.

Kalmijin, Matthijs. 1993. "Trends in Black/White Intermarriage." *Social Forces* 72: 119-146.

Kalmijin, Matthijs. 1998. "Intermarriage and Homogamy: Causes, Patterns, and Trends." *Annual Review of Sociology*, 24:395–421.

Kirk, Dudley. 1946. *Europe's Population in the Interwar Years*. League of Nations.

Kitano, Harry H.L., Wai-Tsang Yeung, Lynn Chai, and Herbert Hatanaka. 1984. "Asian-American Interracial Marriage." *Journal of Marriage and the Family*, 46:179–190.

Levin, Michael J. and Reynolds Farley. 1982. "Historical Comparability of Ethnic Designations in the United States." *Proceedings of the American Statistical Association 1982 Social Statistics Section*, pp. 4–14. Washington, D.C.: American Statistical Association.

Lieberson, Stanley. 1993. "The Enumeration of Ethnic and Racial Groups in the Census: Some Devilish Principles." In Statistics Canada and U.S. Bureau of the Census. 1993. *Challenges of Measuring an Ethnic World: Science, Politics, and Reality*, pp. 23–35. Washington, DC: U.S. Government Printing Office.

Lieberson, Stanley and Lawrence Santi. 1985. "The Use of Nativity Data to Estimate Ethnic Characteristics and Patterns." *Social Science Research*, 14:31–46.

Lieberson, Stanley and Mary Waters. 1988. *From Many Strands: Ethnic and Racial Groups in Contemporary America*. New York: Russell Sage.

Lott, Juanita Tamayo. 1998. *Asian Americans: From Racial Categories to Multiple Identities*. Walnut Creek, CA: Altamira Press.

McKenney, Nampeo R. and Arthur R. Cresce. 1993. "Measurement of Ethnicity in the United States: Experiences of the U.S. Bureau of the Census." In Statistics Canada and U.S. Bureau of the Census, *Challenges of Measuring an Ethnic World: Science, Politics, and Reality*, pp. 173–221. Washington, DC: U.S. Government Printing Office.

Murguia, Edward and W. Parker Frisbie. 1977. "Trends in Mexican American Intermarriage: Recent Findings in Perspective." *Social Science Quarterly*, 58:374–389.

Office of Management and Budget. 1995. Standards for the Classification of Federal Data on Race and Ethnicity. *Federal Register*, vol. 60, no. 166, August 28, 1995/Notices, pp. 44674–44693.

Office of Management and Budget. 1997a. "Recommendations from the Interagency Committee for the Review of the Race and Ethnic Standards to the Office of Management and Budget Concerning Changes to the Standards for the Classification of Federal Data on Race and Ethnicity." *Federal Register*, vol. 62, no. 131, Wednesday, July 9, 1997/Notices, pp. 36874–36946.

Office of Management and Budget. 1997b. "Revisions to the Standards for the Classification of Federal Data on Race and Ethnicity." *Federal Register*. vol. 62, no. 210, Thursday, October 30, 1997/Notices, pp. 58782–58790.

Pagnini, Deanna and S. Philip Morgan. 1990. "Intermarriage and Social Distance Among U.S. Immigrants at the Turn of the Century." *American Journal of Sociology,* 96:405–432.

Passel, Jeffrey S. and Barry Edmonston. 1994. "Immigration and Race: Recent Trends in Immigration to the United States." In Barry Edmonston and Jeffrey S. Passel, eds., *Immigration and Ethnicity: The Integration of America's Newest Arrivals*, pp. 31–71. Washington, DC: The Urban Institute Press.

Perlmann, Joel. 1997. *Reflecting on the Changing Face of America: Multiracials, Racial Clasification, and American Intermarriage*. Public Policy Brief no. 35. The Jerome Levy Economics Institute of Bard College, Annandale-on-Hudson, NY.

Petersen, William. 1997. *Ethnicity Counts*. New Brunswick, NJ: Transaction Publishers.

Preston, Samuel H. 1993. "Demographic Change in the United States, 1970–2050." In Kenneth G. Manton, Burton H. Singer, and Richard M. Suzman, eds., *Forecasting the Health of Elderly Populations*, pp. 51–77. New York: Springer-Verlag.

Rodriguez, Clara E. 1992. "Race, Culture, and Latino 'Otherness' in the 1980 Census." *Social Science Quarterly,* 73:930–937.

Sandefur, Gary. 1986. "American Indian Intermarriage." *Social Science Research,* 15:347–371.

Schnore, Leo F. 1961. "Social Mobility in Demographic Perspective." *American Sociological Review,* 26:407–423.

Shinagawa, Larry Hajime and Gin Young Pang. 1996. "Asian American Panethnicity and Intermarriage." *Amerasia Journal,* 22:127–152.

Shryock, Henry S. and Jacob S. Siegel. 1971. *The Methods and Materials of Demography*. 2 vols. Washington, DC: U.S. Government Printing Office.

Smith, James P. and Barry Edmonston. 1997. *The New Americans: Economic, Demographic and Fiscal Effects of Immigration*. Washington, DC: National Academy Press.

Snipp, C. Matthew. 1989. *American Indians: The First of the This Land*. New York: Russell Sage.

Statistics Canada and U.S. Bureau of the Census. 1993. *Challenges of Measuring an Ethnic World: Science, Politics, and Reality*. Washington, DC: U.S. Government Printing Office.

Sung, Betty Lee. 1990. "Chinese American Intermarriage." *Journal of Comparative Family Studies*, 21:337–352.

U.S. Bureau of the Census. 1975. *Historical Statistics of the United States, Colonial Times to 1970, Bicentennial Edition, Part 2*. Washington, DC: U.S. Government Printing Office.

U.S. Bureau of the Census. 1990. *Census of Population and Housing (1990), Content Determination Reports, 1990 CDR-6: Race and Ethnic Origin*. Washington, DC: U.S. Government Printing Office.

U.S. Bureau of the Census. 1997. *Results of the 1996 Race and Ethnic Targeted Test*. Population Division Working Paper no. 18. Washington, DC: Bureau of the Census.

Warren, Robert and Jeffrey S. Passel. 1987. "A Count of the Uncountable: Estimates of Undocumented Aliens Counted in the 1980 Census." *Demography*, 24:375–393.

Waters, Mary. 1990. *Ethnic Options: Choosing Identities in America*. Berkeley: University of California Press.

Woodrow, Karen A. 1992. "A Consideration of the Effect of Immigration Reform on the Number of Undocumented Residents in the United States." *Population Research and Policy Review*, 11:117–144.

Wong, Morrison G. 1989. "A Look at Intermarriage among the Chinese in the United States in 1980." *Sociological Perspectives*, 32:87–107.

Part II

Basic Demographic Processes and Diversity

Chapter 3

The New Immigration and Ethnicity in the United States

Douglas S. Massey

As anyone who walks the streets of America's largest cities knows, there has been a profound transformation of immigration to the United States. Not only are there more immigrants, but increasingly they also speak languages and bear cultures that are quite different than those brought by European immigrants in the past. The rapidity of the change and the scale of the movement have led to much consternation about what the "new immigration" means for American society.

Some worry about the economic effects of immigration, although quantitative analyses generally show that immigrants do not compete directly with native workers and do not have strong effects on U.S. wages rates and employment levels (Borjas and Tienda, 1987; Borjas, 1990; Borjas and Freeman, 1992). Others worry about the social welfare burden caused by immigrants, but studies again suggest that, with the exception of some refugee groups, immigrants do not drain public resources (see Blau, 1984; Simon, 1984; Tienda and Jensen, 1986; Borjas, 1994; but Rothman and Espenshade [1992] show that local fiscal effects may be significant). Observers also express fears of linguistic fragmentation, but research indicates that immigrants generally shift into English as time passes and that their children move decisively into English if they grow up in the United States (Grenier, 1984; Stevens, 1985; Veltman, 1988).

Despite this reassuring evidence, however, considerable disquiet remains about the new immigration and its consequences (see Espenshade and Calhoun, 1993). Indeed, an immigrant backlash appears to be gathering force. English-only amendments have passed in several locales; federal immigration law has grown steadily more restrictive and punitive; and politicians have discovered the political advantages that may be gained by blaming immigrants for current social and economic problems. Given the apparent animus toward immigrants and the imperviousness of public perceptions to the influence of research findings, one suspects that deeper forces are at work in the American psyche.

This consternation may have less to do with actual facts about immigration than with unarticulated fears that immigrants will somehow create a very different society and culture in the United States. Whatever objective research says about the prospects for individual assimilation, the ethnic and racial composition of the United States is clearly changing, and with it the sociocultural world created by prior European immigrants and their descendants. According to some demographic projections, European Americans will become a minority in the United States sometime during the next century (Edmonston and Passel, 1991), and this projected shift has already occurred in some urban areas, notably Los Angeles and Miami. In other metropolitan areas, such as New York, Chicago, Houston, and San Diego, the transformation is well under way.

This demographic reality suggests the real nature of the anti-immigrant reaction among non-Hispanic Whites: a fear of cultural change and a deep-seated worry that European Americans will be displaced from their dominant position in American life. Most social scientists have been reluctant to address this issue, or even to acknowledge it (nonacademics, however, are not so reticent—see Lamm and Imhoff, 1985; Brimelow, 1995). As a result, analyses by academic researchers have focused rather narrowly on facts and empirical issues: how many undocumented migrants are there, do they displace native workers, do they drive down wage rates, do they use more in services than they pay in taxes?

Answers to these questions do not get at the heart of the matter, however. What the public really wants to know (at least, I suspect, the native White public) is whether or not the new immigrants will assimilate into the Euro-American society of the United States, and how that society and its culture might change as a result of this incorporation. While social scientists have analyzed the state of the trees, the public has worried about the future of the forest, and no amount of empirical research has quieted these anxieties. In this chapter, I assess the prospects for the assimilation of the new immigrant groups and judge their likely effects on the society, culture, and language of the United States.

I begin by placing the new immigration in historical perspective and pointing out the distinctive features that set it apart from earlier immigrations. I then appraise the structural context for the incorporation of today's immigrants and argue that because of fundamental differences, their assimilation will not be as rapid or complete as that achieved by European immigrants in the past. I conclude by discussing how the nature of ethnicity will change as a result of a new immigration that is linguistically concentrated, geographically clustered, and temporally continuous into an American society that is increasingly stratified and unequal.

The New Immigration in Historical Perspective

The history of U.S. immigration during the twentieth century can be divided roughly into three phases: a **classic era** of mass European immigration stretching from about 1901 to 1930; a **long hiatus** of limited movement from 1931 to 1970; and a **new regime** of large-scale, non-European immigration that began around 1970 and continues to the present. The cutpoints 1930 and 1970 are to some extent arbitrary, of course, but they correspond roughly to major shifts in U.S. immigration policy. The 1924 National Origins Act, which imposed strict country quotas, took full effect in 1929; and the 1965 Amendments to the Immigration and Nationality Act, which repealed those quotas, took effect in 1968 (see Jasso and Rosenzweig, 1990:26–97).

Information on the size and composition of immigrant flows during the three periods is presented in Table 3.1. Actual counts of immigrants by region and decade (the data from which the table was derived) are presented in Table 3.2. In both tables, the figures refer to legal immigrants enumerated upon entry; they do not include undocumented migrants (see Massey and Singer [1995] for recent annual estimates), nor do they adjust for return migration, which studies have been shown to be significant in both the classic era (Wyman, 1993) and during the new regime (Warren and Kraly, 1985; Jasso and Rosenzweig, 1990).

The classic years 1901 to 1930 are actually part of a sustained 50-year period of mass immigration that began some time around 1880. During this period some 28 million immigrants entered the United States and, except for two years at the end of World War I, the yearly total never fell below 200,000 immigrants, and in most years it was above 400,000. The largest flows occurred in the first decades of the Twentieth century. From 1901 to 1930 almost 19 million people arrived on American shores, yielding an annual average of 621,000 immigrants (see Table 3.1). The peak occurred in 1907 when some 1.3 million immigrants arrived. Until recently, these numbers were unequalled in American history.

The vast majority of these people came from Europe. Although the composition shifted from Northern and Western Europe to Southern and Eastern Europe as time progressed and industrialization spread across the face of the continent (see Massey, 1988; Morawska, 1990), the composition throughout the first three decades of the century remained overwhelmingly European, averaging 79% for the entire period. As a result, the United States became less Black, more White, and more firmly European in culture and outlook.

Douglas S. Massey

Table 3.1
Patterns of Immigration to the United States during
Three Periods of the Twentieth Century

	Classic Era 1901-1930	Long Hiatus 1931-1970	New Regime 1971-1993
Whole period			
Region of origin (percent)			
Europe	79.6	46.2	13.0
Americas	16.2	43.6	49.6
Asia	3.7	8.6	34.5
Other	0.5	1.6	2.9
Total	100.0	100.0	100.0
Total immigration (thousands)	18,638	7,400	15,536
Annual average (thousands)	621	185	675
Peak year	1,907	1,968	1,991
Peak immigration (thousands)	1,285	454	1,827
First ten years			
Region of origin (percent)			
Europe	91.6	65.9	17.8
Americas	4.1	30.3	44.1
Asia	3.7	3.2	35.3
Other	0.6	0.6	2.8
Total	100.0	100.0	100.0
Total immigration (thousands)	8,795	528	4,493
Annual average (thousands)	880	53	449
Last ten years			
Region of origin (percent)			
Europe	60.0	33.8	10.2
Americas	36.9	51.7	54.0
Asia	2.7	12.9	32.7
Other	0.4	1.6	3.1
Total	100.0	100.0	100.0
Total immigration (thousands)	4,107	3,322	9,293
Annual average (thousands)	441	332	929

Source: U.S. Immigration and Naturalization Service 1994, Table 3.2

This period of mass immigration gave rise to some of the nation's enduring myths: about the struggle of immigrants to overcome poverty, about the
achievement of economic mobility through individual effort, about the importance of group solidarity in the face of ethnic prejudice and discrimination,
and about the inevitability of assimilation into the melting pot of American
life. In the words of one influential social scientist at mid-century, the first
decades of the century offer *The Epic Story of the Great Migrations that Made
the American People* (Handlin, 1951). Although a reaction against the melting
pot myth later arose in the second and third generations, this was largely a symbolic opposition by people who had watched their parents and grandparents

suffer under the yoke of Northern European dominance, but who by the 1960s had largely penetrated arenas of power, prestige, and influence and wanted to get back at their former tormentors (see Glazer and Moynihan, 1970; Greeley, 1971; Novak, 1971).

The classic era of mass immigration was followed by a long, 40-year hiatus during which immigration levels fell to very low levels and the predominance of European immigrants came to an end. From 1931 to 1970, average annual immigration fell to 185,000 and the share arriving from the Americas increased substantially, eventually equalling that from Europe. Over the entire hiatus period, 44% of all immigrants came from the Americas, compared with 46% from Europe and 9% from Asia (the latter region, according to the Immigration and Naturalization Service, includes the Middle East, which has contributed a small number of immigrants over the years, compared with countries such as China, Korea, the Philippines, and Japan). By the last decade of the hiatus, 52% of all immigrants were from the Americas and only 34% came from Europe; the peak year of immigration occurred in 1968, when 454,000 people were admitted for permanent residence.

Table 3.2
Immigrants to the United States from Major World Regions:
Numbers by Decade 1901–1990 and for 1991–1992 (thousands)

	REGION OF ORIGIN				
	Europe	*Americas*	*Asia*	*Other*	*Total*
1901–10	8,056	362	324	53	8,795
1911–20	4,322	1,144	247	23	5,736
1921–30	2,463	1,517	112	15	4,107
1931–40	348	160	17	3	528
1941–50	621	356	37	21	1,035
1951–60	1,326	997	153	39	2,515
1961–70	1,123	1,716	428	55	3,322
1971–80	800	1,983	1,588	122	4,493
1981–90	762	3,615	2,738	223	7,338
1991–93	466	2,104	1,032	103	3,705
1900–93	20,287	13,954	6,676	657	41,574

Source: U.S. Immigration and Naturalization Service, 1994, Table 3.2.

As I have already admitted, the dividing points of 1930 and 1970 are somewhat arbitrary and were chosen partly for convenience, since decennial years are easy to remember and correspond to the standard tabulations favored by demographers. Evidence of the coming hiatus was already apparent in the last decade of the classic era, when immigration levels were a third below their 1901–1930 average (441,000 rather than 621,000) and about half the average that prevailed in the first decade of the century (880,000). Moreover, by the end of the classic era, immigrants' origins were already shifting toward the Americas. Whereas 92% of all immigrants in the first decade of the century were European, by the 1920s the percentage had dropped to 60%. Although it was not recognized for many years, the era of massive European immigration was already beginning to wind down.

The termination of mass immigration around 1930 is attributable to many factors. The one that scholars most often credit is the passage of restrictive immigration legislation. In response to a public backlash against immigrants, Congress passed two new "quota laws" in 1921 and 1924 that were designed to limit the number of immigrants and shift their origins from Southern and Eastern Europe back to Northern and Western Europe (where they belonged, at least in the view of the nativist voters of the time—see Higham, 1963; Hutchinson, 1981).

Although the national origins quotas, combined with earlier bans on Asian immigration enacted in 1882 and 1917, did play a role in reducing the number of immigrants, I believe their influence has been overstated. For one thing, the new quotas did not apply at all to immigrants from the western Hemisphere, leaving the door wide open for mass entry from Latin America, particularly Mexico. Indeed, beginning in the decade of the teens, employers in northern industrial cities began to recruit extensively in Mexico, and immigration from that country mushroomed from 50,000 in the first decade of the century, to 220,000 in the second, to 460,000 in the third (see Cardoso, 1980). Were it not for other factors, the change in immigration law would, at most, have shifted the national origins of immigrants more decisively toward the Americas in the 1930s, but it would not have halted immigration per se.

More than any change in legislation, it was the outbreak of World War I in 1914 that brought a sudden and decisive halt to the flow of immigrants from Europe. During the first half of the decade, the outflow proceeded apace: 926,000 European immigrants arrived in the United States during 1910, 765,000 in 1911, and just over 1 million came in both 1913 and 1914. During the first full year of the war, however, total immigration dropped to 198,000, and it fell every year thereafter to reach a nadir of 31,000 in 1918. As a result, during the decade of the teens, immigration from Europe was halved compared with the prior decade (Ferenczi, 1929).

During the 1920s, however, European immigration began to revive, despite the restrictive immigration quotas. Some 412,000 immigrants arrived from Germany during 1921–1930, 455,000 came from Italy, 227,000 from Poland, and 102,000 from Czechoslovakia. These entries supplemented large numbers arriving from European countries that were not limited by the new quotas: 211,000 from Ireland, 340,000 from Britain, and 166,000 from Norway and Sweden. One country, however, was notably absent from

European immigrant flows of the 1920s: Russia, or as it was thereafter known, the Soviet Union (Immigration and Naturalization Service, 1994:27).

Prior to World War I, immigration from Russia had been massive: 1.6 million Russian immigrants entered the United States during the first decade of the century, and 921,000 managed to get in during the subsequent decade despite the outbreak of war in 1914. The great majority of these people were Jews escaping the rampant antisemitism and pogroms of Czarist Russia (see Nugent, 1992:83–94); but with the Bolshevik Revolution of 1917 and the consolidation of the world's first communist state, the Russian Pale was abruptly disconnected from the capitalist west and emigration was suppressed by a new state security apparatus. As a result, immigration from Russia fell to only 62,000 in the 1920s and to just 1,400 during the 1930s. The flow of Russian immigrants did not exceed 2,500 again until the 1970s (Immigration and Naturalization Service, 1994: 27-28).

Just as immigration from non-Russian Europe was gaining ground during the 1920s, however, another cataclysmic event halted all global movement: the Great Depression. From a total of 241,000 immigrants in 1930, the flow dropped to 23,000 three years later. With mass unemployment in the United States, the demand for immigrant workers evaporated, and during the 1930s total immigration fell below 1 million for the first time since the decade of the 1830s. Only 528,000 immigrants entered the United States from 1931 to 1940, yielding an annual average of about 53,000.

Before the Great Depression had ended, World War II broke out to add yet another barrier to international movement. During the years of World War II, the flow of immigrants to the United States fell once again. From a Depression-era peak of 83,000 in 1939, the number of immigrants fell to only 24,000 in 1943; and during six years of warfare, the number of immigrants averaged only 43,000 per year, lower even than during the Depression years of 1930–1939 (Immigration and Naturalization Service, 1994: 27-28).

With the termination of hostilities in 1945, immigration from Europe finally resumed, but by 1945 the face of Europe had changed dramatically. The Cold War had begun and the communist orbit had shifted westward. In addition to the Soviet Union, Eastern Europe was now cut off from the capitalist economy of the west. Countries such as Czechoslovakia, Hungary, Romania, and Yugoslavia, which had sent large numbers of immigrants just before the onset of the Depression, contributed few after 1945. Although 228,000 Polish immigrants came to the United States during the 1920s, only 10,000 entered during the 1950s.

Just as the avenues for emigration From eastern Europe were cut off, the countries of Western Europe began to seek workers to rebuild their war-shattered economies. The wave of investment and economic growth triggered by the Marshall Plan created a strong demand for labor that by the 1950s began to exceed domestic supplies in most countries (Kindleberger, 1967). As the postwar economy expanded and the pace of growth quickened, Germany, France, Britain, Belgium, and the Netherlands not only stopped sending migrants abroad, they also all became countries of immigration themselves, attracting large numbers of immigrants from Southern Europe, and then as these sources dried up, from the Balkans, Turkey, North Africa, and Asia (see Stalker, 1994). The era of mass European migration to the United States was finally and decisively over.

Although immigrants were no longer available in large numbers from Europe, the postwar boom in the United States nonetheless created a strong demand for labor there. With Eastern Europe cut off and Western Europe itself a magnet for immigration, this new demand was met by Latin Americans, whose entry was unregulated under the quotas of the 1920s. The number of Mexican immigrants rose from 61,000 in the 1940s to 300,000 in the 1950s to 454,000 during the 1960s. This expansion of immigration was not limited to Mexico. During the last decade of the hiatus period, some 200,000 Cubans entered the United States, along with 100,000 Dominicans and 70,000 Colombians. A new era of non-European immigration was clearly on the rise.

It has now become conventional to date the emergence of the new regime in U.S. immigration from the passage of the 1965 Amendments to the Immigration and Nationality Act, which were phased in and implemented fully in 1968. In keeping with the civil rights spirit of the times, this legislation abolished the discriminatory national origins quotas and ended the ban on Asian entry. It put each nation in the eastern hemisphere on an equal footing by establishing a uniform limit of 20,000 per country; it set an overall hemispheric cap of 170,000 immigrants; and it established a "preference system" of family and occupational categories to allocate visas under these limits. The Amendments exempted immediate relatives of U.S. citizens from the numerical caps, however, and nations in the western hemisphere were subject only to a hemispheric cap of 120,000 immigrants, not a 20,000 per-country limit.

Although this legislation contributed to the creation of the new immigration regime, it was neither the sole nor even the most important cause of the increase in numbers or the shift in origins. As with the National Origins Quotas, I believe scholars have generally overstated the role of the 1965 Amendments in bringing about the new immigration. The Act was in no way responsible for the drop in European immigration, since this trend was clearly visible before 1965 and followed from other conditions described above.

Nor did the 1965 Act increase the level of immigration from Latin America. On the contrary, by placing the first-ever cap on immigration from the western hemisphere, the legislation actually made it *more difficult* for Latin Americans to enter the United States. Since 1965, additional amendments have further restricted entry from nations in the western hemisphere, placing them under the 20,000-per country limit, abolishing the separate hemispheric caps, eliminating the right of minor children to sponsor the immigration of parents, and repealing the "Texas Proviso" that exempted employers from prosecution for hiring undocumented migrants. Rather than promoting the shift toward Latin American origins, then, the 1965 Act and its successor amendments actually inhibited the transformation. The shift in origins occurred in spite of the legislation, not because of it.

The one effect that the 1965 Act did have was to remove the ban on Asian entry and thereby unleash an unprecedented and entirely unexpected flow of immigrants from Korea, Taiwan, China, the Philippines, and other Asian countries (see Glazer, 1985). At the time, the legislation was seen as a way of redressing past wrongs that had been visited upon Eastern and Southern Europeans and of mollifying the resentments of their children and grandchildren, who had risen to become powerful members of the Democratic Party. Rather than opening the country to immigration from countries such as Italy and Poland as legislators such as Peter Rodino and Dan Rostenkowski had intended, its principal effect was to initiate large-scale immigration from Asia.

As Table 3.1 shows, the percentage of Asians rose from under 10% of immigrants during the classic and hiatus eras, to around 35% under the new regime that began about 1970. Whereas only 35,000 Chinese, 35,000 Indians, and 34,0000 Koreans were admitted as immigrants during the 1960s, by the 1980s these numbers had become 347,000, 251,000, and 334,000, respectively (Immigration and Naturalization Service, 1994: 27-28). As a result of this sharp and sudden increase in Asian immigration, the percentage of Asians in the U.S. population began rising for the first time in more than a century.

Yet by themselves the 1965 Amendments cannot explain the remarkable surge in Asian immigration. Another key factor was the loss of the Vietnam War and the subsequent collapse of the U.S.-backed governments in Indochina. With the fall of Saigon in 1975, the United States faced new demands for entry by thousands of military officers, government officials, and U.S. employees fearful of reprisals from the new Communist authorities. As economic and political conditions deteriorated during the late 1970s and early 1980s, larger numbers of soldiers, minor officials, and merchants took to the seas in desperate attempts to escape.

For both political and humanitarian reasons, the United States had little choice but to accept these people outside the numerical limits established under the 1965 Act. Although only 335 Vietnamese entered the United States during the 1950s and 4,300 arrived during the 1960s, 172,000 were admitted during the 1970s and 281,000 arrived during the 1980s. In addition to the Vietnamese, the U.S. misadventure in Indochina also led to the entry of thousands of Cambodian, Laotian, and Hmong refugees, who collectively totalled 300,000 by 1990. All told, about a third of Asian immigrants since 1970 can be traced to the failed intervention of the United States in Indochina (Immigration and Naturalization Service, 1994: 28).

For different reasons, therefore, immigration from Asia and Latin America has surged over the past two decades. According to official statistics, the total annual flow of immigrants averaged 675,000 during the period 1971–1993, a rate that exceeds the 621,000 observed during the classic era from 1901 to 1930. Unlike the earlier period, moreover, these 15.5 million new immigrants were overwhelmingly non-European: about half came from Latin America and a third originated in Asia; only 13% were from Europe. The peak year occurred in 1990, when 1.8 million persons were admitted for permanent residence in the United States.

As large as the annual flow of 675,000 immigrants is, both absolutely and relative to earlier periods in U.S. history, it nonetheless constitutes an underestimate of the true level of immigration, for it does not capture the full extent of undocumented migration to the United States, a category that became increasingly important during the 1970s and 1980s. Although the figures summarized in Table 3.1 include 3.3 million former undocumented migrants who were legalized under the 1986 Immigration Reform and Control Act, they do not include other illegal migrants who failed to qualify for the Amnesty Program or who entered after 1986.

Woodrow-Lafield (1993) estimates that about 3.3 million undocumented immigrants lived in the United States as of 1990, bringing the total number of immigrants for the period 1971–1993 to around 854,000 per year. This figure still understates the true size of the flow, however, because her estimate does not include immigrants who entered illegally and subsequently died, or those who subsequently emigrated. Full incorporation of all undocumented migrants into the figures of Table 3.1 would boost the relative share of Latin Americans even more, given the predominance of Mexicans in this population. Among undocumented migrants counted in the 1980 Census, estimates suggest that 55% were Mexican (Warren and Passel, 1987), and of those legalized under IRCA, 75% were from Mexico (Immigration and Naturalization Service, 1991).

Whatever allowance one makes for undocumented migration, it is clear that the United States has embarked on a new regime of immigration that marks a clear break with the past. The new immigration is composed of immigrants from Asia and Latin America, a large share of whom are undocumented and who are arriving in substantially larger numbers compared with earlier periods of high immigration. Although the 1965 Amendments to the Immigration and Nationality Act played some role in creating this new regime, ultimately the effect of U.S. immigration policy has been secondary, and the dramatic change reflects more powerful forces operating in the United States and elsewhere in the world.

The New Immigration and the Future of Ethnicity

No matter what one's opinion of the melting pot ideology, the remarkable amalgamation of European immigrants into the society and culture of the United States must be acknowledged. The disparate groups that entered the country in great numbers between 1880 and 1930—Italians, Poles, Czechs, Hungarians, Lithuanians, and Russian Jews—were not only quite different from prior waves of immigrants from Northern and Western Europe, they were also quite different from each other in terms of language, literacy, culture, and economic background. After several generations of U.S. residence, however, the differences are largely gone, and the various groups have to a great extent merged together to form one large, amorphous class of mixed European ancestry.

By 1980, most people reporting ancestry in Southern or Eastern Europe were in their third or fourth generation of U.S. residence, and as a result of extensive intermarriage in earlier generations, they were increasingly of mixed origins. Over half of those reporting Polish, Russian, Czech, or Hungarian ancestry on the 1980 Census were of mixed parentage; and the rate of intermarriage was 60% for women of Italian and Russian origin, 70% for Polish women, 83% for Czech women, and 88% for Hungarian women. For all women, the odds of intermarriage rose sharply as one moved from older to younger cohorts, and intergroup differences with respect to income, education, and occupation had all but disappeared (Lieberson and Waters, 1988).

As a result of rapid growth in the population of mixed European ancestry, White Americans are gradually losing contact with their immigrant origins. Research by Alba (1990) shows that such people do not regularly cook or consume ethnic foods; they report experiencing little or no ethnic prejudice or discrimination; they are largely uninvolved and uninterested in ethnic politics; they are unlikely to be members of any ethnic social or political organization; and they tend not to live in ethnic neighborhoods.

Although most White Americans identify themselves ethnically, the labels are growing increasingly complex and the percentage who call themselves "American" or "nothing at all" is rising (Lieberson and Waters, 1988; Alba, 1990). In the late Twentieth century social world of European Americans, where intermarriage is pervasive, mixed ancestries are common, economic differences are trivial, and residential mixing is the norm, ethnicity has become largely symbolic (Gans, 1979), a choice made from a range of "ethnic options" that are only loosely tied to ancestry (Waters, 1990).

Compared to the ascriptive ethnicity of the past, the descendants of European immigrants are moving into "the twilight of ethnicity" (Alba, 1981), and rather than signalling a lack of assimilation, the use of ethnic labels proves how far it has come. The amalgamation of European ethnic groups has now proceeded to such an extent that expressions of ethnic identity are no longer perceived threats to national unity. On the contrary, the use of ethnic labels has become a way of identifying oneself as American (Alba, 1990).

It is natural to view the process of European assimilation as a model for the incorporation of Asians and Latin Americans into U.S. society. Present fears of ethnic fragmentation are assuaged by noting that similar fears were expressed about the immigration of Italians, Poles, and Jews. Nativist worries are allayed by showing that today's immigrants appear to be assimilating much as in the past. According to available evidence, income and occupational status rise with time spent in the United States; fertility, language, and residential patterns come to resemble those of natives as socioeconomic status and generations increase; and intermarriage becomes increasingly common with each succeeding generation and increment in income and education (Massey, 1981; Jasso and Rosenzweig, 1990).

Focusing on individual patterns of assimilation, however, ignores the structural context within which the assimilation occurs. By focusing on micro-level analyses of immigrant attainment, we lose sight of the fact that the remarkable incorporation of European immigrants in the past was facilitated, and to a large extent enabled, by a set of historical conditions that no longer prevail. Compared with the great European immigrations, the new immigration differs in several crucial respects that significantly alter the prospects for assimilation and, hence, the meaning of ethnicity for the next century.

The first unique historical feature of European immigration is that it was followed by a long hiatus when few additional Europeans arrived. Although 15 million immigrants entered the United States in the three decades between 1901 and 1930, for the next 60 years the flow fell to the functional equivalent of zero. Compared with an annual average of 495,000 European immigrants from 1901 to 1930, only 85,000 arrived each year from 1930 through 1969, and most of these were not Poles, Italians, or Russian Jews, the big groups before 1930. Although overall immigration revived after 1970, the flow from Europe remained small at around 88,000 per year.

Thus, after taking in large numbers of Europeans for a space of about 50 years, the flow suddenly stopped and for the next 60 years—roughly three generations—it was reduced to a trickle. The cutting off of immigration from Europe eliminated the supply of raw material for the grist mill of ethnicity in the United States, ensuring that whatever ethnic identities existed would be solely a function of events, processes, and mechanisms operating within the United States.

Without a fresh supply of immigrants each year, the generational composition of people labeled "Italians," "Poles," and "Czechs" inexorably shifted: first foreigners gave way to the native-born, then natives yielded to the children of natives, and more recently the children of natives have given way to the grandchildren of natives. Over time, successive generations dominated the populations of European ethnic groups and came to determine their character. With each generational transition, ethnic identities and the meaning of ethnicity itself shifted until finally most groups moved into the "twilight of ethnicity."

This pattern of assimilation was made possible by the long hiatus in European immigration. What it did, in essence, was give the United States a "breathing space" within which slow-moving social and economic processes leading to assimilation could operate. The long hiatus shaped and constrained the meaning of ethnicity by limiting the generational complexity underlying each group's ethnic identity: the ending of European immigration in 1930 meant that for all practical purposes, ethnic groups would never include more than three generations at any point in time.

In addition to generational change, the other engine of immigrant assimilation is social mobility, and a second historical feature of European immigration is that it was followed by a sustained economic expansion that offered unusual opportunities for socioeconomic advancement. From 1940 through 1973, incomes rose, productivity increased, unemployment fell, income inequality diminished, poverty rates declined, rates of college attendance grew, and housing improved as the U.S. standard of living seemed to rise effortlessly each year (Galbraith, 1963; Levy, 1987; 1995). First- and second-generation immigrants from Southern and Eastern Europe rode this wave of prosperity to achieve full economic parity with Northern and Western Europeans by 1980.

Thus, two structural conditions—the long hiatus in immigration and the economic boom that accompanied it—are primarily responsible for the remarkable assimilation of European immigrants into the United States. Were either of these two factors lacking, the story of immigrant, arrival, adaptation, and ultimate absorption might have had a very different conclusion than movement into the twilight of ethnicity or the emergence of symbolic ethnicity. Neither of these two structural conditions, however, is likely to hold for the new immigrants from Asia and Latin America, and the patterns and outcomes of assimilation are likely to be quite different as a result.

Rather than having the luxury of a 60-year "breathing space" within which to absorb and accommodate large cohorts of immigrants, the United States will more likely become a country of perpetual immigration. Unlike the European ethnic groups of the past, today's Latin Americans and Asians can expect to have their numbers continuously augmented by a steady supply of fresh arrivals from abroad. Rather than being a one-time historical phenomenon, immigration has become a permanent structural feature of the postindustrial society of the United States.

Although the relative influence of the different causes is a matter of some debate (Massey et al., 1993), it is clear that international migration stems from a complex interplay of forces operating at several levels (Massey et al., 1994; 1998). Wage differentials between poor and affluent countries provide incentives for individuals to migrate to reap higher lifetime earnings at the destination (Todaro, 1976; Todaro and Maruszko, 1987). Households send migrants to work in foreign labor markets as a means of self-insuring against risk and overcoming capital constraints created by market failures at home (Stark, 1991). A demand for immigrants arises in post-industrial societies because market segmentation creates a class of jobs with low pay, little status, and few mobility prospects that native workers will not accept (Piore, 1979); and the penetration of market forces into developing societies itself creates a mobile population prone to international movement (Sassen, 1988).

Once begun, migratory flows tend to acquire a momentum that is resistant to management or regulation (Massey, 1990a). Networks of social ties develop to link migrants in destination areas to friends and relatives in sending regions (Massey et al., 1994). Branch communities eventually form in the receiving society and give rise to enclave economies that act as magnets for additional immigration (Portes and Bach, 1985; Portes and Manning, 1986; Logan et al., 1994). Large-scale emigration causes other social and economic changes within both sending and receiving societies that lead to its cumulative causation over time (Massey, 1990b).

Thus, current knowledge about the forces behind international migration suggest that movement to the United States will grow, not decline. None of the conditions known to play a role initiating international migratory flows—wage differentials, market failures, labor market segmentation, the globalization of the economy—is likely to end any time soon. Moreover, once begun, the forces that perpetuate international movement—network formation, cumulative causation—help to ensure that these flows will continue into the foreseeable future.

To a great extent, these forces are beyond the immediate reach of U.S. policy, particularly immigration policy. Despite the passage of more restrictive immigration laws and the enactment of increasingly punitive policies, illegal migration from Mexico (and elsewhere) has continued to grow and shows no signs of diminishing (Donato et al., 1992; Massey and Singer, 1995). Although politicians call for even more restrictive measures (Lamm and Imhoff, 1985), the forces producing and perpetuating immigration appear to be of such a magnitude that the new regime of U.S. immigration may continue indefinitely.

The belief that immigration flows can be controlled through legislation stems from a misreading of U.S. history. Although the cessation of European immigration in 1930 is widely attributed to the implementation of restrictive quotas in the early 1920s, I argue that the cutoff actually occurred because of a unique sequence of cataclysmic events: World War I, the Bolshevik

Revolution, the Great Depression, and World War II. A similar string of destructive and bloody events might well arise to extinguish the powerful migratory flows that have become well established throughout Latin America and Asia, but for the sake of the world we should hope they do not.

In all likelihood, therefore, the United States has already become a country of perpetual immigration, one characterized by the continuous arrival of large cohorts of immigrants from particular regions year after year. This basic fact will inevitably create a very different structure of ethnicity compared with that prevailing among European immigrant groups in the past. Populations of Latin Americans and Asians will grow not only through assimilative processes such as generational succession and intermarriage, but also through the countervailing process of net in-migration. Unlike European ethnics, the ranks of Latin American and Asian ethnics will be augmented continuously with new arrivals from abroad, constantly replenishing the supply of raw material for the grist mill of ethnicity.

Rather than creating relatively homogenous populations spanning at most three generations, the new regime will produce heterogeneous ethnic populations characterized by considerable generational complexity. Processes of social and economic assimilation acting upon earlier arrivals and their children, when combined with the perpetual arrival of new immigrants, will lead to the fragmentation of ethnicity along the lines of class, generation, and ancestry. Rather than a slow, steady, and relatively coherent progression of ethnicity toward twilight, it will increasingly stretch from dawn to dusk.

Moreover, because the social and economic forces that produce assimilation operate slowly, and those promoting immigration work quickly, the rate at which ethnic culture is augmented by raw material from abroad will tend to exceed the rate at which new ethnic culture is created through generational succession, social mobility, and intermarriage in the United States. As a result, the character of ethnicity will be determined relatively more by immigrants and relatively less by later generations, shifting the balance of ethnic identity toward the language, culture, and ways of life in the sending society.

The future state of ethnicity in the United States is now seen most clearly in the Mexican American population. Upon the annexation of northern Mexico into the United States in 1848, fewer than 50,000 Mexicans became U.S. citizens (Jaffe et al., 1980). Virtually all Mexican Americans today are descendants of immigrants who arrived in the 100 years between 1890 and the present. During this time, the United States experienced continuous immigration from Mexico except for a brief, 10-year span during the 1930s, thereby replicating the condition of perpetual immigration that will probably characterize other groups in the future (Hoffman, 1974; Cardoso, 1980; Massey et al., 1987).

As a result of the long history of immigration from Mexico, Mexican Americans find themselves distributed across a variety of generations, socioeconomic classes, legal statuses, ancestries, languages, and, ultimately, identities (Bean and Tienda, 1987). Rather than the relatively coherent ethnicity that arose among European ethnics, Mexican identity is rife with internal divisions, conflicts, contradictions, and tensions (Browning and de la Garza, 1986; Nelson and Tienda, 1985). The fragmented state of Mexican ethnicity is symbolized by the fact that the Census Bureau must use three separate identifiers to capture it in its Spanish Origin question—Mexican, Mexican American, and Chicano—each of which corresponds to a different conception of Mexican identity (Garcia, 1981).

Not only will perpetual immigration create a new, complex, and fragmented kind of ethnicity, but the new immigrants and their decedents will also encounter a very different economy compared with that experienced by the European immigrants and their children. Rather than rising prosperity and structural occupational mobility, current economic trends point in the opposite direction. Since 1973 wages have stagnated and income inequality has grown (Phillips, 1990; Levy, 1995); the long decline in U.S. poverty rates has come to an end (Smith, 1988); and immobility in the occupational structure has increased (Hout, 1988). Moreover, just at the point when public schools used by immigrants have fallen into neglect, the importance of education in the U.S. stratification system has increased (Hout, 1988; DiPrete and Grusky, 1990; Levy, 1995), particularly for Hispanics (Stolzenberg, 1990).

Thus, not only will the United States lack the luxury of an extended space within which to absorb and integrate an unprecedented number of new immigrants, one of the basic engines of past assimilation may also be missing: a robust economy that produces avenues of upward mobility for people with limited education. Perpetual immigration will expand the relative influence of the first generation in creating ethnic culture, while the rigidification of the U.S. stratification system will slow the rate of socioeconomic advancement among the second and third generations and make them look more like the first. Both of these structural conditions will act to increase the relative weight of the sending country's language and culture in the definition of ethnic identity.

The new immigration also differs from European immigration in other respects likely to influence the creation and maintenance of ethnicity in the United States. Although the flow of immigrants from 1971 to 1993 is actually *smaller* relative to the size of the U.S. population than the flow during the classic era, it is also more concentrated, both geographically and linguistically. As Table 3.3 shows, the per capita rate of legal immigration (3.0 per thousand) is presently less than half that observed during the classic era (6.3 per thousand); and even making a generous allowance for undocumented migration (raising the total flow to 830,000) does not erase the differential (it increases the rate only to 3.8 per thousand per capita).

Table 3.3
Indicators of the Relative Size and Concentration of U.S. Immigration
in Two Periods of the Twentieth Century

	Classic Era 1901-1930	New Regime 1971-1993
Rate of immigration (per 1,000 population)	6.3	3.0
Rate of immigration (including undocumented migrants)	6.3	3.8
Share of largest national group (percent)	19.4	23.6
Share of largest linguistic group (percent)	19.4	38.4
Share of the five most important destination states, 1910 and 1990 (percent)[1]	54.0	78.2
Share of the five most important urban destinations, 1910 and 1990 (percent)[2]	35.6	47.9

[1] In 1910 the five most important destination states were New York, Pennsylvania, Illinois, Massachusetts, and New Jersey; in 1990 they were California, New York, Texas, Illinois, and Florida.

[2] In 1910 the five most important urban destinations were New York. Chicago, Philadelphia, Cleveland, and Boston; in 1990 they were Los Angeles, New York, Chicago, Anaheim-Santa Ana, and Houston.

Sources: U.S. Immigration and Naturalization Service 1991, 1993, Tables 2, 17, and 18; U.S. Bureau of the Census 1913, Tables 15 and 16.

Despite its smaller relative size, however, the new immigration is far more concentrated in terms of national origins and language. Whereas the largest nationality of the classic era (Italians) represented only 19% of the total flow of immigrants, the largest group under the new regime (Mexicans) constitute 24% of the flow. Moreover, whereas the language most often spoken by immigrants in the classic era (Italian) was confined to immigrants from one country who comprised only 19% of the flow, the most important language among the new immigrants (Spanish) is spoken by migrants from a dozen countries who together comprise 38% of all arrivals.

Thus, although European immigrants were relatively larger in number, they were scattered across more national origin groups and languages, thereby reducing their salience for native White Americans and limiting the possibilities for linguistic segmentation in the United States. For European immigrants during the classic era, the only practical lingua franca was English, but since nearly 40% of the new immigrants speak the same language, Spanish becomes viable as a second language of daily life, creating the possibility of movement toward a bilingual society.

The new immigrants are not only more concentrated linguistically, they are also more clustered geographically. In 1910 the five most important immigrant-receiving states took in just 54% of the total flow, whereas the five most important urban destinations received 36%. By 1990, in contrast, the five most important immigrant-receiving states comprised 78% of the flow, and the five most important urban areas received nearly half of all entering immigrants. The metropolitan areas receiving these immigrants—New York, Chicago, Miami, and Los Angeles—were the most important centers of communication and media in the country, guaranteeing that the new immigration would be seen in Dubuque and Peoria as well as in cosmopolitan centers of the east and west coasts.

The increasing concentration of Spanish-speaking immigrants in a few metropolitan areas will inevitably change the process of assimilation itself. Through the new immigration, large communities of Spanish speakers will emerge in many U.S. urban areas, lowering the economic and social costs of not speaking English and raising the benefits of speaking Spanish. As a result, the new immigrants from Latin America will be less likely to learn English than were their European counterparts at the turn of the century (Jasso and Rosenzweig, 1990). The emergence of immigrant enclaves—a process already well advanced in many areas—also reduces the incentives and opportunities to learn other cultural habits and behavioral attributes of Euro-American society.

Conclusion

The new immigration from Asia and Latin America that has become increasingly prominent since 1970 has several distinctive features that set it apart from the older European immigration of the early Twentieth century. First, the new immigration is part of an ongoing flow that can be expected to continue indefinitely, making the United States a country of perpetual immigration rather than a nation of periodic entry. Second, the new immigrants will most likely enter a more highly stratified society characterized by high income inequality and growing labor market segmentation that will provide fewer opportunities for upward mobility. Third, the national origins and geographic destinations of the new immigrants are highly concentrated, creating distinctive linguistic and cultural communities in many areas of the United States.

As a result of these conditions, the experience of European immigrants provides a poor model for the future assimilation and incorporation of new immigrants from Asia and Latin America. Rather than relatively homogenous ethnic groups moving steadily toward assimilation with the American majority, the new immigration will instead create complex ethnic groups fragmented along the lines of generation, class, ancestry, and, ultimately, identity. Rather than ethnic populations moving toward the twilight of ethnic identity, ethnicity itself will be stretched out across the generations to reach from dawn to dusk.

The perpetual immigration of immigrants from Latin America will also increase the prevalence and influence of the Spanish language and Latin culture in the United States. Large Spanish-speaking communities have already emerged in the gateway cities of New York, Los Angeles, Houston, and Chicago, and Latinos have become the majority in Miami, San Antonio, and in most cities along the Mexico–U.S. border. The combination of continuous immigration and high regional and linguistic concentration will produce more such communities and will move the United States toward bilingualism and biculturalism. Assimilation will become much more of a two-way street, with Euro-Americans learning Spanish and consuming Latin cultural products as well as Latins learning English and consuming Anglo-American products. Increasingly, the economic benefits and prospects for mobility will accrue to those able to speak both languages and move in two cultural worlds.

Since these trends will occur in an increasingly rigid, stratified, and unequal society, growing antagonisms along class and ethnic lines can be expected, both within and between groups. Given the salience of race in American life, the acceleration of Black immigration from Africa and the Caribbean, and the history of racial conflict and hostility in the United States, the relationship between native Blacks and the new immigrants is likely to be particularly conflict-ridden (see Portes and Stepick, 1993; Portes and Zhou, 1993).

Although these trends are now most apparent with respect to Latin Americans, especially Mexicans, the latent potential for immigration and ethnic transformation is probably greater in Asia, where immigration has just begun. The potential for Chinese immigration alone is enormous. Already the Chinese make up 7% of all legal immigrants, not counting the ethnic Chinese from various southeast Asian countries, and Chinatowns have arisen and expanded in many cities around the United States. Since theory and empirical evidence suggests that large-scale emigration is created by economic development and market penetration (Massey, 1988; Hatton and Williamson, 1992), China's movement toward markets and rapid economic growth may contain the seeds of an enormous future migration.

Even a small rate of emigration, when applied to a population of more than a billion people, would produce a flow of immigrants that would dwarf levels of migration now observed from Mexico. Social networks linking China and the United States are now being formed and in the future will serve as the basis for mass entry. Immigration from China and other populous, rapidly developing nations in Asia have an unrecognized and latent potential to transform the ethnic composition of the nation and to alter even more dramatically the meaning and conception of ethnicity in the United States.

References

Alba, Richard D. 1981. "The Twilight of Ethnicity among American Catholics of European Ancestry." *Annals of the American Academy of Political and Social Science*, 454:86–97.

———. 1990. *Ethnic Identity: The Transformation of White Identity*. New Haven: Yale University Press.

Bean, Frank D. and Marta Tienda. 1987. *The Hispanic Population of the United States*. New York: Russell Sage Foundation.

Blau, Francine D. 1984. "The Use of Transfer Payments by Immigrants." *Industrial and Labor Relations Review* 37:222-239.

Borjas, George J. 1990. *Friends or Strangers: The Impact of Immigrants on the U.S. Economy*. New York: Basic Books.

———. 1994. "Immigrants and the U.S. Welfare System." Paper presented at 1994 Symposium on Immigration, Population Studies and Training Center, Brown University, March 11.

Borjas, George J. and Marta Tienda. 1987. "The economic consequences of immigration." *Science* 235: 645–651.

Borjas, George J. and Richard B. Freeman, eds. 1992. *Immigration and the Workforce: Economic Consequences for the United States and Source Areas*. Chicago: University of Chicago Press.

Brimelow, Peter. 1995. *Enough is Enough: Common Sense About Immigration*. New York: Random House.

Browning, Harley L. and Rodolfo de la Garza, eds. 1986. *Mexican Immigrants and Mexican Americans: An Evolving Relation*. Austin, TX.: Center for Mexican American Studies, University of Texas.

Cardoso, Lawrence. 1980. *Mexican Emigration to the United States: 1897–1931*. Tucson: University of Arizona Press.

DiPrete, Thomas A. and David B. Grusky. 1990. "Structure and Trend in the Process of Stratification for American Men and Women." *American Journal of Sociology,* 96:107–121.

Donato, Katharine M., Jorge Durand, and Douglas S. Massey. 1992. "Stemming the Tide? Assessing the Deterrent Effects of the Immigration Reform and Control Act." *Demography* 29:139–157.

Edmonston, Barry and Jeffrey Passel. 1991. "The Future Immigrant Population of the United States." Paper presented at the Conference on Immigration and Ethnicity, The Urban Institute, Washington, DC, June 17–18.

Espenshade, Thomas J. and Charles A. Calhoun. 1993. "An Analysis of Public Opinion Toward Undocumented Immigration." *Population Research and Policy Review* 12:189–224.

Ferenczi, Imre. 1929. *International Migration, vol. I, Statistics*. New York: National Bureau of Economic Research.

Galbraith, John K. 1963. *The Affluent Society*. New York: Dutton.

Gans, Herbert J. 1979. "Symbolic Ethnicity: The Future of Ethnic Groups and Cultures in America." *Ethnic and Racial Studies,* 2:1–20.

Garcìa, John A. 1981. "Yo Soy Mexicano: Self-Identity and Sociodemographic Correlates." Social Science Quarterly, 62:88–98.

Glazer, Nathan. 1985. *Clamor at the Gates: The New American Immigration*. San Francisco, CA: Institute for Contemporary Studies Press.

Glazer, Nathan and Daniel P. Moynihan. 1970. *Beyond the Melting Pot: The Negroes, Puerto Ricans, Jews, Italians, and Irish of New York City*. Cambridge: MIT Press.

Greeley, Andrew. 1971. *Why Can't They Be Like Us?* New York: Dutton.

Grenier, Gilles. 1984. "Shifts to English as Usual Language by Americans of Spanish Mother Tongue." *Social Science Quarterly,* 65:537–550.

Handlin, Oscar. 1951. *The Uprooted: The Epic Story of the Great Migrations that Made the American People*. Boston: Little, Brown.

Hatton, Timothy J. and Jeffrey G. Williamson. 1992. "International Migration and World Development: A Historical Perspective." Historical Paper 41. National Bureau of Economic Research, Cambridge, MA.

Higham, John. 1963. *Strangers in the Land: Patterns of American Nativism. 1896–1925*. New York: Atheneum.

Hoffman, Abraham. 1974. *Unwanted Mexican Americans in the Great Depression: Repatriation Pressures 1929–1939*. Tucson: University of Arizona Press.

Hout, Michael. 1988. "More Universalism, Less Structural Mobility: The American Occupational Structure in the 1980s." *American Journal of Sociology,* 93:1358–1401.

Hutchinson, Edward P. 1981. *Legislative History of American Immigration Policy, 1798-1965*. Philadelphia: University of Pennsylvania Press.

Immigration and Naturalization Service. 1991. *1990 Statistical Yearbook of the Immigration and Naturalization Service*. Washington, DC: U.S. Government Printing Office.

————. 1994. *1993 Statistical Yearbook of the Immigration and Naturalization Service*. Washington, DC: U.S. government Printing Office.

Jaffe, A.J., Ruth M. Cullen, and Thomas D. Boswell. 1980. *The Changing Demography of Spanish Americans.* New York: Academic Press.

Jasso, Guillermina and Mark R. Rosenzweig. 1990. *The New Chosen People: Immigrants in the United States.* New York: Russell Sage.

Kindleberger, Charles P. 1967. *Europe's Postwar Growth: The Role of Labor Supply.* New York: Oxford University Press.

Lamm, Richard D. and Gary Imhoff. 1985. *The Immigration Time Bomb: The Fragmenting of America.* New York: Dutton.

Levy, Frank. 1987. *Dollars and Dreams: The Changing American Income Distribution.* New York: Russell Sage.

———. 1995. "Incomes and Income Inequality." In Reynolds Farley, ed., *State of the Union—America in the 1990s, Volume One: Economic Trends.* New York: Russell Sage, pp. 1–58.

Lieberson, Stanley and Mary C. Waters. 1988. *From Many Strands: Ethnic and Racial Groups in Contemporary America.* New York: Russell Sage.

Logan, John R., Richard D. Alba, and Thomas L. McNulty. 1994. "Ethnic Economies in Metropolitan Regions: Miami and Beyond." *Social Forces,* 72:691–724.

Massey, Douglas S. 1981. "Dimensions of the New Immigration to the United States and the Prospects for Assimilation." *Annual Review of Sociology,* 7:57–85.

———. 1988. "International Migration and Economic Development in Comparative Perspective." *Population and Development Review,* 14:383–414.

———. 1990a. "Social Structure, Household Strategies, and the Cumulative Causation of Migration." *Population Index,* 56:3–26.

———. 1990b. "The Social and Economic Origins of Immigration." *Annals of the American Academy of Political and Social Science,* 510:60–72.

Massey, Douglas S., Rafael Alarcon, Jorge Durand, and Humberto Gonzalez. 1987. *Return to Aztlan: The Social Process of International Migration from Western Mexico.* Berkeley and Los Angeles: University of California Press.

Massey, Douglas S., Joaquin Arango, Graeme Hugo, Ali Kouaouci, Adela Pellegrino, and J. Edward Taylor. 1993. "Theories of International Migration: A Review and Appraisal." *Population and Development Review,* 19:431–466.

———. 1994. "An Evaluation of International Migration Theory: The North American Case." *Population and Development Review* 20:699-752.

____. 1998. *Worlds in Motion: Understanding International Migration at Century's End.* Oxford: Oxford University Press.

Massey, Douglas S. and Audrey Singer. 1995. "New Estimates of Undocumented Mexican Migration and the Probability of Apprehension." *Demography,* 32:203–213.

Morawska, Ewa. 1990. "The Sociology and Historiography of Immigration." In Virginia Yans-McLaughlin, ed., *Immigration Reconsidered: History, Sociology, and Politics.* New York: Oxford, pp. 187–240.

Nelson, Candace and Marta Tienda. 1985. "The Structuring of Hispanic Ethnicity: Historical and Contemporary Perspectives." *Ethnic and Racial Studies,* 8:49–74.

Novak, Michael. 1971. *The Rise of the Unmeltable Ethnics.* New York: Macmillan.

Nugent, Walter. 1992. *Crossings: The Great Transatlantic Migrations, 1870–1914.* Bloomington: Indiana University Press.

Phillips, Kevin. 1990. *The Politics of Rich and Poor: Wealth and the American Electorate in the Reagan Aftermath.* New York: Random House.

Piore, Michael J. 1979. *Birds of Passage: Migrant Labor in Industrial Societies.* New York: Cambridge University Press.

Portes, Alejandro and Robert L. Bach. 1985. *Latin Journey: Cuban and Mexican Immigrants in the United States.* Berkeley and Los Angeles: University of California Press.

Portes, Alejandro and Robert D. Manning. 1986. "The Immigrant Enclave: Theory and Empirical Examples." In Susan Olzak and Joane Nagel, eds., *Competitive Ethnic Relations.* Orlando, FL: Academic Press, pp. 47–68.

Portes, Alejandro and Alex Stepick. 1993. *City on the Edge: The Transformation of Miami.* Berkeley and Los Angeles: University of California Press.

Portes, Alejandro and Min Zhou. 1993. "The New Second Generation: Segmented Assimilation and its Variants." *Annals of the American Academy of Political and Social Science,* 530:74–96.

Rothman, Eric S. and Thomas J. Espenshade. 1992. "Fiscal Impacts of Immigration to the United States." *Population Index,* 58:381–415.

Sassen, Saskia. 1988. *The Mobility of Labor and Capital: A Study in International Investment and Labor Flow.* Cambridge: Cambridge University Press.

Simon, Julian L. 1984. "Immigrants, Taxes, and Welfare in the United States." *Population and Development Review,* 10:55–69.

Smith, James P. 1988. "Poverty and the Family in the United States." In Gary D. Sandefur and Marta Tienda, eds., *Divided Opportunities: Minorities, Poverty, and Social Policy.* New York: Plenum, pp. 141–172.

Stalker, Peter. 1994. *The Work of Strangers: A Survey of International Labour Migration.* Geneva: International Labour Office.

Stark, Oded. 1991. *The Migration of Labor.* Cambridge: Basil Blackwell.

Stevens, Gillian. 1985. "Nativity, Intermarriage, and Mother-Tongue Shift." *American Sociological Review,* 50:74–83.

Stolzenberg, Ross M. 1990. "Ethnicity, Geography, and Occupational Achievement of Hispanic Men in the United States." *American Sociological Review,* 55:143–154.

Tienda, Marta and Leif Jensen. 1986. "Immigration and Public Assistance Participation: Dispelling the Myth of Dependency." *Social Science Quarterly,* 15:372–400.

Todaro, Michael P. 1976. *International Migration in Developing Countries.* Geneva: Inernational Labor Office.

Todaro, Michael P. and Lydia Maruszko. 1987. "Illegal migration and U.S. Immigration Reform: A Conceptual Framework." *Population and Development Review,* 13:101–114.

Veltman, Calvin. 1988. "Modelling the Language Shift Process of Hispanic Immigrants." *International Migration Review,* 22:545–562.

Warren, Robert, and Ellen P. Kraly. 1985. *The Elusive Exodus: Emigration from the United States.* Population Reference Bureau Occasional Paper 8. Washington, DC: Population Reference Bureau.

Warren, Robert and Jeffrey S. Passel. 1987. "A Count of the Uncountable: Estimates of Undocumented Aliens Counted in the 1980 United States Census." *Demography* 24: 375–393.

Waters, Mary C. 1990. *Ethnic Options: Choosing Identities in America.*Berkeley and Los Angeles: University of California Press.

Woodrow-Lafield, Karen A. 1993. "Undocumented Residents in the United States in 1989–1990: Issues of Uncertainty in Quantification." Paper presented at the Annual Meetings of the Population Association of America, Miami Beach, FL.

Wyman, Mark. 1993. *Round Trip to America: The Immigrants Return to Europe 1880–1930.* Ithaca, NY: Cornell University Press.

Chapter 4

Racial and Ethnic Fertility Differentials in the United States

Gray Swicegood and S. Philip Morgan

Introduction

The racial and ethnic composition of the U.S. population is changing. This is "old news" that demographers have been delivering for some time now, but their message has been largely understood in terms of the high volume of immigration from Latin America and Asia during the last two decades. The contribution of differential childbearing patterns across racial and ethnic groups to the ongoing diversification of the American population is often overlooked.

In this paper we examine the impact, extent, and nature of fertility differentials and highlight several key issues drawn from the research literature on this topic. In the first section, we demonstrate that current fertility differentials substantially affect the growth rates of racial/ethnic groups. Next, we provide a descriptive account of recent fertility differences across various segments of the population along with some historical perspectives on these differences. Third, we consider the childbearing patterns of immigrant groups in the United States and the disparate fertility regimes of Black and White American women. Immigration has greatly increased the presence of many national origin groups with widely disparate fertility levels, while the African American population provides an example of demographic divergence after decades of expected and to some extent actual convergence. Focusing on these groups further illustrates the range of childbearing patterns in the country and provides a platform for introducing some of the theoretical issues involved in the explanation of this variation. In the final section of the paper, we assess the current state of research in this area. This body of literature is large, and undoubtedly, we will not comment on or even allude to all the important work. Our goal is to provide an overview of the main features of past studies and to identify some emerging lines of inquiry.

The major points we develop are:

- Childbearing varies considerably across racial and ethnic groups in the United States.

- Differential fertility contributes substantially to the growth of some racial/ethnic groups.

- Diminution of fertility differentials is *not* inevitable. Indeed, we discuss recent examples of diverging fertility among some groups.

- Adequate explanation of differential fertility requires greater attention to sociological factors that generate and sustain both structural differentiation and distinctive cultural environments.

The Impact of Differential Fertility
on Changing Population Composition

Figure 4.1
Population Percentages by Race, 1810-2050

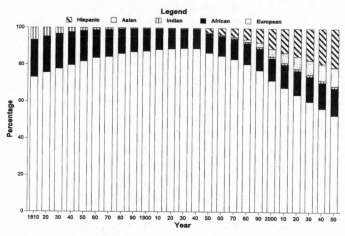

Source: McDaniel 1995.

Figure 4.1 places current discussions of population composition in historical perspective (McDaniel, 1995). Initially, we focus on five racial/ethnic categories: Hispanic, Asian, American Indian (Native American), African, and European. In the Nineteenth Century the largest non-European groups were

Indians and Africans. Their proportions declined due to the decimation of the American Indian population by warfare and disease and due to the large influx of Northern and, later, of Southern Europeans. The proportion of Europeans surpassed 80% early in the Twentieth Century. Ironically, this is the period when concerns about the composition of the population reached their peak. Many in this period were concerned about the increasing proportion of the population of Southern European origin. The 1950-1990 period shows large increases in the proportion of the population which was Hispanic and Asian which correspond to a greater attention to large flows of Hispanic and Asian immigrants. The 2000 to 2050 estimates are U.S. Census Bureau projections that will be discussed below.

How important is differential fertility across these categories in producing changes in the U.S. population composition? We noted above that mortality increase was a key factor leading to population decline for Native Americans in the Nineteenth Century. Immigration was clearly important to the historical growth of the European population as well as the contemporary increases in the country's Hispanic and Asian populations. Theoretically, fertility differences across groups can also be a powerful source of differential growth. The demographers' balancing equation shows that population growth equals the net migration rate plus the difference in crude birth and death rates (e.g., births and deaths per 1,000 population). Thus, an important impact on differential growth depends on substantial differences in fertility between groups.

Table 4.1
Total Fertility Rates by Race and Hispanic Origin: 1995 to 2050

			RACE/HISPANIC ORIGIN			
				Not of Hispanic Origin		
		Hispanic	*White*	*African American*	*Native American*	*Asian*
Year:	1995	2,650	1,850	2,450	2,900	2,300
	2000	2,650	1,850	2,450	2,900	2,300
	2010	2,591	1,850	2,450	2,900	2,252
	2030	2,472	1,850	2,450	2,900	2,152
	2050	2,358	1,850	2,450	2,900	2,057

Source: U.S. Bureau of the Census, 1992: Table J.

To assess the role of differential fertility for future changes in population composition, we ask the hypothetical question: If other groups had the fertility of non-Hispanic Whites, how much slower (or faster) would those minority groups grow? Or stated differently, How much of the projected population growth can be attributed to the higher fertility of minority groups? To answer this question, we use the group-specific population projections made by the U.S. Bureau of the Census for the years 1995–2050 (U.S. Bureau of the Census, 1992. For nontechnical discussions of these projections and their limitations see Ahlburg, 1993 and Hirschman page 51.) These projections provided the estimates shown in Figure 1 for the years 2000-2050.

We use the "middle series" projections that are based on the following assumptions (U.S. Bureau of the Census 1992:xxiv–xxix):

1. Age-specific fertility rates are held constant at slightly below 1990 levels for the non-Hispanic Whites, non-Hispanic Blacks and non-Hispanic Indian, Eskimo, and Aleut. A 10% reduction in fertility after the year 2000 is assumed for the Hispanic and Asian populations. (These total fertility rates are shown in Table 4.1.)

2. Life expectancy is assumed to increase in the middle series from 75.8 years in 1992 to 82.1 years in 2050. Sub-population differentials are assumed to remain constant.

3. Current net immigration is assumed to remain constant at 800,000 per year until 2050. The composition of the net immigration is assumed to be the same as that in 1990.

Table 4.2
Percent Female for Racial/Ethnic Groups by Age: 1995

	RACE/HISPANIC ORIGIN				
Age:	*White*	*Hispanic*	*African American*	*Native American*	*Asian*
0–14	9.65	14.39	13.46	14.67	11.87
15–39	17.79	21.05	21.19	20.14	21.85
40+	23.70	13.77	18.08	15.85	17.19

Ratio of percent of women of prime childbearing age (15-39) compared to whites:

White	*Hispanic*	*African American*	*Native American*	*Asian*
1.00	1.18	1.19	1.13	1.23

Sources: Calculated from *Current Population Reports*: Population Projections of the United States, by Age, Sex, Race, and Hispanic Origin: 1992 to 2050 (Bureau of the Census: P25-1092, Table 2 of p. 19).

Note: Persons of Hispanic origin may be of any race; Indians include American Indians, Eskimo, and Aleut; Asians include Asians and Pacific Islanders.

The Census Bureau's middle series projection shows the population size in each year (1992–2050), the yearly growth rate, and the components of change: crude net migration, birth, and death rates (U.S. Bureau of the Census, 1992: Table 4.1). These estimates are produced for the five major race/Hispanic origin groups. In essence, we substitute the non-Hispanic White fertility rate for the fertility rate of each of the other groups. Then we assess the impact of this fertility adjustment on projections. However, there is a complication. We cannot simply substitute the crude birth rate of the non-Hispanic group for the others because this rate reflects two components: an effect of the underlying age-specific fertility rates and an effect of age structure. Table 4.2 shows that the age structures of the minority populations are quite different with minority groups. They contain a higher proportion of females in the prime childbearing ages (i.e 15-39) than the non-Hispanic white population. For instance, the proportion of Hispanic women in the 15-39 age range is 18% greater than for non-Hispanic whites. We adjust for the effect of age structure and replace each groups crude birth rate with the one that would obtain if they had the age-specific rates of non-Hispanic whites.[1]

Table 4.3
Effect of Differential Fertility on Growth Rates
of Racial and Ethnic Groups

		RACE/HISPANIC ORIGIN				
		White	*Hispanic*	*African American*	*Native American*	*Asian*
Year:	1995	1.000	1.284	1.574	1.917	1.072
	2000	1.000	1.304	1.618	1.960	1.084
	2010	1.000	1.321	1.641	1.986	1.096
	2020	1.000	1.332	1.731	2.070	1.103
	2030	1.000	1.339	1.843	2.124	1.105
	2040	1.000	1.347	1.940	2.149	1.102
	2050	1.000	1.354	1.940	2.143	1.096

Sources: Calculated from Current Population Reports: Population Projections of the United States, by Age, Sex, Race, and Hispanic Origin: 1992 to 2050 (Bureau of the Census: P25-1092, Table 1).

Note: See Table 2.

The results of this exercise are shown in Tables 4.3 and 4.4. They provide evidence of the importance of group differences in childbearing. The entries in Table 4.3 are factor increases in growth rates that result from differential fertility. They are calculated by taking the ratio of the projected growth rate with differential fertility (published in U.S. Bureau of the Census, 1992: Table 4.1) to the growth rate we calculate in the absence of differential fertility. Note that the impact of differential fertility varies across groups. It is greatest for Native Americans and African Americans. By the year 2000, these ratios are nearly 2 (implying that fertility differences double the growth rate) for Native Americans and are over 1.6 for African Americans. Effects for Hispanics are also substantial ranging from 1.28 to 1.35 across the series while the effects on the Asian/non-Hispanic White ratio is smaller. The impact of differential fertility on differential growth rates tends to increase in the projections for later years for all comparisons except those involving the Asians.

Table 4.4 shows the effects of differential fertility on the absolute size of populations in the period 1995–2050. Row 1 shows the projected populations under the assumption of *no* differential fertility across this period. Row 2 shows the Bureau of the Census's projections, which incorporate the fertility differences shown in Table 4.1. The projected population size of the Hispanic population in 2050 is over 80 million. This figure is about one-third larger than it would be (about 60 million) if the Hispanic population had the same fertility levels as the non-Hispanic White population.

Differential fertility has similarly large effects on African American and American Indian populations. However, the impact of fertility differences on the Asian population growth is considerably smaller. Note that all populations will continue to grow in the absence of differential fertility—due to net immigration and favorable age structures. Although much of that population increase tends to result from these other sources, our exercise clearly shows that differential fertility has substantial effects on minority population growth.

Table 4.4
Projected Size of Racial Population in 2050,
with and without Differential Fertility

	RACE/HISPANIC ORIGIN			
	Hispanic	*African American*	*Native American*	*Asian*
1. Without Fertility Differential (1):	60,128	43,932	2,735	33,833
2. With Fertility Differential (2):	80,350	57,309	4,053	38,581
3. Ratio [(2)/(1)]:	1.336	1.304	1.482	1.140

Sources: See Table 3.
Note: See Table 2.

Patterns and Trends in Racial and Ethnic Childbearing

The orthodox view of fertility differentials sees them as transitional or time-bound. As Ryder (1973:66) explains:

> The essence of the position is that groups that still have higher-than-average fertility have not yet become modern. The inference is that, as they come to participate more fully and equally in modern life, and as the secular values of primacy of the individual...permeate the entire social system, their fertility will also decline.

Thus, differentials are explained within the framework commonly called on to account for the transition from high to low birth rates. That is, modernization/industrialization propel the demographic transition. (See for instance, Freedman 1961/62:56.) Immigrants and groups beyond the "mainstream" may lag behind. But eventually all will assimilate, and convergence with dominant group patterns will be complete.

Interestingly, the recent Census Bureau projections that we just examined do not assume that White–black and White–Indian fertility differentials will narrow in the future, and only minor declines in White–Hispanic and White–Asian fertility are forecast. The projection of relatively stable differentials was made, not on the basis of revised theory, but on the basis of empirical evidence from the 1980s that showed little diminution of intergroup fertility differentials. We will review this evidence and, in a subsequent section, return to the issue of explanations for stable differentials. In brief, two decades ago Campbell (1974) argued that it was time to move "beyond the demographic transition" and modernization theory if one was to account for contemporary fertility trends. Time is past due for a similar conclusion vis-à-vis differential fertility.

Our descriptive survey begins with a brief look at racial and ethnic differences in cumulative fertility (the number of children ever born) based on published figures from the 1980 Census and our own calculations from the 1990 Census Public Use samples. These data are useful because they provide a wide coverage of more specific racial and ethnic groups along with relatively accurate measurement of family size. The main feature of Table 4.5 is the sizable variation in levels of childbearing across the racial and ethnic groups. Note also that much of this variation is observed within the broad categories previously defined, especially for those of Hispanic origin, for Asian and Pacific Islander, and even for European ancestry, in the case of the 1980 data. Although they do not always occupy the maximum and minimum positions in the distributions, the Mexican American and Japanese American groups provide good illustrations of the range of fertility variation. In 1980, the oldest cohort (35–44) of Mexican-origin women averaged nearly 40% more children than Whites while Japanese women had about 25% fewer children than Whites.

Table 4.5
Children Ever Born Per 1,000 Women by Age and Racial/Ethnic Origin, 1980 and 1990

	1980			*1990*		
Ages	*15–24*	*25–34*	*35–44*	*15–24*	*25–34*	*35–44*
Race/Ethnicity						
White	269	1404	2544	257	1232	1853
Black	540	1859	3185	548	1614	2257
Hispanic Origin	475	1922	3202	475	1752	2544
Mexican	528	2105	3646	521	1913	2824
Puerto Rican	548	1986	3202	535	1718	2435
Cuban	192	1189	2033	169	1143	1674
Other Hispanic	337	1567	2640	346	1480	2179
Native American	529	2014	3462	559	1903	2484
Asian / Pacific Islander	217	1233	2272	166	1092	1931
Japanese	106	908	1872	80	686	1429
Chinese	82	939	2233	78	740	1681
Filipino	278	1270	2216	171	1094	1808
Korean	229	1244	2045	70	1069	1833
Asian Indian	236	1336	2197	—	—	—
Vietnamese	305	1775	3397	175	1367	2484
Hawaiian	431	1880	3325	356	1657	2633
Guamanian	408	1885	3700	350	1633	3179
Samoan	453	2400	4276	308	2166	3478
Other	433	1694	2723	—	—	—
European Origin						
English	353	1532	2558			
French	360	1567	2797			
German	294	1446	2589			
Irish	290	1432	2662			
Italian	182	1223	2362			
Polish	215	1230	2404			

Source: U.S. Bureau of the Census. *United States Summary, 1980 General Social and Economic Characteristics Vol. I.* and computations from the 1990 PUMs, U.S. Bureau of the Census.

The figures in Table 4.5 summarize childbearing that occurred over varying spans of individual ages and during different historical periods, depending
upon which age cohort is under consideration. For 1980, the cumulative fertility of the 35–44-year-old women reflects 20 or more years of experience,
much of which transpired during the years of the baby boom. For this reason
the average number of children for this age group appears high for almost all
of the groups when compared with the period fertility rates of the 1980s and
1990s. As can be seen in the 1990 columns, the younger age cohorts of 1980
will end up with smaller family sizes than the older women. Yet, while the fertility levels of all groups declined over the decade, the substantial relative differences between racial and ethnic groups remained in 1990. The average
number of children ever born to 35–44-year-old Mexican American women
was about 50% higher than that of non-Hispanic White women while the
cumulative fertility of Japanese American women remained nearly 25% lower.
These data clearly indicate a persistence of substantial variation in childbearing across racial and ethnic groups in the United States. Again, recent Census
Bureau estimates have begun to accept the persistence of these observed differences and to incorporate them into future projections.

Figure 4.2
Total Fertility Rates by Race/Origin: U.S., 1960-1995

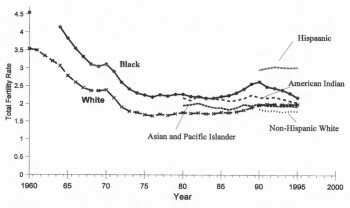

Current racial and ethnic differences in levels of childbearing along with
recent trends can also be viewed in terms of period fertility rates reported by the
National Center for Health Statistics (NCHS).[2] Figure 4.2 shows the time series
of annual total fertility rates by race since 1960.[3] In 1995, the TFR was 2.02 for
the country as a whole. The White rate for this year is 1.99 while the Black rate
was only about 10% higher at 2.18. Rates for the Asian Americans and
American Indians are even closer to the White rate. Only the Hispanic TFR of

3.02 distinctly departs from replacement level fertility. The most prominent elements of the time series are well known; the high fertility levels of the baby boom, the baby bust, a modest rebound in the 1980s, and general stability in the 1990s. The trends for the various groups tend to move in tandem.

Only the Black–White differential can be observed across the entire series. It is evident that rates for Blacks have been consistently higher than those for Whites throughout the decades. Periods of both minor convergence and divergence can be observed. Note for example, that the Black–White differential was increasing during the latter half of the 1980s. The Black period fertility rate was about 18% higher than that for Whites in 1985 but about 24% higher in 1990. This divergence is noteworthy because several widely cited accounts of differential fertility patterns have emphasized the racial convergences of the early 1980s (Evans, 1986; Cherlin, 1990). These convergences led to expectations of further convergence through the end of the decade that did not occur. The time series in Figure 4.2 does appear to show a narrowing of the gap between the Black and White rates between 1990 and 1995, but much of this apparent convergence follows from the increasing Hispanic component of the White population. The non-Hispanic Black TFR in 1995 was nearly 26% higher than the non-Hispanic White rate (2.25 versus. 1.79), a much wider racial gap than the 10% figure mentioned above that did not take Hispanic ethnicity with its associated higher fertility levels into account.

Changing fertility levels during the 1980s were accompanied by an accentuation of the long-standing racial differences in the timing of fertility (Chen and Morgan, 1991). In Table 4.6, we can see that the relative increase in Black childbearing during that decade was most pronounced in the younger age categories. By 1990 the age-specific birth rate for 15–19-year-olds was nearly 2.7 times higher for Blacks than for Whites, and for 20–24-year-olds, it was nearly 1.7 times higher. In contrast to this early stage of the childbearing years, the rates for Blacks and Whites are very similar for 25–29-year-old women, and by 1990 the rates for Black women ages 30–39 were actually lower than those recorded for White women. In sum, the rise in American period fertility rates during the latter part of the 1980s occurred in much different fashion for the two racial groups. Among Whites, increases are observed only for older cohorts whose earlier years had been characterized by record levels of delayed childbearing (Rindfuss, Morgan, and Swicegood, 1988). By contrast, the increases for Blacks were more concentrated among younger cohorts where group-specific fertility rates were already the highest. Since 1990, fertility rates have fallen moderately for most age groups of women of both races. These decreases are sharpest for young Black women, but their fertility rates remain substantially higher than those of their White counterparts.

Now we consider the annual proportion of births by race as recorded in the U.S. vital statistics. The relative quantity of births each year has the most direct bearing on the contribution of race and ethnic fertility to the increasing diversity of the country's population. This way of examining racial and ethnic childbearing brings into focus the extent of ethnic and racial variation in our youngest cohorts and complements our earlier analysis of the impact of differential fertility on the changing racial and ethnic composition of the population.

Table 4.6
Age-Specific Fertility Rates for White and Black Women, 1970–1995

Age Group	1995 [a]	1990 [a]	1980	1970
10–14	0.4	0.5	0.6	0.5
15–19	39.3	42.5	44.7	57.4
20–24	90.0	97.5	109.5	163.4
25–29	106.5	115.3	112.4	145.9
30–34	82.0	79.4	60.4	71.9
35–39	32.9	30.0	18.5	30.0
40–44	5.9	4.7	3.4	7.5
45–49	0.3	0.2	0.2	0.4

Age-Specific Fertility Rates for Black Women, 1970–1995

Age Group	1995 [a]	1990 [a]	1980	1970
10–14	4.3	5.0	4.3	5.2
15–19	99.3	116.2	97.8	140.7
20–24	141.7	165.1	140.0	202.7
25–29	102.0	118.4	103.9	136.3
30–34	65.9	70.2	59.9	79.6
35–39	29.4	28.7	23.5	41.9
40–44	6.1	5.6	5.6	12.5
45–49	0.3	0.3	0.3	1.0

[a] Rates for 1990 and 1995 are for non-Hispanic whites and non-Hispanic blacks respectively.

Sources: Ventura, S.J., Martin, J.A., Curin, S.C., and Matthews, T.J. Report of Natality Statistics, 1995. Monthly Vital Statistics Report. Vol. 45, No. 11(S), June 10, 1997. Hyattsville, MD: National Center for Health Statistics.

National Center for Health Statistics. 1988. Vital Statistics of the United States, 1988 (Vol.1) Natality. Washington, D.C.: U.S. Department of Health and Human Services.

Table 4.7 shows the racial and ethnic profile for all U.S. births in 1995. Of the 3.9 million births for the year, about 79.5% were classified as White, 15.5% Black, slightly more than 4% Asian and Pacific Islander, and just under 1% Native American. All states in the vital registration system now classified births according to Hispanic parentage. These births made up 17.4% of the total for the country as a whole in 1995. The White non-Hispanic population is frequently viewed as the "majority group" or basis for comparison in racial and ethnic studies. Here we see that when Hispanic births are removed from the counts, the percentage of all births that were White drops to 61%. Thus, by 1995 nearly two of every five births were a potential minority group member. If the Census Bureau projections discussed above were to hold by 2050, only 42% of annual births would occur to non-Hispanic Whites. Hispanic, African, Asian, and Native Americans, respectively, would account for about 26%, 20.5%, 10% and 1.5% of all births in that year.

Table 4.7
Distribution of 1995 Births by Race and Hispanic Origin

	Number	*Percent*
White	3,098,885	79.47
Black	603,139	15.47
Native American	37,278	.96
Asian and Pacific Islander	160,287	4.11
Chinese	27,380	.70
Japanese	8,901	.23
Filipino	30,551	.78
Hawaiian	5,787	.15
Other API	87,668	2.25
Hispanic Origin	679,768	17.43
Mexican	469,615	12.04
Puerto Rican	54,824	1.41
Cuban	12,473	.32
Central and South Am.	94,996	2.44
Other and Unknown Hispanic	47,860	1.23
White–Non-Hispanic	2,382,638	61.10
Black–Non-Hispanic	587,781	15.07
U.S. Total	3,899,589	

Source: Ventura, S.J., Martin, J.A., Curin, S.C., and Matthews, T.J. Report of Natality Statistics, 1995. Monthly Vital Statistics Report, Vol. 45, No. 11(S), June 10, 1997. Hyattsville, MD: National Center for Health Statistics.

The birth data shown in Figure 4.3 demonstrate quite succinctly that the relative size of the non-White population has already been shifting steadily for some time. Here we have plotted the time series of the percentage of annual births that were non-White and the percentage of all births that were Black from 1960–1990. Both measures show a sustained increase over the period.

The series does not take into account the percentage of births to Hispanic mothers, a percentage that has risen dramatically in the last decade. That phenomenon has tended to dampen the percentage increases in non-White births because most Hispanic births occur to women who are classified as White by the vital statistics system. This simple depiction of the changing racial/ethnic mix of annual births makes it clear that even if immigration were somehow halted entirely, the distinct fertility regimes and age compositions of the groups that we have already examined will ensure a continuing increase in the proportion of each new cohort who are minority group members.[4]

Figure 4.3
Percentage of All Births that Were Black and Non-White, 1960-1990

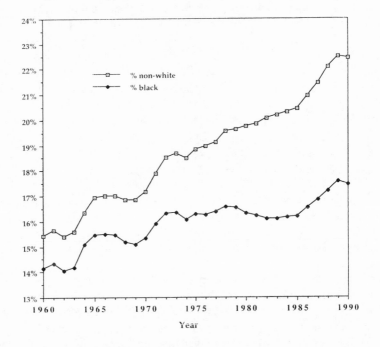

Reproductive Patterns of Immigrants

Issues of differential racial and ethnic fertility are intertwined with the patterns and flows of immigration into the country. Our historical record reveals a recurring interest in the relative reproductive levels of the latest round of immigrants vis-à-vis that of the native-born population (King and Ruggles, 1990). Indeed a sound argument can be made that the racial/ethnic categories under which official population data are recorded reflect in part prior concerns over the changing character of immigrant streams. Many of the racial and ethnic groupings examined in the earlier descriptive analysis have relatively high proportions of foreign-born persons. Not surprisingly, the recent explosion of popular and scholarly interest in immigration has been accompanied by studies focusing on the fertility behavior of immigrants. Most studies have implicitly followed an assimilation perspective, a view very similar to the "modernization/industrialization" perspective outlined earlier. The general expectation has been that with passage of time (either individual or generational), immigrant groups and their descendants will become increasingly assimilated on a variety of dimensions, and as a consequence their fertility patterns will come to resemble those of their new country.

The interpretation of fertility differences between immigrant and native-born populations may be complicated by two factors that are less directly linked to the assimilationist perspective. First, immigrants may postpone or forgo childbearing as a result of spousal separation, stress, reallocation of resources, or other disruptions associated with the migration process. Second, the selectivity of the immigrant streams with respect to fertility-related characteristics must be considered when examining variation in fertility patterns across immigrant groups from different origins or the change in fertility patterns across successive immigration cohorts.

Several studies have provided indirect support for selection effects. Changes over time in the selectivity of immigrants both within and across origin countries have resulted in relatively higher fertility among the immigrant population than would otherwise have been the case. For example, Blau's (1992) analysis of 1980 Census samples showed that recent immigrants reported more children than either the native-born or immigrants of longer residence. Similarly, there is evidence that disruption effects do occur around the time of immigration (Bean and Swicegood, 1985; Blau, 1992; Kahn, 1995; Stephen and Bean, 1992). Although the magnitudes of these effects are difficult to specify with precision, they do appear to occur for many immigrant groups.[5]

The difficulties involved with gauging the overall impact of disruption processes arise in part from the complexity of immigrant fertility experiences after arrival into the United States. Pace and quantity of childbearing are conditioned by factors that are specific to the country of origin of the immigrant and by individual characteristics such as human capital and language facility. Kahn's work provides several illustrations of this complexity. Her analysis of recent CPS data (Kahn, 1995) produced patterns consistent with disruption effects, but subsequent to immigration, some groups tend to make up for the disruption while others do not. Among women who were recent immigrants in

1980, the gap between the Mexican-born and the native-born populations grew much wider over the remainder of the decade while the fertility of Asian women fell further behind the referent group. Kahn (1988) further shows that while fertility levels prevailing in the country of origin continue to influence childbearing in the United States, the extent of this influence varies. As one might expect, childbearing patterns more typical of the country of origin are most pronounced among the least educated, least assimilated immigrants.

The differential fertility patterns that have been observed across national-origin groups of women carry several implications. Recent trends in immigration are likely to reinforce current racial and ethnic and fertility differences. In this volume (page 85) Massey argues that the new immigration will have a different meaning for ethnicity and race in American life than early European waves because it is grounded in fundamentally different structural circumstances. Flows of new immigrants are expected to be more continuous across a longer duration of time, creating a state of more or less "permanent immigration." Geographic concentration of the new immigration has created and sustained distinctive language and cultural communities on an unprecedented scale. To the extent that sustained immigrant streams can reinforce ethnicity, any distinctive norms about childbearing may also be reinforced among the entire ethnic community, including the native-born generations. This may be especially true for a group like the Mexican Americans. Their immigration originates from a higher fertility context. Their proximity to the receiving areas of the United States is relatively close; their migration patterns frequently involve return episodes; and numerous large Spanish-language communities are available as destination points.

Over the last 25 years, the largest immigrant stream to the United States has come from Mexico, and numerous studies have examined the distinctively high fertility of this ethnic group. These studies underscore several of the processes discussed above. Even for this high fertility group, there is some evidence of disrupted childbearing, especially among those women who are relatively young at the time of their arrival (Bean and Swicegood, 1985; Stephen and Bean, 1992). But the gap between their fertility and that of the non-Hispanic White population appears to widen with length of residence in the United States (Stephen and Bean, 1991).

A particular issue of recurring interest in the literature on the Mexican-origin population concerns how childbearing levels shift across generational groupings. To what extent if any do the childbearing patterns of native-born Mexican Americans of native-born parents approach that of the majority White population? Does demographic assimilation occur across generations? The answer to these questions depends upon the historical period under review. Peter Uhlenberg (1973) first looked at this issue with 1960 Census data and found virtually no differences in cumulative fertility between

Mexican-born women, second generational women, and native-born Mexican-origin women of native-born parents. All three generational groupings had comparatively high levels of childbearing. In 1970 the pattern of *net* fertility differences between the generational groups tended to be curvilinear with the lowest Mexican American fertility being observed for the first generation, the highest fertility among the second generation, and with the intermediate level being occupied by the third generation. This pattern of differentials suggests that several decades ago immigration was either more disruptive or that the immigrant population was more selected on low-fertility behavior. At this time, the adjusted cumulative fertility levels of immigrant women were actually at or below those of non-Hispanic White women. By 1980 Mexican-born women still tended to have lower net cumulative fertility than their native-born Mexican-origin counterparts but higher levels of current fertility, and in contrast to 1970, the immigrant generation had considerably higher net fertility than non-Hispanic White women on both measures[6] (Bean and Swicegood, 1985; Stephen and Bean, 1992).

During the 1980s, a new generational pattern emerged in the Mexican-origin population in which the highest fertility levels (both unadjusted and net) are observed for the first generation and the lowest levels for the second generation (Bean, Swicegood, and Berg, 1998). The fertility levels of the third-or-later generational Mexican-origin women now run counter to the hypothesis of generational convergence. Not only are they generally higher than those of the second generation, they also tend to be closer to the levels of Mexican-born women than to those of non-Hispanic Whites. These recent findings clearly indicate that the increased length of residence in the country need not result in behavioral assimilation with respect to childbearing.

The fertility patterns discussed in this section (except where otherwise indicated) were obtained from multivariate models in which numerous statistical controls were applied to the comparisons. Such controls tend to reduce differences between immigrant and native-born women.[7] For virtually every country-of-origin group, the fertility of immigrants is higher than that of women of the same descent group. However, it is important to remember that it is unadjusted differences that will directly affect change in the population composition. Overall, the proportional differences between the fertility levels of the native and foreign-born components of the population may now be as great or greater than at any time in the past. Much of the literature on immigrant fertility is based on data from 1980 or earlier. The assessment of differentials for this period is generally based on cohorts of foreign-born women who were on average more likely than is currently the case to have immigrated to the United States from a relatively low fertility society. The fertility of these foreign-born women is compared with the fertility of native-born women, many of whom completed childbearing during the baby boom era and of course, had births at both a faster pace and at higher levels than is typical of native-born women today. As a result, much of the existing research tends to understate the extent of currently prevailing immigrant–native-born differences in childbearing.

Black–White Differences in Childbearing

Next, we further examine the distinctive childbearing regimes of the Black and White populations. Although a rich store of demographic and social information is available for these two populations, there is much we don't fully understand about how their different fertility patterns emerged and continue to evolve. However, both theoretical and empirical work support the notion that the disparate demographic regimes of Blacks and Whites in America are grounded in the dynamics of intergroup relations.

Historically Blacks have entered into parenthood at a somewhat earlier average age than Whites, and as noted earlier, this difference has been widening in the past several decades. Rindfuss, Morgan, and Swicegood (1988, chapter 6) have documented a clear racial divergence in trends toward delayed childbearing during the 1970s. This divergence was most pronounced among women with the highest education. Since this finding contradicts expectations generated by an assimilationist perspective, we offered a relative socioeconomic status interpretation of the pattern. Our interpretation was based on the observation that better-educated Blacks had experienced real economic improvement over the period, while Whites had not. Whites responded to the relatively poor economic times by sharply delaying parenthood. Alternatively, educated Blacks had reason to interpret their economic circumstances more favorably. The dynamics of race relations of the era led to social programs and legislation that provided the basis for improving the economic status of Blacks. As it turned out, the impact of this race-conscious social action proved to be most advantageous to better-educated minority group members. It appears that this effort to attain economic equity had the unanticipated consequence of promoting demographic divergence. Chen and Morgan (1991) have shown that the racial divergence in first-birth timing has continued into the 1980s, but it is most unlikely that the same explanation can account for this more recent divergence. Meanwhile, as attention has been drawn to the much earlier pace of parenthood among Blacks, the comparative racial and ethnic studies have begun to concentrate on fertility-related behavior during adolescence.

After some years of research emphasis on adolescent fertility behavior, we now know a good deal about the factors leading to the earlier average entry of Black women into parenthood (Hogan and Kitagawa, 1985; Hayes, 1987; Moore, Simms, and Betsey, 1986) There is evidence for intergenerational transmission of a constellation of behaviors that result in premarital births to teenage women. Factors associated with this outcome are disproportionately distributed in the Black population.

A less well-developed story involves how and why Black women postpone and forego second-order births more often than Whites. Johnson (1988) and St. John and Grasmick (1985) identified this pattern in research motivated by the minority group status hypothesis. This hypothesis is motivated towards identifying the circumstances associated with the distinctively low fertility of specific segments of the minority group. The basic idea is that at some point in the assimilation/incorporation process, minority group members may reduce their fertility relative to majority counterparts in order to overcome the additional barriers to socioeconomic achievement that they face (Goldscheider and Uhlenberg, 1969). It does appear that for recent cohorts of Black women, the link between timing of first birth and cumulative number of children has weakened. This may account in part for Furstenberg's findings that the consequences of adolescent childbearing may not be as deleterious as commonly believed (Furstenberg, Gunn and Morgan, 1987; Hoffman, Foster and Furstenberg, 1993). Still, there is much we don't know about the how the pace of subsequent fertility is slowed among Black women. It may be useful, as has often proved the case, to identify the proximate determinants through which this process is operating.

There is some evidence that racial differences in abortion play an important role (Kochanek,1991). Vital registration data for the fourteen states reporting induced abortion indicate that the abortion ratio (the number of abortions per one thousand live births) for Black women of all ages was 2 1/4 times higher than for Whites. The rates for 15–19-year-olds is very similar for both races, and the greatest differences by race occur for women 25–34. Racial differences in the likelihood of terminating a pregnancy also interact with marital status and education. The abortion ratio for unmarried black women is actually lower than that for white women (776.6 versus. 1,131:1) while among married women the abortion ratio is nearly four times higher than for Whites (261.3 versus. 68.1). It is clear that understanding how these patterns arise will require some investigation of how marital dynamics differ in the Black and White populations. The pattern of abortion ratios by education also varies in a way that is consistent with the minority group status hypothesis. The greatest differences by race occur for women with a college education.

One final set of racial differences we mention concerns the prevalence of unwanted and mistimed births. In 1988 for ever-married women, the proportion of births in the previous five years that were unwanted was over twice as high for Black women as compared with Whites (22.8% versus 8.8%). The propensity for births to be unwanted increased for both races between 1982 and 1988, but especially so for Blacks. Another quarter of the births to both races can be described as mistimed. A similar racial difference held for never-married women. In 1988, 36% of all Black births in the previous five years were reported as unwanted compared to about 15% of the births to White women. A majority of the remaining births to both races was reported as mistimed (Williams and Pratt, 1990). Here we see yet another dimension on which racial differences tended to widen rather than converge.

Main Currents of Old and New Lines of Research

Below, we provide a brief overview of the research literature in this area, including a few remarks about some promising lines of inquiry. In recent years, social demographers have devoted somewhat less attention to the topic of differential racial and ethnic fertility than in earlier periods. We've already alluded to several reasons why this might be the case. First, there is the matter of data constraints. Surveys rarely contain sufficient numbers of women from specific racial and ethnic groups to sustain detailed analysis beyond the comparisons of the Black, White, and in some instances Mexican-origin populations. In many surveys ethnicity is not even assessed. Conversely, data sources that may contain richer information about the concepts that we hypothesize as central to ethnicity may have little information about childbearing attitudes and behaviors. The public-use samples from the decennial Census circumvents the numbers problem to some extent, but these samples contain relatively little information on either fertility-related behavior or ethnicity.

On the theoretical side, studies grounded in minority group status hypotheses have generally run their course. Distinctively low fertility of specific segments (e.g., the best educated) of a minority group has become less evident in recent fertility surveys and reports, especially in the African American and Hispanic American populations. The lack of specificity of the connection between the operative mechanisms (e.g., discrimination and social and psychological insecurity) implied by the hypothesis and the proximate determinants of fertility have also been criticized (Forste and Tienda, 1996). Understandably, substantive interests have been shifting toward other topics, such as the more socially compelling issue of adolescent fertility behavior.

To some extent the research on racial and ethnic fertility differentials may have received lower priority because of the ascendancy of economic perspectives in the modeling of demographic behavior. Research grounded in the microeconomics of fertility decision making has been particularly prevalent.

Clearly, economic perspectives have relevance to the question of racial and ethnic differentials. The concept of opportunity costs of childbearing would seem especially useful for explaining racial and ethnic differentials (e.g., Swicegood et al., 1988). But, the search for what Freedman and Thornton (1982) have termed the "elusive income-fertility relationship" has followed a path of ever more homogeneous samples. Ethnic populations have not been generally considered to provide the most appropriate applications of the "new home economics." They may have tastes for quantities or qualities of children that are different from the majority group. Their more complex marital histories undercut the assumptions of the model. Moreover, the limitations of any model of fertility behavior that is focused on married persons are increasingly apparent. Rindfuss and Parnell (1989) have presented evidence that the major axes of fertility differentiation that we think of as characterizing U.S. society, that is race and education, are primarily a consequence of the childbearing patterns of unmarried women.

Despite the influence of economic perspectives in fertility research, some researchers have continued to emphasize sociological factors in the interpretation of their results. Sorenson (1988) makes a strong case that the association between a husband's language characteristics and the fertility of his wife reflect the cultural influence of pronatalist norms. The net association between the fertility rate of the sending country and the childbearing patterns of immigrants to the United States has similarly been interpreted as the impact of the sending country's norms, values, and attitudes (Kahn, 1988). St. John and Rowe (1990) have taken on the task of measuring the presence of norms more directly at the individual level. In their study of racial differences in the antecedents of adolescent pregnancy, they obtained measures of the perceived problems associated with a premarital pregnancy and the moral and social disapproval that might accompany premarital sexual activity. Their results led them to conclude that even among college educated women, Blacks were more likely to hold norms favorable to early childbearing. Each of these normative interpretations may be accurate. The evidence they provide is certainly more convincing than the still frequent practice of attributing residual fertility differences between groups to cultural factors. However, their evidence for the independent role of norms is indirect and leaves us wanting to know more about the content and operation of these norms.

Efforts to reintroduce the idea of culture into demographic theory have proceded on a more theoretical front that could be useful for explaining variation in fertility behavior across social groups (e.g., Hammel, 1990; Watkins, 1990). "Culture may explain why....persons living under apparently identical economic conditions but differing in language or tradition, often behave very differently demographically...(or) why the population of a geographic region or linguistic area continues to behave demographically in much the same way...even though economic conditions change, (or)...why demographic differentials between populations persist even as the level of some demographic measure for all of them exhibits similar change over time" (Hammel, 1990: 455). These are exactly the kind of questions that we are left with after we apply our statistical controls to regression models and group differentials stubbornly remain. How can demographers use this notion of culture? Hammel's prescriptions are complex and demanding. One begins by identifying "the network of social actors that are directly involved in the processes that have demographic import." For Watkins this might involve the delineation of a gossip circle that discusses the appropriate practices of breast-feeding or an elaboration of the changing boundaries of a particular marriage market. If culture is maintained and transformed in the context of networks, then subcultures associated with race and ethnicity can be examined in terms of distinctive social networks.

Calvin Goldscheider (1995) has also argued that conceptualizing ethnicity in terms of network linkages is a potentially important avenue to understanding its demographic significance. Some of the promise of this orientation can be seen in its connections with prior empirical studies of racial and ethnic fertility patterns. Research along these lines has suggested how kinship and friendship circles in the Black community may provide support for adolescent childbearing, and how a women's adolescent fertility experiences may influence the childbearing pattern of her younger sister (Hogan and Kitagawa, 1985). Brewster (1994) has also shown how wider community characteristics influence fertility-related behavior across racial boundaries. The conjugal partners of the women are one obvious set of network members whose influence on fertility-related behavior is usually unexamined. This influence may be especially important for fertility outcomes in minority groups. Sorenson (1989), for example, has shown that the statistical association of husband's characteristics and couple fertility is much stronger in the case of Mexican Americans than non-Hispanic Whites. Of course, we need to know much more about what is transpiring between partners before we can confirm the operation of a cultural effect, and this is just the direction that this new work is pointing towards.

The idea that distinctive cultural factors may shape demographic behavior in the African American population seems particularly plausible considering even the partial listing of differences in Black and White reproductive regimes that we outlined earlier. Given the long history of unfavorable structural conditions of Blacks and the persistence of high levels of residential and educational segregation, it would hardly be surprising for unique cultural patterns to be sustained. These patterns, however, are likely to be both rooted in the past structures and elaborated upon by new circumstances. Whatever the nature of this cultural system, it almost certainly amounts to something more complex than a set of pronatalist norms. While such norms might account for early initiation of parenthood, they are hard to reconcile with the comparatively high levels of unwanted births and abortions that have been recorded for the African American population.

Discussion

Our goal has been to highlight the differential fertility patterns of racial and ethnic groups in the United States. Published statistics from government agencies along with numerous analytical studies document the substantial fertility differences that prevail within American society. We demonstrate, by modifying Census Bureau projections, that differential fertility can contribute substantially to the growth of minority populations and consequently shift the racial and ethnic composition of the population.

Intergroup variation in fertility levels are long-standing. In an earlier comprehensive overview of American fertility, Rindfuss and Sweet (1977) made this point while emphasizing the remarkable extent to which nearly ever social group participated in postwar fertility trends. The "ubiquitous" nature of these trends does not strictly imply eventual convergence across groups, but given the implicit assimilationist/modernization bent of much of the writing on this topic, it is easy to see how their finding might be given this twist. A convergence hypothesis also follows easily from the multivariate statistical techniques of modern social science. Statistically controlling for education, family background, and similar factors usually reduces group differentials, often by a substantial amount. In real life, however, all of these factors continue to differentiate racial and ethnic groups and certainly contribute to the observed cross-sectional variation in fertility behavior. Moreover, they are likely to interact with cultural factors, to produce the instances of divergent trends that we have discussed.

One can, of course, take another view and emphasize similarities as opposed to differentials. The fertility levels observed by all American ethnic populations are relatively low by historical and international standards, and it is always possible that periods of divergent patterns will be quickly followed by periods of convergence. For many individual women/couples, the difference between two and three children may seem relatively small. However, the patterns of differences discussed here have potential consequences and, thus, their importance should not be minimized.

At the individual level, similar completed family sizes may be produced by quite different patterns of timing of births across the life course. These timing differences may impact on many social and economic outcomes for all family members, and they are a key distinguishing feature of black and white fertility schedules. Clearly, part of the Black–White differential results from differential unwanted and mistimed childbearing. As a result, policies and programs designed to facilitate effective family planning may reduce the racial differences in both timing and numbers of births.[8] Unfortunately, we know much less about the intentions status for births in Hispanic, Asian and Native American groups because they are not represented in sufficient numbers in the standard fertility surveys.

At the societal level, differential racial and ethnic fertility could have significant implications. Over time, differential reproduction has helped change the relative size of racial and ethnic groups in the United States. The momentum built into the current demographic regime suggests that the contribution of differential childbearing to future racial and ethnic diversity will accelerate, as our earlier tabulations showed. Shifts in group size could have important consequences for intergroup relations. Prior research has demonstrated a link between the relative size of minority groups and various aspects of racial and ethnic relations, including discrimination, inequality, and racial attitudes of the majority group (Fossett and Kiecolt, 1989; Lieberson, 1980; Frisbie and Niedert, 1977). But the translation of changing population size or composition into *particular* outcomes, via theories of "demographic determinacy," can prove to be very misleading.[9] Consequences may, for instance, be mediated by another correlate of increasing diversity—intermarriage. Because intergroup marriage and mating have been so prevalent in the United States, many children have mixed ethnic/racial backgrounds. The extent of this phenomenon is substantial. Stevens (1990), for example has examined the extent to which children ages 0–13 in 1976 of various reported ethnic/racial backgrounds actually have homogeneous or mixed-ethnic parentage. For most of the European ancestry groups, the percentage of children with mixed background exceeded 75%. One of every five children classified as Mexican ancestry had parents with different ethnic backgrounds as compared with only 1 in 20 of the Black children. Increased levels of intermarriage since 1976 means that the portion of children with mixed ethnic background is even greater today.

This complexity of background has not yet been fully addressed in the demography of race and ethnicity although this situation is changing (especially see the chapters by Hirschman page 51 and Waters page 25). Researchers have usually assumed that the birth of a child to a woman of a particular race or ethnicity changes the population composition accordingly. The vital statistics system classified births according to race of child (until the late 1980s) and the ethnicity of the parents. The Census Bureau largely allows people to report these attributes for themselves and their children. However, the children may grow to identify with neither the race nor ethnicity of that classification. Thus, one birth recorded as Japanese in the vital statistics does not imply a new member of the Japanese ethnic group.[10] The figures cited above and in the Waters and Hirschman chapters demonstrate just how indeterminate our classification schemes may be. Mixed backgrounds are now so prevalent in the United States that the long-term implications for racial and ethnic diversity of the fertility differentials examined here will depend on how these mixed ancestries are sorted out. The "blurring" of racial/ethnic lines may reduce the social distance between groups.

Finally, differential fertility and fertility patterns may be most important for their "alleged" as opposed to "objective" effects. In the divisive debates about racial/ethnic inequalities, one often hears claims that the family/fertility behavior of a group, such as the teenage childbearing of African Americans, is responsible for the group's disadvantaged position. In this view, the behavior of the group is seen as producing the group's disadvantaged position.[11] Such arguments often direct attention away from other structural factors, such as discrimination or residential segregation, that may benefit the dominant group. The dominant group might well seize evidence of differential fertility behavior as a more palatable explanation for inequality compared to structural features that benefit the majority. Clearly, we cannot resolve this debate here. But it is näive to ignore the likely uses of evidence on differential fertility.

Notes

1. We adjust for age structure in the following way: For each year we know both the crude birth rate (CBR) and the total fertility rate (TFR). The ratio, CBR/TFR, provides a metric for age structure effects. This ratio for a minority population divided by the ratio for non-Hispanic Whites provides an appropriate adjustment for the pronatalist effects of the minority group age structure.

2. NCHS has long reported a wide array of birth statistics separately for Whites, Blacks, and persons of all races other than Whites including a time series of total fertility rates. Until relatively recently, only less refined measures have been reported for a more detailed racial/ethnic classification that also includes separate measures for Hispanics.

3. The total fertility rate (TFR) is the summation of the age-specific fertility rates for the year and represents the average number of children a hypothetical woman (or cohort of women) would have if she bore children throughout her life at the age-specific rates observed for the time period under consideration. This measure eliminates the effects of differential age composition on comparisons across time or groups.

4. This inference assumes that changes in differential mortality will not overwhelm the fertility dynamics already in force, a possibility that seems unlikely.

5 Indochinese refugees may be an exception. Weeks and his colleagues (1989) present evidence of very high fertility for this group immediately following their arrival in the United States in the 1980s.

6. These patterns hold except at the very youngest age cohorts of women where disruption effects again appear to be operating to suppress immigrant fertility.

7. Even the direction of differences can change after statistical controls. For example, in all of the Mexican origin studies cited above, the unadjusted fertility levels of immigrant women of Mexican-origin were always higher than their native-born counterparts and substantially higher than those for the non-Hispanic white population.

8. Of course, restricting access to abortion and cutting back programs that facilitate family planning may widen existing differentials.

9. Take for example Preston's (1984) account of the consequences of the growth in the elderly population in recent decades. Straightforward application of Malthusian concepts suggests that more elderly would produce greater demands on fixed resources. Instead, the elderly became a powerful political force and enlarged the resources available to the elderly.

10. Obviously, racial or ethnic identification is not a matter of open choice. Choice is constrained by parental backgrounds and pressures, interactions with peers, and encounters with social institutions, all factors that are shaped in turn by the prevailing climate of intergroup relations. The choice of persons of African American ancestry are especially likely to be constrained.

11. Perhaps the most famous instance of such an argument is the Moynihan Report (1965), which traced the current socioeconomic position of Blacks to a "weaknesses" in the Black family.

References

Ahlburg, Dennis A. 1993. "The Census Bureau's new projections of the U.S. population." *Population and Development Review,* 19:159–74.

Bean, Frank D. and Gray Swicegood. 1985. *Mexican American Fertility Patterns.* Austin: The University of Texas Press.

Bean, Frank D., Gray Swicegood, and Ruth Berg. 1998. "Assimilationist and Ethnic Resilience Factors in Mexican Origin Fertility: A Multi-Generational Study." Presented at the Annual Meetings of the American Sociological Association, San Francisco, CA.

Blau, Francine D. (1992). "The Fertility of Immigrant Women: Evidence from High Fertility Source Countries." In George J. Borjas and Richard B. Freeman eds., *Immigration and the Work Force: Economic Consequences for the United States and Source Areas.* Chicago: University of Chicago Press, pp. 93–133.

Brewster, Karin L. 1994. "Race Differences in Sexual Activity among Adolescent Women: The Role of Neighborhood Characteristics." *American Sociological Review* 59: 408–24.

Campbell, A.A. 1974. "Beyond the Demographic Transition." *Demography,* 11:549–561.

Chen, Renbao and S. Philip Morgan. 1991. "Recent Trends in the Timing of First Births in the United States." *Demography,* 28: 513–533.

Cherlin, Andrew. 1990. "Recent Changes in American Fertility, Marriage and Divorce." *The Annals, AAPSS,* 510:145–154.

Evans, M.D.R. 1986. "American Fertility Patterns: A Comparison of White and Non-White Cohorts Born 1903–56." *Population and Development Review,* 12:267–293.

Forste, Renata and Marta Tienda. 1996. "What's Behind Racial and Ethnic Fertility Differentials?" In John B. Casterline, Ronald D. Lee, and Karen A. Foote, eds. *Fertility in the United States: New Patterns, New Theories. Population and Development Review.* A Supplement to Volume 22. New York: The Population Council, pp. 109–133.

Fossett, Mark A. and K. Jill Kiecolt. 1989. "The Relative Size of Minority Populations and White Racial Attitudes." *Social Science Quarterly,* 70:820–835.

Freedman, Deborah S. and Arland Thornton. 1982. "Income and Fertility: The Elusive Relationship." *Demography,* 19:65–78.

Freedman, Ronald C. 1961/62. "The Sociology of Human Fertility: A Trend Report and Bibliography." *Current Sociology,* 10/11:35–68.

Frisbie, W. Parker and Lisa J. Niedert. 1977. "Inequality and the Relative Size of Minority Populations: A Comparative Analysis." *American Journal of Sociology* 82:1007–1030.

Furstenberg, Frank F., Jr., J. Brooks-Gunn and S. Philip Morgan. 1987. *Adolescent Mothers in Later Life.* Cambridge: Cambridge University Press.

Goldscheider, Calvin. 1995. *Population, Ethnicity, and Nation-Building.* Westview Press.

Goldscheider, Calvin and Peter Uhlenberg. 1969. "Minority Group Status and Fertility." *American Journal of Sociology,* 74:361–372.

Hammel, E. A. 1990. "A Theory of Culture for Demography." *Population and Development Review,* 16:455–485.

Hayes, Cheryl D., ed. 1987. *Risking the Future: Adolescent Sexuality, Pregnancy and Childbearing.* Volume I. National Research Council. Washington, DC: National Academy Press.

Hoffman, Saul D., E. Michael Foster, and Frank F. Furstenberg, Jr. 1993. "Re-evaluating the Costs of Teenage Childbearing." *Demography,* 30:1–15.

Hogan, Dennis P. and Evelyn M. Kitagawa. 1985. "The Impact of Social Status, Family Structure, and Neighborhood on the Fertility of Black Adolescents." *American Journal of Sociology,* 90:825–855.

Johnson, Nan E. 1988. "The Pace of Births over the Life Course: Implications for the Minority Group Status Hypothesis." *Social Science Quarterly,* 69:95–107.

Kahn, Joan R. 1995. "Immigrant and Native Fertility in the U.S. in the 1980s: Adaptation and Expectations for the Future." *International Migration Review,* 28:501–519.

————. 1988. "Immigrant Selectivity and Fertility Adaptation in the United States." *Social Forces,* 67:108–127.

King, Miriam and Steven Ruggles. 1990. "American Immigration, Fertility and Race Suicide at the Turn of the Century." *Journal of Interdisciplinary History,* 20:347–369.

Kochanek, Kenneth D. 1991. "Induced Terminations of Pregnancy: Reporting States, 1988." *Monthly Vital Statistics Report,* vol. 39, no. 12, Suppl. Hyattsville, MD: National Center for Health Statistics.

Lieberson, Stanley. 1980. *A Piece of the Pie: Blacks and White Immigrants Since 1880.* Berkeley: University of California Press.

McDaniel, Antonio. 1995. "The Dynamic Racial Composition of the United States." *Daedalus,* 124:179–198.

Moore, Kristin A., Margaret C. Simms, and Charles L. Betsey. 1986. *Choice and Circumstance.* New Brunswick, NJ: Transaction Books.

Moynihan, Daniel Patrick. 1965. The Negro Family: The Case for National Action. Washington DC: Department of Labor; Office of Policy Planning and Research.

Preston, Samuel H. 1984. "Children and the Elderly: Divergent Paths for America's Dependents." *Demography* 21:435–437.

Rindfuss, Ronald R., S. Philip Morgan, and Gray Swicegood. 1988. *First Births in America: Changes in the Timing of Parenthood.* Berkeley: University of California Press.

Rindfuss, Ronald R. and James Sweet. 1977. *Postwar Fertility Trends and Differentials in the United States.* New York: Academic Press.

Rindfuss, Ronald R. and Allan M. Parnell. 1989. "The Varying Connection between Marital Status and Childbearing in the United States." *Population and Development Review,* 15:447–470.

Ryder, Norman B. 1973. "Recent Trends and Group Differences in Fertility." Westoff, Charles et al., *Toward the End of Growth.* Englewood Cliffs, NJ: Prentice Hall pp. 57–68.

St. John, Craig and Harold Grasmick. 1985. "Decomposing the Black/White Fertility Differential." *Social Science Quarterly,* 66:132–146.

St. John, Craig and David Rowe. 1990. "Adolescent Background and Fertility Norms: Implications for Racial Differences in the Early Childbearing." *Social Science Quarterly,* 71:152–162.

Sorenson, Ann M. 1988. "The Fertility and Language Characteristics of Mexican-American and Non-Hispanic Husbands and Wives." *Sociological Quarterly,* 29:111–130.

———. 1989. "Husbands' and Wives' Characteristics and Fertility Decisions: A Diagonal Mobility Model." *Demography,* 26:125–135.

Stephen, Elizabeth H. and Frank D. Bean. 1992. "Assimilation, Disruption and the Fertility of Mexican Origin Women in the United States." *International Migration Review,* 26: 67–88.

Stevens, Gillian. 1990. "The Ethnic and Linguistic Backgrounds of U.S. Children." Presented at the annual meetings of the Southern Demographic Association. Louisville, KY, October 18–20.

Swicegood, Gray, Frank D. Bean, Elizabeth H. Stephen, and Wolfgang Opitz. 1988. "Language Usage and Fertility in the Mexican-Origin Population of the United States." *Demography,* 25:17–33.

Uhlenberg, Peter. 1973. "Fertility Patterns Within the Mexican American Population." *Social Biology,* 20:30–39.

Ventura, S.J., J.A. Martin, S.C. Curin, and T.J. Matthews, Report of Natality Statistics, 1995. *Monthly Vital Statistics Report,* Vol. 45, No. 11(S), June 10, 1997. Hyattsville, MD: National Center for Health Statistics.

Watkins, Susan Cotts. 1990. "The Transformation of Demographic Regimes in Western Europe, 1870–1960." *Population and Development Review,* 16:241–272.

Weeks, John R., Ruben G. Rumbaut, Claire Brindis, Carol C. Korenbrot, and Donald Minkler. 1989. "High Fertility among Indochinese Refugees." *Public Health Reports* 104:143–150.

Williams, Linda B. and William F. Pratt. 1990. "Wanted and Unwanted Childbearing in the United States: 1973–88." *Advance Data from Vital and Health Statistics,* no. 189. Hyattsville, MD: National Center for Health Statistics.

U.S. Bureau of the Census. 1992. *Population Projections of the United States, by Age, Sex, Race and Hispanic Origin: 1992 to 2050.* Current Population Reports, P25-1092. Washington, DC: U.S. Government Printing Office.

Chapter 5

Mortality Differentials in a Diverse Society

Richard G. Rogers

Introduction

This chapter explores ethnic differences in mortality. It begins by providing a general framework from which to examine mortality. It then reveals mortality variations both among and within ethnic groups. Finally, it uncovers some of the factors that lead to these differences.

The Significance of Mortality

Understanding mortality trends is important from demographic, public policy, public health, and social perspectives. Measures of mortality, especially of infant mortality and of life expectancy, are gauges of the population's general health. Differences in mortality by age, sex, race, and ethnicity suggest dissimilar access to education, employment, and health care; differential exposure to hazardous substances; and diverse lifestyle patterns. Mortality and fertility are the driving forces behind natural increase, or the growth of the population. These factors, along with migration, affect population size and composition, including sex ratios, racial composition, age structure, cohort effects, and family formation and composition. In fact, high mortality can create higher rates of widowhood, or single-parent families, and more households arranged around extended families. Therefore, information on the current and future mortality of racial and ethnic groups is crucial to understanding the dynamics of our society.

Conceptual Considerations

Most mortality research has focused on how demographic characteristics—age, sex, race, and ethnicity—affect overall and cause-specific mortality.

Although demographic factors are important, so too are social relations, cultural factors, health behaviors, and biological influences (Rogers, Hummer, and Nam, 2000). For example, Blacks may exhibit higher rates of cancer because of greater genetic predispositions, risky health behaviors such as cigarette smoking, or lower likelihoods of seeking medical care. American Indians may suffer more fatal accidents because they live in more dangerous environments, or because, in general, lower socioeconomic status increases a person's risk of accidents.

Contextual effects—which include social support and stress, social order and disorder, and environmental amenities and insults—affect life chances (LeClere, Rogers, and Peters 1997; 1998). The protection against mortality that cohesive family and community relations can bestow on individuals is called the "Roseto Effect," after a small community in Pennsylvania, which had been settled by Italian immigrants in 1882 (Egolf et al., 1992). In the mid-1950s, Roseto exhibited remarkably low mortality from myocardial infarction relative to other like towns in the area. Several studies attributed Roseto's low rates of heart attack and relatively great individual longevity to its stable social structure, close family ties, ethnic and social homogeneity, and community support (Egolf et al., 1992). In the 1960s, as Roseto youth abandoned many of the traditions—family-centered life, absence of ostentation, patronage of local business, and ethnic intramarriages—for more contemporary behavior—looser family and community ties, more materialist orientation, greater rates of ethnic intermarriage—myocardial infarction morbidity and mortality rates climbed.

Contextual effects can contribute to mortality: areas with high rates of crime, poverty, drug and alcohol abuse, marital disruption, sub-standard housing, overcrowding, illiteracy, unemployment, and air and water pollution may predispose residents to unusually high mortality due to cancer, accidents, such infectious diseases as AIDS and tuberculosis, respiratory disease, cirrhosis of the liver, and homicide (see Feingold, 1994; Haan, Kaplan, and Camacho, 1987; Jenkins et al., 1977; McCord and Freeman, 1990; Wilson, 1987). Moreover, these social strains may produce individual stress and hostility—a distrust of and antagonistic behavior toward others—which contributes to heart disease and premature mortality (Adler et al., 1994). As early as 1971, Nesser, Tyroler, and Cassel found that familial and social disorganization and poverty at the county level increased the risk of stroke mortality among Blacks.

Compositional effects, including nativity, can contribute to ethnic differences in mortality. International migration selects motivated, healthy individuals who engage in healthy behaviors—low rates of cigarette smoking, moderate to low rates of alcohol consumption, increased seat belt use in automobiles, and dietary practices that lead to less obesity (Hummer, Rogers, Nam, and LeClere, 1999). Compared to native-born individuals, foreign-born individuals experience about 20% lower mortality. This lower mortality is witnessed for most all ethnic groups, including foreign-born Blacks and Whites. Because foreign-born persons generally experience lower mortality than native-born persons, those ethnic groups with the highest percentages of foreign-born individuals experience lower mortality than groups with high proportions of native-born individuals (Hummer, Rogers, Nam, and LeClere, 1999).

Race and ethnicity have both social and genetic components. Although different racial and ethnic groups may die from the same diseases, some groups may be at greater risk, less resistant, more likely to develop comorbidities, less tolerant of medical or pharmaceutical therapy, or in an environment that triggers the disease. Thus, the same disease may run its course differently for different people. Ignoring biological factors may impede researchers from examining the association of rare but life-threatening diseases. Exploring biological differences among ethnic groups in resistance to disease and in disease processes may help increase life expectancies for those groups.

Sickle cell anemia—a disease in which red blood cells are damaged—is more common among Blacks than among Whites (Cooper and David, 1986). Tay-Sachs disease—a disease that creates severe mental retardation, progressive neurologic deterioration, and early childhood mortality—occurs more frequently among the Ashkenazi (Eastern European descent) Jewish population (Weiss, 1993). Cystic fibrosis, which leads to chronic lung obstruction and childhood and young adult disability, is more common among European Caucasians (U.S. Dept. of Health, Education, and Welfare, 1979). Gallbladder disease is high among several American Indian tribes, including the Apache, Arapaho, Chippewa, Shoshone, and Sioux, and is also high among some Hispanic groups (Morris et al., 1978). Devor and Buechley (1979; 1980) discovered that the high rates of gallbladder disease and cancer among New Mexican Hispanics were associated with the genetic admixture between Hispanics and Indians.

Thus, although there are some genetically linked causes of death, they are rare (Farley and Allen, 1987), they often display more variation within than between races (Williams, Lavizzo-Mourey, and Warren, 1994), are not always aligned along racial boundaries, and are interrelated with race, environmental, cultural, and social influences. Genetic differences by race are difficult to discern because of past and current mass migration, discordant rather than concordant human variation, and high rates of ethnic intermarriage. Over time, rates of intermarriage have increased for Asians, Mexicans, and Native Americans, which has blurred ethnic boundaries and created more complex individual ethnic identities (see Hirschman, 1994). Indeed, between 1960 and 1980, the number of interracial couples grew by 535% (Waters, page 35). Discordant human variation suggests that even though two groups may exhibit similar skin color, they may vary in predisposition to different diseases (Cooper and David, 1986). Moreover, even though skin color may be inherited, it is not a genetic indicator of disease (see Keil et al., 1992).

Methodological Considerations

Data Sources and Ethnic Identification

Mortality rates are usually derived from two sources: Vital Statistics and Census data. The definition and identification of ethnic groups is fundamental to mortality research, yet ethnicity is not always well defined or consistently measured among federal agencies, or properly provided by individuals (see, for example, Gimenez, 1989; Hahn and Stroup, 1994; Hayes-Bautista and Chapa, 1987; Trevino, 1982). Ethnic groups can be identified on questionnaires on the basis of political need, social interest, or special interest lobbying, rather than solely on scientific merit (see Hahn and Stroup, 1994; Hirschman, page 63).

Surveys, censuses, and Vital Statistics have not identified ethnic groups consistently over time (Rogers, 1989; Rogers, Carrigan, and Kovar, 1997). In 1930, the U.S. Census classified "Mexicans" as a separate race. Beginning in 1940, Hispanics were classified White (Williams, Lavizzo-Mourey, and Warren, 1994). Currently, Hispanics[1] can be of any race: Vital Statistics and Census ascertain Hispanic origin first, then ask for race. Therefore, comparisons contrast the Hispanic population with non-Hispanic Blacks and non-Hispanic Whites, or Anglos[2]. Nevertheless, the way to define Hispanics remains unclear. Hispanics can be identified as such through Spanish surname or through self-identification based on Hispanic origin. Self-identification based on Hispanic origin has the disadvantage that individuals may report their origin differently at different times. Identifying individuals on the basis of surname requires the use of a computer program that can identify ethnic names. Some Vital Statistics departments have used the program GUESS, or Generally Useful Ethnic Search System, which identifies Spanish surnames through linguistic structure (Buechley, 1976). The U.S. Census Bureau has used a list of Spanish surnames prepared by Passel and Word (1980). Death rates created for persons of Spanish surname will have consistent numerators and denominators. But some Spanish surnames are also common among non-Spanish persons, for instance, American Indians, Italians, and Portuguese (see Rosenwaike and Bradshaw, 1988). And not all Hispanic or partly Hispanic persons have Spanish surnames. High rates of intermarriage of Hispanic women who do not retain their Spanish surnames, and of their children, will reduce the effectiveness of this method over time. For example, the San Antonio Heart Study found that 7% of Mexican American women had non-Spanish surnames, while 11% of non-Hispanic White women had Spanish surnames (Hazuda et al., 1986). Moreover, identification of Hispanics by surname overlooks the heterogeneity of Hispanics.

Hispanic subpopulations differ in culture, social relations, economic status, lifestyle, and geographic residence. For example, Mexican Americans are concentrated in the Southwest, Puerto Ricans in New York and New Jersey, and Cubans in Florida (Rogers, 1991). In Northern New Mexico and Southern Colorado, some Hispanics identify themselves as "Spanish," or "Hispano," descendants of Sixteenth- or Seventeenth-century Spanish people who settled in what is now the Southwestern United States (Rosenwaike and Bradshaw, 1988).

The identification with a particular ethnic group can be rather fluid. Hazuda et al. (1986) examined ethnic identification based on ethnicity of the respondent's grandparents. They found that of those respondents with three Mexican-origin grandparents, 17% reported themselves as non-Hispanic; of those with two Mexican-origin grandparents, 38% reported themselves as non-Hispanic. The distinction between American Indian and Hispanic is often unclear. American Indians may in fact contribute as much as 40% to the Hispanic gene pool in Southern Colorado and Northern New Mexico (Devor and Buechley 1979; 1980). Through intermarriage and adoption of Hispanic practices, many Indians in New Mexico become assimilated into Hispanic culture. Some Indians, especially during the Spanish colonial period in New Mexico (1598–1821), spoke Spanish, were baptized with Spanish names, relinquished their tribal affiliation, and adopted village life and other social and cultural practices of the Spanish colonists (Devor and Buechley, 1979). Thus, some "Hispanics" identify themselves as Hispanic only, some as Hispanic and Indian, and others as Indian only.

In some publications, for instance those by the National Center for Health Statistics (NCHS), Hispanics are subdivided into Mexicans, Puerto Ricans, Cubans, and Other Hispanics. NCHS reports of mortality for these groups are based on 45 states, New York state (excluding New York City), and the District of Columbia. Data from New York City are excluded because over 10% of the death certificates there code ethnicity as "unknown origin." In 1990, these reporting areas accounted for 92% of the Cuban population, almost 90% of the Mexican, and 81% of the "Other Hispanic," but only 58% of the Puerto Rican population (NCHS, 1993). Because a large proportion of Puerto Ricans die in New York City, the exclusion of this city affects estimates of Puerto Rican mortality.

Some individuals, especially those of mixed races, may be reported of one race through the Census and of another race for Vital Statistics. When inconsistencies arise, it is usually individuals who were coded as Hispanic, American Indian, and Asian on surveys who are coded White at death (Poe et al., 1993; Sorlie, Rogot, and Johnson, 1992). These inconsistent codes can artificially lower life expectancy estimates for Whites and artificially raise them for other ethnic subpopulations. Similar problems in the reporting of ethnicity on the birth and death certificates often lead to an overestimate of

White infant mortality and underestimates of Black, Hispanic, Indian, and Asian infant mortality (Hahn, Mulinare, and Teutsch 1992; Rumbaut and Weeks, 1989).

Such results suggest that researchers should make greater use of linked files, where racial information can be followed, checked, and, if need be, modified through multiple records. But because linked files provide small samples, surveys using them must oversample small racial and ethnic groups or risk unstable mortality estimates. Furthermore, because of the difficulty described above in creating national mortality estimates by ethnicity, many such estimates are provided for specific subpopulations or specific geographic areas, such as states or census regions. In this chapter, I cull information from linked files, select geographic areas, and the nation as a whole to sketch a picture of the current mortality status of ethnic groups in the United States.

Mortality Estimates

Infant Mortality

The infant mortality rate—or the number of deaths to babies during their first year of life per 1,000 births—represents a crude measure of the quality of life of the population (see Nam, 1994). As such, it is frequently employed and often publicized. Infant mortality can be further divided into mortality occurring within the first month of life, or neonatal mortality, and mortality between the first month of life and the twelfth month, or postneonatal mortality. Table 5.1 presents infant mortality rates for the years 1985–1987 for the United States from the National Linked Files of Live Births and Infant Deaths (NCHS, 1994). Currently, the total Hispanic neonatal, postneonatal, and infant mortality rates parallel Anglo rates. But as recently as 1957, the Hispanic postneonatal mortality rate was over three times larger than the Anglo rate in San Antonio, Texas (Frisbie, Forbes, and Rogers, 1992). The decline in Hispanic postneonatal mortality is due to increased access to medical care and public health improvements (Forbes and Frisbie, 1991). Table 5.1 reveals substantial variations among Hispanics; there is significantly more variation among Hispanics than there is between Hispanics and Anglos. Compared to other Hispanic subpopulations, Puerto Ricans consistently demonstrate the highest neonatal, postneonatal, and infant mortality rates. Much of the excess mortality may be attributed to the birth weight distributions. For example, fewer than 6% of the Mexican American, Cuban, and Central and South American births are of low weight, compared to over 9% of Puerto Rican births (NCHS, 1994).

Table 5.1

**Neonatal, Postneonatal, and Infant Mortality Rates by Race and
Ethnicity: U.S. Birth Cohorts, 1985-87 (rates per 1,000 live births)[1,2]**

Race/Ethnicity of Mother	Mortality Rates		
	Neonatal	Postneonatal	Infant
HISPANIC	5.5	3.0	8.5
Mexican American	5.2	2.9	8.1
Puerto Rican	7.3	3.6	10.9
Cuban	5.5	2.2	7.7
Central and South American	5.2	2.6	7.8
Other and Unknown Hispanic	5.7	3.4	9.1
ASIAN OR PACIFIC ISLANDER	4.7	2.9	7.6
Chinese	3.4	2.6	6.0
Japanese	3.9	2.7	6.6
Filipino	4.7	2.5	7.2
Other Asian or Pacific Islander	5.2	3.2	8.3
AMERICAN INDIAN AND ALASKAN NATIVE	6.1	7.2	13.3
BLACK	11.6	6.3	17.9
ANGLO	5.4	3.0	8.4
Grand Total	6.6	3.6	10.1

Source: NCHS 1994, Table 18.

1 Neonatal and postneonatal rates may not add to equal infant rates due to rounding.

2 Rates for Hispanics, non-Hispanic Black, and non-Hispanic White are shown only for states with an Hispanic-origin item on their birth certificates.

Asian and Pacific Islanders display some of the lowest infant mortality rates in the United States. These low rates may be due in part to low proportions of low birthweights. The Chinese reveal the lowest infant mortality rates of any ethnic group, at 6.0, and only have 5.1% of low weight births. They are followed by the Japanese, at 6.6, with 5.9% of low weight births, and the Filipinos, at 7.2, with 7.3% low weight births (see Table 5.1 and NCHS, 1994). These low infant mortality rates are due to both low neonatal and postneonatal mortality.

Infant mortality rates are also low for Indochinese refugees. Rumbaut and Weeks (1989) found that in San Diego County, California, the infant mortality rates are 6.6 for all Indochinese, 5.5 for Vietnamese, 5.8 for Khmer, 7.2 for Lao, and 9.1 for Hmong subpopulations. Differences among Indochinese infant mortality rates can be partly explained by differences in socioeconomic status, prior residential location, and time in the United States. Compared to the Vietnamese, the Hmong came to the United States with lower educational and income levels, from more rural backgrounds, after spending more time in refugee camps before their resettlement. For example, Hmong parents averaged three years in refugee camps in Thailand before their resettlement, compared to a little more than half a year for the Vietnamese (Rumbaut and Weeks, 1989).

Infants of Indochinese refugees may be expected to experience higher mortality than other subpopulations in the United States because many of their parents have low socioeconomic status and have migrated from countries with high infant mortality. For instance, in 1985, mortality rates for infants in Vietnam and Laos were 76 and 110, respectively (World Health Organization, 1985). Low levels of education, low proportions in white-collar occupations, and high rates of poverty can translate into inadequate medical care and housing, and overcrowding. But the Indochinese infant mortality rates are low— lower than the general population's, other Asian's, Anglo's, and Hispanic's, and much lower than Black's—and have continued to decline over time. These low rates are partly due to migration selectivity, low rates of maternal smoking and alcohol use, familial and community social support, and low proportions of teenage childbearing.

The Vietnamese and Khmer display the lowest infant mortality rates and have only 5% teenage mothers, compared to the Hmong, who have high mortality and 16.5% of their births to teenage mothers, and to the Blacks, who have the highest mortality and 19% of their births to teenagers. Although Indochinese men report high levels of smoking, women report exceptionally low rates: 13% of the Cambodian, less than 2% of the Hmong, and none of the Laotian and Vietnamese women were smokers. Moreover, 97% of the Indochinese women abstained from drinking alcohol. Further, these migrants do not represent their general population of origin, but, because they migrated, they are a select subpopulation that is more resourceful, ambitious, and healthy. For instance, before refugees were admitted to the United States, they had to pass medical and psychiatric screenings (Rumbaut and Weeks 1989).

Although American Indian infant mortality is relatively high, it has witnessed steady declines; the rate was halved in the 15 years between 1973 and 1988 (U.S. Department of Health and Human Services, 1991, 1993). Nevertheless, Indians display the highest mortality rates for the postneonatal period, the period when infants are most susceptible to infectious diseases and accidents. Blacks exhibit the highest neonatal and infant mortality rates. Black rates are generally twice as high as those of other ethnic groups. For example, the Black infant mortality rate, at 17.9, is higher than the American

Indian rate, and is over twice as high as the Anglo rate, at 8.4, the Hispanic rate at 8.5, or the Asian rate at 7.6.

Although most policies have focused on reducing Black mortality through socioeconomic solutions, the Asian experience suggests that Black mortality could also be reduced through the following social and behavioral measures: low rates of maternal smoking, drinking, and drug use; low levels of teenage childbearing; high rates of prenatal care; and institutional support (Rumbaut and Weeks, 1989; Williams, Lavizzo-Mourey, and Warren, 1994). Indeed, compared to Whites, Black babies are born into households with half the income to mothers with half the education; they are four times more likely to be born to single mothers, and twice as likely to be of low weight and to have a teenage mother (Hummer, 1993; U.S. Department of Health and Human Services, 1985).

Life Expectancy

Table 5.2 reveals life expectancies—or the average years of life remaining to a group of people attaining a specific age—for different U.S. ethnic groups for circa 1980 and 1990 (see Nam, 1994). Bear in mind that life expectancies for each group have witnessed remarkable increases. In 1900, the average life expectancy in the United States was just 47 years; today it is over 75 years.

The relative positions of ethnic groups have also changed over time. Compared to other subpopulations, Asians now display the highest life expectancies. In 1990, the life expectancies were 84 for Asians and 76 for Anglos. This is a switch from earlier in the Twentieth century. For example, in 1920, Anglos showed higher life expectancies than each of the three Asian subpopulations (see Barringer, Gardner, and Levin, 1993). Among Asians circa 1990, the Japanese exhibit the highest life expectancies, at 82.1, followed closely by the Chinese at 81.7, and the Filipinos at 80.6. Japanese in the United States have a long history of high life expectancies, dating back to at least the 1940s (Barringer, Gardner, and Levin, 1993).

High Asian life expectancies could be a result of misreporting of race and ethnicity on different data sources (see Kitagawa and Hauser, 1973), of immigration selectivity—many Asian in-migrants have been highly educated professionals (Yu, 1982)—or of emigration selectivity—some older and/or dying Asians may return to their country of origin. Hahn (1995) terms this latter relation the "moribund migration effect." Before they leave the country, such sick and dying Asians may respond to a decennial Census, but information on their eventual death would be missed by the U.S. Vital Statistics system.

Table 5.2
Life Expectancies at Birth by Race and Ethnicity,
1980 and 1990, United States

Racial and Ethnic Group	Life Expectancies	
	1980	*1990*
Anglo	74.4	76.1
Black	68.1	69.1
Hispanic	74.8	76.0
American Indian and Alaskan Native	71.1	71.5
Asian and Pacific Islander[1]	81.9	83.9
Chinese	80.2	81.7
Japanese	79.7	82.1
Filipino	78.8	80.6
TOTAL	73.7	75.4

[1] Chinese, Japanese, and Filipino life expectancies in 1980 are from the state of Hawaii only; for 1990, life expectancies for these three groups are based on 1992 data for seven reporting states with the largest API populations: California, Hawaii, Illinois, New Jersey, New York, Texas, and Washington.

Sources: Life expectancies for: Indians in 1980 from HHS (1991); Indians in 1988 from HHS (1993); Asian and Pacfic Islanders in 1979–1981 from Gardner (1994); Asian and Pacific Islanders in 1990 and calculated as the average male and female life expectancies from Hahn (1995); Chinese, Japanese and Filipino in 1992 from Hoyert and Hsiang-Ching Kung (1997); Hispanics in 1980 for Texas Mexican Americans and calculated as the average male and female life expectancies of Spanish origin from Sullivan et al. (1984); Hispanics in 1990 for New Mexico and calculated as the average male and female life expectancies from New Mexico Dept. of Health (1993).

Nevertheless, Asian life expectancies are high, even with adjustments to possible death undercounts. Moreover, the Chinese and Japanese in Hawaii exhibit higher life expectancies than the average expectancies in China and Japan (see World Health Organization, 1985). And the 1990 Asian American life expectancy exceeds the overall life expectancy in Japan, touted as the highest national life expectancy in the world (Hahn, 1995).

Hispanics and Anglos have similar life expectancies, even though a greater proportion of Hispanics live in poverty and lack health insurance (Sorlie et al., 1993). This incongruity between socioeconomic status and mortality has been termed the "epidemiological paradox" (Markides and Coreil, 1986). American Indian life expectancies are intermediate to Anglos and Blacks.

Of the subpopulations portrayed here, Blacks show the lowest life expectancies, at 69.1 years. There is enormous national concern about the high mortality among Blacks. For example, one of the five major health goals of the nation is to reduce the racial disparity in life expectancy from over 6 years to no more than 4 years by the year 2000 (U.S. Department of Health and Human Services, 1989). The Black/White gap in life expectancy, which had been slowly closing over the past century, slowly but consistently widened between 1985 and 1989. The Black/White gap in life expectancy at birth was 14.6 years in 1900, declined to 5.8 years in 1984, but was up to 7.1 years by 1989. The recent divergence is due both to small increases in White life expectancy and to small decreases in Black life expectancy, which declined from a high of 69.5 years in 1984 to 68.8 years in 1989. Causes contributing to the decrease in black life expectancy—HIV infection, homicide, accidents, diabetes, and pneumonia—obscured improvements in mortality from other causes—most notably, heart disease (Kochanek, Maurer, and Rosenberg, 1994). Preliminary figures show narrowing of the large gap for 1990 (NCHS, 1993). The gap is generally larger at younger ages and smaller at older ages (Sorlie et al., 1992).

Life expectancies have witnessed tremendous historical improvements. Between 1910 and 1980, life expectancies for Chinese and Japanese in Hawaii increased by about 50% and 60%, respectively. Between 1910 and 1990, White life expectancy increased by around 50%. But Blacks posted some of the largest gains in life expectancy; between 1910 and 1990, they witnessed over a 90% gain in length of life (see Gardner, 1984; NCHS, 1986; 1993)[3] Thus, although Black life expectancies lag behind Whites, they have witnessed the most impressive relative increases over time. The gap, which is still large, may be due to a host of social, cultural, and environmental factors. Another way to determine which factors are most important is to look at age-specific mortality.

Age-Specific Mortality

Table 5.3 presents age-specific and age-adjusted mortality rates for different ethnic groups[4]. The age-specific mortality rates, which summarize mortality for multiple age groups and adjusts for the age composition of the population, demonstrates that Asians exhibit the lowest overall mortality, followed by Hispanics, American Indians, Whites, and Blacks.

Mortality patterns by age generally mirror the age-adjusted mortality rates. For instance, Asians display the lowest age specific mortality rates for all ages, save the age group 85 and over, where American Indians display a lower rate. The low Indian age-adjusted mortality rate is due to the low mortality rates at ages 45 and above. These rates are most likely underestimates, reflected by a 45% increase in the American Indian population between 1980 and 1990 and the increased propensity for individuals to identify themselves as Indian in 1990 (NCHS 1994).

Table 5.3 reveals the race-crossover effect: Blacks have higher mortality than Whites until ages 85 and over, where White mortality is higher (see also Nam 1995). But there are also crossovers for Hispanics and Whites, Indians and Whites, and Indians and Asians. Some of these crossovers most likely indicate differences in selectivity; other crossovers suggest problems with the quality of the data.

Table 5.3
Death Rates by Age and Ethnicity, U.S., 1989–1991[1,2]

Age	All Ethnicities	White	Black	Asian	American Indian	Hispanic
All ages, age adjusted	519.9	492.5	790.4	289.7	452.6	395.8
1–14 years	31.4	28.4	48.3	22.7	37.3	30.2
15–24 years	99.1	89.3	161.9	50.1	142.0	103.3
25–44 years	178.3	153.8	373.8	76.1	214.3	162.2
45–64 years	805.2	752.9	1,374.9	380.4	712.8	566.8
65–74 years	2,650.8	2,574.6	3,734.7	1,458.7	2,083.4	1,874.8
75–84 years	5,979.2	5,931.1	6,962.0	3,859.6	4,121.2	4,282.5
85 years and over	15,231.2	15,367.5	14,336.4	11,058.3	9,122.4	11,021.7

[1] Whites, Blacks, Asians, and Indians include Hispanic and non-Hispanic persons; Hispanics include individuals of any race.

[2] The death rates are per 100,000. Age-adjusted rates are calculated from the direct method using the 1940 U.S. population as the standard.

Cause–Specific Mortality

Table 5.4 compares the age-adjusted cause-specific mortality ratios of Hispanics, Asians, American Indians, and Blacks to Whites[5]. Although Hispanic total mortality is lower than Anglo mortality, it results from different causes. Compared to the Anglos, Hispanics are generally less likely to die from heart disease, cerebrovascular disease, cancer, pneumonia and influenza, suicide, and chronic obstructive pulmonary diseases and allied conditions (COPD), several of the major causes of death, but are generally more likely to die from diabetes, homicide, and cirrhosis of the liver. Hispanics are also at risk of death from human immunodeficiency virus infection (HIV). Table 5.5 shows that Hispanics aged 45–64 are twice as likely as Anglos to die from HIV.

Table 5.4

Ratios of Age-Standardized Cause-Specific Mortality Rates of Hispanics, Asian-Americans, Indians, and Blacks, Compared to U.S. Whites[1]

Cause of Death	Hispanic				Asian-American			Indian	Black
	Cuban	Mex-Am	P.R.	Total	Chinese	Japanese	Filipino		
					Compared to U.S. White Population				
All causes	0.8	0.8	0.8	0.8	0.6	0.5	0.4	1.2	1.6
Diseases of heart	0.7	0.7	0.7	0.7	0.5	0.4	0.4	0.9	1.5
Cerebrovascular diseases	0.5	0.9	0.9	0.8	0.8	0.8	0.4	1.0	1.9
Malignant neoplasms	0.7	0.6	0.6	0.6	0.8	0.6	0.4	0.7	1.4
Accidents	0.7	1.1	0.9	1.1	0.3	0.4	0.4	2.7	1.3
Chronic liver disease and cirrhosis	0.9	2.1	1.9	1.9	0.4	0.3	0.3	3.3	1.9
Diabetes mellitus	1.0	1.9	1.4	1.6	0.8	0.6	0.5	2.9	2.5
Pneumonia and influenza	0.7	0.9	0.8	0.8	0.8	0.7	0.6	1.5	1.4
Suicide	0.8	0.5	0.7	0.6	0.6	0.6	0.3	1.5	0.6
Homicide	3.5	3.4	3.3	3.8	—	—	—	1.7	9.4
Chronic obstructive pulmonary diseases and allied conditions	0.5	0.4	0.6	0.4	0.5	0.3	0.3	0.7	0.8

— indicates no data available.

[1] For the cause-of-death classification, see NCHS (1993).

Source: Data for Hispanics and for Blacks compared to Whites are for 1990 (rates courtesy of Jeff Maurer, NCHS); for Indians compared to Whites are for 1988 (HHS 1993); for Chinese, Japanese, and Filipino, compared to Whites for 1980 (Barringer, Gardner, and Levin 1993).

Table 5.5
Death Rates for Human Immunodeficiency Virus Infection (HIV)
by Age and Ethnicity, U.S., 1989-91 [1,2]

Age Group	All Races	White	Black	Asian	Indian	Hispanic[3]
25–44 years	23.4	18.8	61.7	4.3	5.6	34.6
45–64 years	11.4	9.6	30.1	3.1	2.8	19.5

Source: NCHS 1994

[1] Whites, Blacks, Asians, and Indians include Hispanic and non-Hispanic persons; Hispanics include individuals of any race.

[2] The death rates are per 100,000.

[3] Data for Hispanics are for 1989 only.

The rates and causes of mortality vary substantially among Hispanic subpopulations: Cubans display the lowest total age-adjusted mortality rates, at 377, followed by Mexicans, at 398, and then Puerto Ricans, at 405[6]. Compared to Anglo rates, the rate of cirrhosis of the liver is the same for Cubans, but about twice as high for Mexican Americans and Puerto Ricans. Alcohol consumption levels for Hispanics generally mirror the rates of cirrhosis of the liver. Although Mexicans drink more beer than Cubans or Puerto Ricans, Puerto Ricans drink more wine and hard liquor than Mexicans, who drink more than Cubans. For instance, of those Hispanic men aged 20–44 who drink, Cubans average about 3 drinks of hard liquor per day, Mexicans 4, and Puerto Ricans almost 6 (Rogers, 1991). Indeed, Island-resident Puerto Ricans are considered to have one of the highest levels of hard liquor per capita consumption in the world (Fernandez, 1975).

Mortality due to diabetes is the same for Cubans and Anglos, higher among Puerto Ricans, and highest among Mexican Americans. Diabetes is associated with obesity, among other factors. Among Hispanics, Cubans are relatively likely to be of normal weight. For example, 80% of Cuban men aged 20–44 are of normal weight. Mexican Americans and Puerto Ricans have a greater tendency to be obese: among women aged 20–44, 31% of the Mexican women are obese, as are 35% of the Puerto Rican women (Hazuda et al., 1988; Rogers, 1991). Not surprisingly, Cubans have a much lower prevalence of diabetes than either Mexicans or Puerto Ricans, and the lower disease prevalence contributes to the differences in diabetes mortality (see Rogers, 1991).

Compared to Anglos, each Hispanic subpopulation exhibits over a threefold excess of homicide mortality. Homicide is especially high at younger ages. Gang violence in Los Angeles, the largest Mexican American community in the United States, contributes to the high rate of homicide among

Mexican American men aged 15–24 years of age (see Loya and Mercy, 1985). Cubans display the highest homicide mortality rates of any Hispanic subpopulation. Rosenwaike and Shai (1989) attribute the high Cuban homicide rates to the 1980 Mariel boatlift. The original purpose of the boatlift was family reunification. But Cuban authorities also released many hard-core criminals from jails, inmates from psychiatric hospitals, and patients from mental institutions. Between 1979 and 1981, the years that bound the boatlift operation, the homicide rate for the Cuban-born population in the United States rose 151%. In 1981, the Mariel migrants may have been responsible for half of all violent crimes in Miami (Rosenwaike and Shai, 1989).

Suicide rates are lower for Hispanics than Anglos. For example, Mexican Americans are only half as likely to kill themselves as are Anglos. Suicide rates for Mexican Americans in Texas and California are also lower than for the general population (see also Rosenwaike and Hempstead, 1990b).

Accidents are high among Mexican Americans, but low among Cubans and Puerto Ricans. The high accident rate among Mexican Americans is most likely due to a variety of factors, but may include lower socioeconomic status, which results in owning older, poorly maintained cars, and living in areas that require more time on the roads and highways. Low incomes may contribute to deteriorating housing and overcrowding, which in turn may increase the risk of nonautomotive accidents (Shai, Rosenwaike, and Rogers, 1991).

Smoking also contributes to mortality variations within the Hispanic subpopulations. Compared to Anglos, Hispanics generally smoke less and therefore have lower mortality due to such smoking-related diseases as heart disease, cancer, and COPD (see Castro, Baezconde-Garbanati, and Beltran, 1985). The age-adjusted rates of death from lung cancer in the United States in 1980 were 32 for the Cuban-born, 29 for the Mexican-born, 23 for the Puerto Rican-born, 48 for Whites, and 59 for Blacks (Rosenwaike, 1987). Cuban men not only smoke more cigarettes than do Mexicans and Puerto Ricans, but they are also more likely to smoke cigars (Rogers 1991).

The three Asian-American subpopulations—Chinese, Japanese, and Filipinos—exhibit lower mortality than Anglos for each cause listed. They achieve their superior life expectancies through reductions in degenerative diseases as well as external causes. Some causes of death may be reduced due to the low rates of substance abuse. "Asian Pacific Americans report the lowest use of cigarettes, alcohol, marijuana, and cocaine and other hard drugs when compared with other ethic groups, particularly Whites" (Zane and Kim, 1994:318). Filipinos display the lowest mortality. Compared to Anglos, they are one-third as likely to die from cirrhosis of the liver, suicide, or COPD. Not only do Asians have lower overall cancer mortality than Anglos, they also enjoy lower mortality from most every cancer site. Stomach cancer is one of the few exceptions where the rate is higher for the Japanese and Chinese than Whites.

Compared to Whites, mortality due to cancer of the stomach is over three times higher. Stomach cancer for the Japanese most likely represents an "'incomplete transition' from high death rates in Japan to the relatively low rates characteristic of U.S. whites" (Gardner, 1994:85–86). Oriental diets include fermented and pickled foods in addition to seasonings high in salt content, like soy sauce, which may contribute to stomach cancer (Smith, 1993).

Compared to Anglos, Asian and Pacific Islanders are also less likely to die from firearms or motor vehicles (Fingerhut, Jones, and Makuc, 1994). Although homicide data were not available for each Asian subpopulation, NCHS (1994) has reported that compared to similarly aged Whites, homicide rates are lower for Asians aged 15–24 and 25–44, but slightly higher for Asians aged 45–64. Furthermore, Asians are less likely than the general population to die from HIV infections (see Table 5.5).

Compared to Anglos, American Indians are less likely to die from cardiovascular diseases, cancer, and COPD, but more likely to die from diabetes, social pathologies, and infectious diseases. Historically, infectious diseases have been a major cause of death for Indians. Indians in the United States exhibit a high rate of tuberculosis, one that is six times higher than average (U.S. Department of Health and Human Services, 1993).

Now intentional and unintentional accidents and violence have replaced infectious diseases as major causes of death among American Indians. Compared to Anglos, Indians are over two-and-one-half times more likely to die from accidents and over three times more likely to die from cirrhosis of the liver. The high rate of cirrhosis of the liver implies that alcohol abuse may contribute to the high accident rate. Indeed, American Indians are over five times more likely to die from alcoholism than others (U.S. Department of Health & Human Services, 1993). On a northeastern Arizona Hopi reservation, pedestrian fatalities, rollover crashes, and falls contribute to high accident mortality (Simpson et al., 1983).

American Indians also experience high rates of suicide and homicide. In fact, compared to Anglos, Indians are 1.6 times more likely to die from firearms (Fingerhut, Jones, and Makuc, 1994). Simpson et al. (1983) have documented the high rates of suicide among the Apache, Blackfeet, Hopi, Northern Cheyenne, Papago, and Shoshone-Bannock. And yet these high rates may be understated: Indian religious and cultural taboos against suicide may lead to an underreporting of it (Simpson et al., 1983).

Compared to Whites, Blacks die more frequently from most causes of death, save COPD and suicide. Although it is commonly acknowledged that Blacks are less likely than Whites to die from suicide, Warshauer and Monk (1978) indicate that more Black than White suicides are underestimated. If true, the advantage that Blacks gain from low suicide mortality would be diminished. Compared to Whites, Blacks are over nine times more likely to die from homicide (see Table 5.4), almost five times more likely to die from firearms (Fingerhut, Jones, and Makuc, 1994), and about three times more likely to die from HIV (see Table 5.5). The high rates of homicide play a large factor in Black mortality, especially for young males. For example, in 1990, guns killed more Blacks aged 15 to 19 than "acquired immunodeficiency syndrome, sickle cell disease, and all other natural causes *combined*" (Kellermann, 1994:541).

Mortality Adjusted by Socioeconomic Covariates

The results I have discussed above are based on the demographic framework that focuses on age and ethnic differences in mortality. While instructive, such a focus overlooks the effects of economic, social, and health factors. A comparison of Black and White mortality illustrates such relations.

The Black/White gap in life expectancy, which is still large, is partly due to the tendency for Blacks to exhibit less healthy lifestyles, to smoke, and to be in disadvantaged social categories. For instance, compared to Whites, Blacks are less likely to be employed, married, or wealthy (Potter, 1991; Rogers, 1992; Schoenborn, 1986). Although Blacks are less likely than Whites to be heavy smokers, they are more likely to die from smoking-related illnesses. This paradoxical finding may be attributed to their use of high-tar, high-nicotine, mentholated cigarettes; to their greater propensity to "wake-up" smoking (smoking within the first few minutes of awakening); and to higher social and environmental stresses and hazards (see Novotny et al., 1988; Royce et al., 1993). Thus, to fully understand racial differences in mortality entails more completely exploring the social, economic, and health factors.

In earlier research, I found that a purely demographic approach demonstrated that compared to Whites, Blacks had higher overall mortality and higher mortality from nearly all causes, save suicide (Rogers, 1992). Once I controlled for differences in age, sex, marital status, family size, and income, however, the race gap in overall mortality was virtually eliminated[7].The adjusted rates showed that compared to Whites, Blacks had lower mortality risk from respiratory diseases, accidents, and suicide; similar risks from circulatory diseases and cancer; and higher risks from infectious diseases, diabetes, and homicide. Centerwall (1984) demonstrates that even the homicide mortality gap closes substantially once household crowding is controlled.

Conclusions

Individuals are a composite of various social, cultural, and biological characteristics that are related to racial and ethnic groups. And racial and ethnic differences do affect mortality. To properly conceptualize the multiple and interacting proximate determinants of mortality by race and ethnicity, researchers must extend the traditional demographic framework of mortality analysis to a more complete, though more complex, model that also incorporates demographic, social, economic, biological, and contextual factors such as availability and quality of medical care, migration selectivity, health behavior, and socioeconomic status (see also Rosenwaike, 1988).

It is important to examine differences in cause of death because social policies aimed at reducing mortality may be most efficient if they target specific causes. Future research could extend knowledge of ethnic variations in death by exploring multiple-cause mortality, which refers to deaths in terms of all of the identifiable medical causes entered on the death certificate (see Nam, 1990). Combinations of causes can be more lethal than single causes and can influence the mortality differentials between subpopulations. As we begin to target specific causes of death, it also becomes more important to examine mortality by ethnic group and subgroup. For example, although a program could screen for diabetes among Hispanics, a group with high rates of diabetes, such screening might not be as cost-effective for Cubans, since they have relatively low rates of diabetes. Thus, knowledge of variations in ethnic groups could enable public health and medical programs to target "at risk" populations and therefore to better serve their constituents.

Biological factors do influence mortality, but their contribution to ethnic variations in mortality is small and difficult to isolate. Because of high levels of intermarriage, the biological factors do not always follow racial boundaries. Therefore, the ethnic codes employed by social scientists usually ascertain a person's self-perceived membership in a social group characterized by common language, ancestry, nationality, culture, or physical appearance.

It is important to recognize diversity in America: Indians are distinguished from Anglos, Blacks, Hispanics, and Asians. But American Indians themselves comprise subgroups that vary by history, geography, language, and custom. For example, the Apache differ from the Navajo, Arapaho, Chippewa, and Sioux. Puerto Ricans, Cubans, and Mexican Americans are different one from the other. Even the surveys that disaggregate major Hispanic populations overlook new and currently small Hispanic groups, including those from Central and South America. Asian subpopulations show marked variations. There are differences between Chinese, Japanese, Koreans, Vietnamese, and Laotians. Although Whites have been treated as a homogeneous group, there are differences by country of origin, language spoken, religion, time since migration, and socioeconomic status. For example, Rosenwaike and Hempstead (1990a) revealed mortality differences among Irish, Italians, and Jews in New York City. They suggested that these differences were due in part to variations in time in the United States—Italian and Jewish immigration occurred between the years 1890 and 1923, while Irish immigration was concentrated between the years 1835 and 1865—in language barriers, drinking patterns, and ethnic community cohesiveness—the Italians and Jews were more likely than the Irish to live in homogeneous neighborhoods (Rosenwaike and Hempstead, 1990a). And researchers must begin examining different black subpopulations, especially as larger numbers of Blacks from the West Indies, Africa, South and Central America, and Europe migrate to the United States. For instance, Black immigrants to the United States numbered just 5,000 in 1954, but grew to over 80,000 in 1984 (Reid, 1986). "The black population from the Caribbean basin countries is diverse and includes Spanish-speaking persons from Cuba, the Dominican Republic, and Panama; French-speaking persons from Haiti and other French-speaking Caribbean areas; Dutch-speaking persons from the Netherlands Antilles; and English-speaking persons from the former British colonies" (Williams, Lavizzo-Mourey, and Warren 1994:33). Foreign-born Blacks may differ from native-born Blacks in language, in cultural practices, and in age, sex, and cause-specific mortality patterns (see Bryce-Laporte 1993).

To create detailed mortality estimates for ethnic subpopulations, however, we need better data. The mortality estimates presented here were hampered by the lack of consistent coding of ethnicity on different records and by the problems associated with linking numerator and denominator data from different records. Mortality estimates for some ethnic groups are currently impossible at the national level, and available only at the regional, state, or in some instances, county level. The U.S. standard certificate of death, the National Health Interview Survey, and the Census ask different questions about race and ethnicity (see Chyba and Washington, 1993; Poe et al., 1993). Data sources could emphasize diversity by including a more detailed set of racial and ethnic groups, and by oversampling small ethnic groups so that their subsequent mortality can be estimated. Moreover, more data sets could link with the National Death Index (for an example, see Rogers et al., 1996). Such linkages will alleviate some of the statistical anomalies that result when individuals report their ethnicity differently on different sources.

Some researchers recommend using Spanish surnames to identify Hispanics (see Rosenwaike and Bradshaw, 1988). But I recommend ethnic self-identification, especially for surveys that can link with death records. In the past, surname identification was the only way to ensure consistent numerators and denominators for mortality research. With surveys that follow-up individuals to death, this is no longer a concern. Instead, social scientists should be concerned with the individual's own identification with a particular group. Thomas and Thomas (1928:572) noted that if you believe something to be true, it is true insofar as it affects your subsequent beliefs and behavior.

Because ethnic identification can affect ties to central social institutions—family, friends, work, school, church—it is important to ascertain self-identification rather than status defined by others. The San Antonio Heart Study captures several facets of ethnicity through a nine-item indicator that uses self-identification, parental surnames and birthplaces, and ethnic backgrounds of all four grandparents (Hazuda et al., 1986).

Finally, it is important to adjust mortality figures for structural covariates. The "Roseto Effect" reduced mortality for the small Pennsylvanian community in the 1950s. Similar processes may operate today. Unfortunately, however, the converse is often found: many poor urban areas with high rates of crime, drug abuse, illiteracy, and unemployment may predispose residents to unusually high mortality. We must examine not only the advantages that a cohesive community can bestow on its members, but also the disadvantages that may be imposed by community strife, conflict, and disorganization. Such structural problems call for institutional remedies. Mortality can be reduced through community- , clinic- , and church-sponsored outreach programs that provide not only food, shelter, and health care, but also security, safety, and stability (see Thomas et al., 1994).

Ethnic differences in mortality have changed and will continue to change over time. And ethnic groups themselves change, through basic demographic processes—differences in fertility, mortality, and migration—and through social processes—differences in how individuals identify with ethnic groups, and different ethnic distributions of education, employment, occupation, household composition, and social relations. America's rich ethnic diversity creates a kaleidoscope of changing patterns that affects our individual and collective life chances.

Notes

1. I use the term "Hispanic" because of convention (see NCHS, 1993). Other researchers have suggested different terms, but Hispanic suits the research purposes, is clear, and lacks the political overtones that other terms can engender.

2. Anglo refers to non-Hispanic Whites.

3. Black life expectancies in 1910 cannot be separated from life expectancies for non-Whites. Therefore, the comparison is somewhat biased. But because Blacks most likely suffered higher mortality at the turn of the Twentieth century than other non-White groups, the percentage gain in life expectancy between 1910 and 1990 would be higher, creating an even more impressive life expectancy gain over time.

4. For ways to calculate these rates, see Shryock and Siegel (1976).

5. The ratios can be contrasted with a specific referent group or with the average, say, the total U.S. population. I selected Whites as the referent group because many of the published reports have done the same. Further, a specific referent group provides a more direct interpretation and discussion.

6. Rates courtesy of Jeff Maurer, NCHS.

7. Other studies have demonstrated similar closures of the overall race gap in mortality with adjustments to socioeconomic status. By age, however, the race gap in mortality is generally largest at the young ages and smallest at the older ages (see Sorlie et al., 1992).

References

Adler, Nancy E., Thomas Boyce, Margaret A. Chesney, Sheldon Cohen, Susan Folkman, Robert L. Kahn, and S. Leonard Syme. 1994. "Socioeconomic Status and Health: The Challenge of the Gradient." *American Psychologist*, 49(1):15–24.

Barringer, Herbert R., Robert W. Gardner, and Michael J. Levin. 1993. *Asians and Pacific Islanders in the United States*. New York: Russell Sage Foundation.

Bryce-Laporte, Roy Simon. 1993. "Voluntary Immigration and Continuing Encounters between Blacks: The Post-Quincenterary Challenge." *The Annals of the American Academy of Political and Social Science*, 530(Nov):28–41.

Buechley, Robert W. 1976. *Generally Useful Ethnic Search System: GUESS*. Albuquerque, NM: University of New Mexico, Cancer Research and Treatment Center.

Castro, Felipe G., Lourdes Baezconde-Garbanati, and Hector Beltran. 1985. "Risk Factors for Coronary Heart Disease in Hispanic Populations: A Review." *Hispanic Journal of Behavioral Sciences*, 7(2):153–175.

Centerwall, Brandon S. 1984. "Race, Socioeconomic Status, and Domestic Homicide, Atlanta, 1971–72." *American Journal of Public Health*, 74(8):813–815.

Chyba, Michele M. and Linda R. Washington. 1993. "Questionnaires from the National Health Interview Survey, 1985–89." *Vital and Health Statistics*, 1(31):1–412.

Cooper, Richard and Richard David. 1986. "The Biological Concept of Race and Its Application to Public Health and Epidemiology." *Journal of Health Politics, Policy and Law*, 11(1):97–116.

Devor, Eric J. and Robert W. Buechley. 1979. "Gallbladder Cancer in Hispanic New Mexicans. II. Familial Occurrence in Two Northern New Mexico Kindreds." *Cancer Genetics and Cytogenetics*, 1:139–145.

———. 1980. "Gallbladder Cancer in Hispanic New Mexicans. I. General Population, 1957–1977." *Cancer*, 45(7):1705–1712.

Egolf, Brenda, Judith Lasker, Stewart Wolf, and Louise Potvin. 1992. "The Roseto Effect: A 50-Year Comparison of Mortality Rates." *American Journal of Public Health*, 82(8):1089–1092.

Farley, Reynolds and Walter R. Allen. 1987. *The Color Life and the Quality of Life in America*, New York: Russell Sage Foundation.

Feingold, Eugene. 1994. "Working on Environmental Justice." (Editorial). *The Nation's Health*. March, p. 2.

Fernandez, Nelson A. 1975. "Nutrition in Puerto Rico." *Cancer Research*, 35:3272–3291.

Fingerhut, Lois A., Cheryl Jones, and Diane M. Makuc. 1994. "Firearm and Motor Vehicle Injury Mortality—Variations by State, Race, and Ethnicity: United States, 1990–91." *Advance Data from Vital and Health Statistics*. 242:1–12.

Forbes, Douglas and W. Parker Frisbie. 1991. "Spanish Surname and Anglo Infant Mortality: Timing and Cause of Death Differentials Over a Half Century." *Demography*, 28(4):639–660.

Frisbie, W. Parker, Douglas Forbes, and Richard G. Rogers. 1992. "Neonatal and Postneonatal Mortality as Proxies for Cause of Death: Evidence from Ethnic and Longitudinal Comparisons." *Social Science Quarterly*, 73(3):535–549.

Gardner, Robert W. 1984. "Life Tables by Ethnic Group for Hawaii, 1980." *Research and Statistics Reports*, 47:1–15. Honolulu: Hawaii State Department of Health.

———. "Mortality." 1994. In Nolan Zane, David Takeuchi, and Kathleen Young, eds, *Confronting Critical Health Issues of Asian and Pacific Islander Americans*, Thousand Oaks, CA: Sage Publications.

Gimenez, Martha E. 1989. "Latino/'Hispanic'—Who Needs a Name: The Case Against a Standardized Terminology." *International Journal of Health Services*, 19(3):557–571.

Haan, Mary, George A. Kaplan, and Terry Camacho. 1987. "Poverty and Health: Prospective Evidence from the Alameda County Study." *American Journal of Epidemiology*, 125(6):989–998.

Hahn, Robert A. 1995. "Life Expectancy in Four U.S. Racial/Ethnic Populations: 1990." *Epidemiology*, 6(4):350–355.

Hahn, Robert A., Joseph Mulinare, and Steven M. Teutsch. 1992. "Inconsistencies in Coding of Race and Ethnicity Between Birth and Death in U.S. Infants: A New Look at Infant Mortality, 1983 Through 1985." *The Journal of the American Medical Association*, 267(2):259–263.

Hahn, Robert A. and Donna F. Stroup. 1994. "Race and Ethnicity in Public Health Surveillance: Criteria for the Scientific Use of Social Categories." *Public Health Reports*, 109(1):7–15.

Hayes-Bautista, David E. and Jorge Chapa. 1987. "Latino Terminology: Conceptual Bases for Standardized Terminology." *American Journal of Public Health*, 77:61–88.

Hazuda, Helen P., Paul J. Comeaux, Michael P. Stern, Steven M. Haffner, Clayton W. Eifler, and Marc Rosenthal. 1986. "A Comparison of Three Indicators for Identifying Mexican Americans in Epidemiologic Research." *American Journal of Epidemiology*, 123(1):96–112.

Hazuda, Helen, Steven M. Haffner, Michael P. Stern, and Clayton W. Eifler. 1988. "Effects of Acculturation and SES Status on Obesity and Diabetes in Mexican-Americans." *American Journal of Epidemiology*, 128:1289–1301.

Hummer, Robert A. 1993. "Racial Differentials in Infant Mortality in the U.S.: An Examination of Social and Health Determinants." *Social Forces*, 72(2):529–554.

Hummer, Robert A., Richard G. Rogers, Charles B. Nam, and Felicia B. LeClere. 1999. "Race/Ethnicity, Nativity, and U.S. Adult Mortality." *Social Science Quarterly*, 80(1):136–153.

Jenkins, C. David, Robert W. Tuthill, Saul I. Tannenbaum, and Craig R. Kirby. 1977. "Zones of Excess Mortality in Massachusetts." *The New England Journal of Medicine*, 296(23):1354–1356.

Keil, J. E., S. E. Sutherland, R. G. Knapp, H.A. Tyroler, and W. S. Pollitzer. 1992. "Skin Color and Mortality." *American Journal of Epidemiology*, 136(11):1295–1302.

Kellermann, Arthur L. 1994. "Annotation: Firearm-Related Violence—What We Don't Know is Killing Us." *American Journal of Public Health*, 84(4):541–542.

Kitagawa, Evelyn M. and Philip M. Hauser. 1973. *Differential Mortality in the United States: A Study in Socioeconomic Epidemiology*. Cambridge, MA: Harvard University Press.

Kochanek, Kenneth D., Jeffery D. Maurer, and Harry M. Rosenberg. 1994. "Why Did Black Life Expectancy Decline from 1984 through 1989 in the United States." *American Journal of Public Health*, 84(6):938–944.

LeClere, Felicia B., Richard G. Rogers, and Kimberley D. Peters. 1997. "Ethnicity and Mortality in the United States: Individual and Community Correlates." *Social Forces*, 76(1):169–198.

————. 1998. "Neighborhood Social Context and Racial Differences in Women's Heart Disease Mortality." *Journal of Health and Social Behavior*, 39(2):91–107.

Loya, Fred and James A. Mercy. 1985. *The Epidemiology of Homicide in the City of Los Angeles 1970–1979*. Department of Health and Human Services, Public Health Service, Centers for Disease Control.

Markides, Kyriakos S. and Jeannie Coreil. 1986. "The Health of Hispanics in the Southwestern United States: An Epidemiological Paradox." *Public Health Reports*, 101:253–265.

McCord, Colin and Harold P. Freeman. 1990. "Excess Mortality in Harlem." *The New England Journal of Medicine*, 322(3):173–177.

Morris, Dexter L., Robert W. Buechley, Charles R. Key, and Marion V. Morgan. 1978. "Gallbladder Disease and Gallbladder Cancer among American Indians in Tricultural New Mexico." *Cancer*, 42(5):2472–2477.

Nam, Charles B. 1990. "Mortality Differentials from a Multiple Cause-of-Death Perspective." In S. D'Souza, A. Palloni, and J. Vallin, eds, Measurement and Analysis of Mortality. London: Oxford Press, pp. 328–342.

————. 1994. *Understanding Population Change*. Itasca, IL: F. E. Peacock Publishers, Inc.

————. 1995. "Another Look at Mortality Crossovers." *Social Biology*, 42(1–2):133–142.

National Center for Health Statistics. 1986. *Vital Statistics of the United States, 1981*, Vol II, Mortality, Part A. Washington, DC: USGPO.

————. 1993. "Advance Report of Final Mortality Statistics, 1990." *Monthly Vital Statistics Report*, 41(7):1–52.

————. 1994. *Health, United States, 1993*, Hyattsville, MD: USGPO.

Nesser, W. B., H. A. Tyroler, and J. C. Cassel. 1971. "Social Disorganization and Stroke Mortality in the Black Population of North Carolina." *American Journal of Epidemiology*, 93(3):166–175.

Novotny, Thomas E., Kenneth E. Warner, Juliette S. Kendrick, and Patrick L. Remington. 1988. "Smoking by Blacks and Whites: Socioeconomic and Demographic Differences." *American Journal of Public Health*, 78(9):1187–1189.

Passel, Jeffrey and David L. Word. 1980. "Constructing the List of Spanish Surnames for the 1980 Census: An Application of Bayes' Theorem." Paper presented at the 1980 Annual Meeting of the Population Association of America.

Poe, Gail S., Eve Powell-Griner, Joseph K. McLaughlin, Paul J. Placek, Grey B. Thompson, and Kathy Robinson. 1993. "Comparability of the Death Certificate and the 1986 National Mortality Followback Survey." *Vital and Health Statistics*, 2(118):1–53.

Potter, Lloyd B. 1991. "Socioeconomic Determinants of White–Black Male Life Expectancy." *Demography*, 28(2):303–321.

Reid, John. 1986. "Immigration and the Future U.S. Black Population." *Population Today*, (Feb):6–8.

Rogers, Richard G. 1989. "Ethnic Differences in Infant Mortality: Fact or Artifact?" *Social Science Quarterly*, 70(3):642–649.

———. 1991. "Health-Related Lifestyles among Mexican-American, Puerto Ricans, and Cubans in the United States." In Rosenwaike, Ira, ed., *Mortality of Hispanic Populations*. NY: Greenwood Press, pp 145–160

———. 1992. "Living and Dying in the USA: Sociodemographic Determinants of Death among Blacks and Whites." *Demography*, 29(2):287–303.

Rogers, Richard G., Jacqueline A. Carrigan, and Mary Grace Kovar. 1997. "Comparing Mortality Estimates Based on Different Administrative Records." *Population Research and Policy Review*, 16(3):213–224.

Rogers, Richard G., Robert A. Hummer, Charles B. Nam. 2000. *Living and Dying in the USA: Behavioral, Health, and Social Differentials of Adult Mortality*. New York: Academic Press.

Rogers, Richard G., Robert A. Hummer, Charles B. Nam, and Kimberley Peters. 1996. "Demographic, Socioeconomic, and Behavioral Factors Affecting Ethnic Mortality by Cause." *Social Forces*, 74(4):1419–1438.

Rosenwaike, Ira. 1987. "Mortality Differentials among Persons Born in Cuba, Mexico, and Puerto Rico Residing in the United States, 1979–81." *American Journal of Public Health*, 77(5):603–606.

———. 1988. "Cancer Mortality among Mexican Immigrants in the United States." Public Health Reports, 103:195–201.

Rosenwaike, Ira and Benjamin S. Bradshaw. 1988. "The Status of Death Statistics for the Hispanic Population of the Southwest." *Social Science Quarterly*, 69(3):722–736.

Rosenwaike, Ira and Katherine Hempstead. 1990a. "Differential Mortality by Ethnicity and Nativity: Foreign- and Native-born Irish, Italians, and Jews in New York City, 1979–1981." *Social Biology*, 37(1–2):11–25.

———. 1990b. "Mortality Among Three Puerto Rican Populations: Residents of Puerto Rico and Migrants in New York City and in the Balance of the United States, 1979–81." *International Migration Review*, 24(4):684–702.

Rosenwaike, Ira, and Donna Shai. 1989. "Changes in Mortality among Cubans in the United States Following an Episode of Unscreened Migration." *International Journal of Epidemiology*, 18(1):152–157.

Royce, Jacqueline M., Norman Hymowitz, Kitty Cobett, Tyler D. Hartwell, and Mario A. Orlandi. 1993. "Smoking Cessation Factors among African Americans and Whites." *American Journal of Public Health*, 82(2):220–226.

Rumbaut, Ruben G. and John R. Weeks. 1989. "Infant Health Among Indochinese Refugees: Patterns of Infant Mortality, Birthweight and Prenatal Care in Comparative Perspective." *Research in the Sociology of Health Care*, 8:137–196.

Schoenborn, C. A. 1986. "Health Habits of U.S. Adults, 1985: The 'Alameda 7' Revisited." *Public Health Reports*, 101:571–580.

Shai, Donna, Ira Rosenwaike, and Richard G. Rogers. 1991. "Mortality by Violence among Mexican Immigrants and Mexican-Americans in California and Texas." In Rosenwaike, Ira, ed., *Mortality of Hispanic Populations*. NY: Greenwood Press.

Shryock, Henry S., Jacob S. Siegel, and Associates. 1973. *The Methods and Materials of Demography*. New York: Academic Press.

Simpson, Sylvia G., Raymond Reid, Susan P. Baker, and Stephen Teret. 1983. "Injuries among the Hopi Indians: A Population-Based Survey." *The Journal of the American Medical Association*, 249(14):1873–1876.

Smith, David W. E. 1993. *Human Longevity*. NY: Oxford University Press.

Sorlie, Paul, Eugene Rogot, Roger Anderson, Norman J. Johnson, and Eric Backlund. 1992. "Black–White Mortality Differences by Family Income." *The Lancet*, 340(8815):346–350.

Sorlie, Paul D., Eugene Rogot, and Norman J. Johnson. 1992. "Validity of Demographic Characteristics on the Death Certificate." *Epidemiology*, 3(2):181–184.

Sorlie, Paul D., Eric Backlund, Norman J. Johnson, and Eugene Rogot. 1993. "Mortality by Hispanic Status in the United States." *The Journal of the American Medical Association*, 270(20):2464–2468.

Thomas, Stephen B., Sandra Crouse Quinn, Andrew Billingsley, and Cleopatra Caldwell. 1994. "The Characteristics of Northern Black Churches with Community Health Outreach Programs." *American Journal of Public Health*, 84(4):575–579.

Thomas, William I. and Dorothy S. Thomas. 1928. *The Child in America*. NY: Alfred A. Knopf.

Trevino, F. M. 1982. "Vital and Health Statistics for the U.S. Hispanic Population." *American Journal of Public Health*, 72:979–981.

U.S. Department of Health, Education, and Welfare. 1979. *Healthy People: The Surgeon General's Report on Health Promotion and Disease Prevention.* Washington, DC: USGPO.

U.S. Department of Health and Human Services. 1985. *Report of the Secretary's Task Force on Black & Minority Health.* Volume I: Executive Summary. Washington, DC: USGPO.

————. 1989. *Promoting Health/Preventing Disease: Year 2000 Objectives for the Nation* (Draft). Washington, DC: USGPO.

————. *Trends in Indian Health, 1991.* 1991. Washington, DC: USGPO.

————. *Trends in Indian Health, 1993.* 1993. Washington, DC: USGPO.

Warshauer, M. Ellen and Mary Monk. 1978. "Problems in Suicide Statistics for Whites and Blacks." *American Journal of Public Health,* 68(4):383–388.

Weiss, Kenneth M. 1993. *Genetic Variation and Human Disease: Principles and Evolutionary Approaches.* Great Britain: Cambridge University Press.

Williams, David R., Risa Lavizzo-Mourey, and Rueben C. Warren. 1994. "The Concept of Race and Health Status in America." *Public Health Reports,* 109(1):26–41.

Wilson, William J. 1987. *The Truly Disadvantaged: The Inner City, the Underclass, and Public Policy.* Chicago: University of Chicago Press.

World Health Organization. 1985. *World Health Statistics.* Geneva: WHO.

Yu, Elena. 1982. "The Low Mortality Rates of Chinese Infants: Some Plausible Explanatory Factors." *Social Science and Medicine,* 16:253–265.

Zane, Nolan and Jeannie Huh Kim. 1994. "Substance Use and Abuse." In Nolan Zane, David Takeuchi, and Kathleen Young, eds. *Confronting Critical Health Issues of Asian and Pacific Islander Americans.* Thousand Oaks, CA: Sage Publications.

Part III

Life Cycle and Diversity

Chapter 6

Housing Segregation:
Policy Issues for an Increasingly Diverse Society

Michael J. White and Eileen Shy

Introduction

There is a well-known maxim in sociology, first attributed to the gifted sociologist and newspaperman of the Chicago School, Robert Park, that "Spatial distance reflects social distance." For that reason, countless sociologists over the decades have examined patterns of population distribution, redistribution, and residential segregation as windows on the social structure of American society. In this chapter, we will draw on that tradition to talk about trends and issues in residential segregation among ethnic groups in America.
We address three broad questions:

1. What have been the trends in residential segregation in the United States? Here we examine the most recent decades but also embed that description in a longer historical framework.

2. How can social science help us understand patterns of segregation and housing discrimination in an increasingly diverse society? To answer that question, we will draw upon the findings of a variety of recent studies that use Census data, mortgage application records, and matched pairs of testers to examine housing patterns in the United States.

3. What can public policy do? We conclude the discussion by reviewing federal enforcement in housing and comparing it to other arenas. We raise some issues for social scientists and policy makers to consider in the Twenty-first century.

Trends in Residential Segregation and Racial Tolerance

First, let us examine some trends in the attitudes of Americans. Attitudes are important because they usually translate into behavior. We might expect

persons expressing prejudice toward those of another ethnic group to discrimi-
nate against them in housing, jobs, and other realms of behavior. Attitudes also
reflect social distance. Thus, we would expect that a society increasingly tolerant of ethnic differences might witness a decline in residential segregation. It is
not necessarily the case that changing attitudes become manifest in new behaviors, but it is an important place to start. On the other hand, policy intervenes
with respect to behavior, and it may ultimately help shape attitudes.

Figure 6.1 reports *trends* in racial tolerance according to three indicators,
as reported by Schuman, et al., in their book, *Racial Attitudes in America*
[1997]. The lines represent the trend in the fraction of Whites expressing more
tolerant sentiments regarding school integration, willingness to vote for a
Black presidential candidate, and racial intermarriage. The trend, of course, is
only in an attitude expressed to an interviewer, and further, represents only
attitudes of adult Whites about Blacks. We have no comparable time trend of
survey responses for opinions about Asian, Latinos, and other groups, nor of
attitudes held by these minority group members about Whites.

Figure 6.1
Trends in Racial Tolerance, 1956-1997

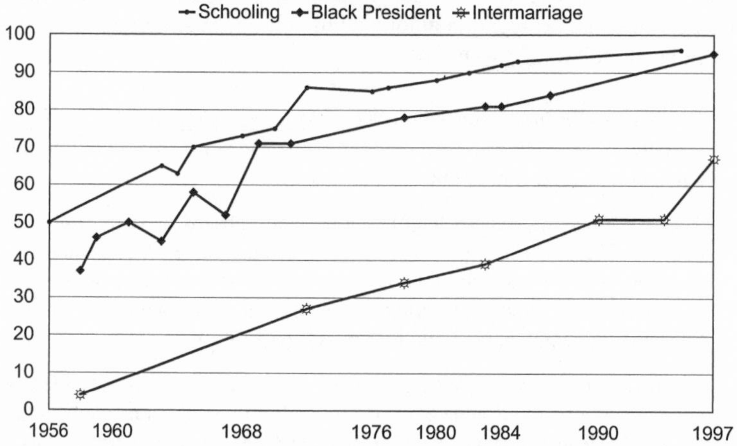

Source: Schuman, Steen, Bobo & Krysan, 1997

The trend suggests a decline in social distance, but what has happened
regarding spatial distance? Specifically, we would like to know:

• what about segregation of Whites versus persons of color?

• how does this fit into a broader historical pattern?

• what about segregation *within* the European ancestry group?

• what predicts level of segregation and its change?

Figure 6.2 presents residential segregation indices for four minority groups (versus non-Hispanic Whites). Data from the 1990 Census reported by Harrison and Weinberg replicate the very high level of segregation for Americans of African descent (Harrison and Weinberg, 1992). For the index used on this chart, the interpretation is that nearly 70% of Black Americans would have to change residence in order to become evenly distributed with respect to Whites. These are averages across many metropolitan areas. Cities themselves vary, with large cities tending to exhibit more segregation. For instance, in the New York metropolitan area Black–White segregation is at 0.82; in Chicago it is 0.86; and in Los Angeles it is 0.73. By contrast, the small metropolitan area of Jacksonville, North Carolina shows a Black–White segregation value of 0.23. Early analyses of similar data from Census 2000 by the Lewis Mumford Center (www.albany.edu/mumford/census) reveal a similar pattern of segregation for major race groups in 2000 and show only modest declines in most metropolitan areas.

Figure 6.2
Residential Segregation from Whites by Race/Ethnicity, 1990

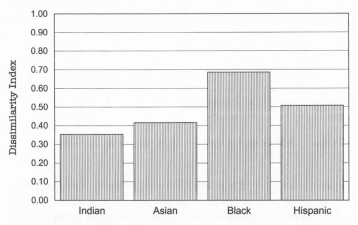

Source: Harrison and Weinberg, 1992.

Across the 318 metropolitan areas, the average segregation index comes in at about 50 for Hispanics, and still less for Asians and American Indians. Blacks are clearly more segregated than other minorities. (In the Los Angles metropolitan area, which has sizable proportions of both Asians and Latinos, the White–Asian segregation index stands at 0.46 and the White–Hispanic index stands at 0.61). All of these groups are more segregated than other European stock groups, such as the French, Germans, Irish, Italian, and Poles (White, 1987)[1]. Residential separation of Blacks from Whites has been so extreme, pervasive, and persistent that Douglas Massey and Nancy Denton could title their 1993 book *American Apartheid* (Massey and Denton, 1993).

In Figure 6.3 we examine the *trend* in residential segregation, limiting our look to Blacks and Whites in the largest 28 metropolitan areas. Between 1960 and 1970 there was no movement at all; between 1970 and 1990 we observe a steady, *but modest,* downward trend in the level of residential segregation in these large urban areas. For Hispanics, the 1980s brought little change in segregation; for Asians, the drop was a little over two points (Farley and Frey, 1994).

Figure 6.3
Change in Residential Segregation, 1980-90, By Race

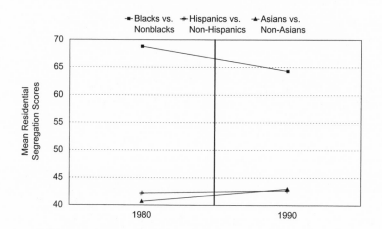

Source: Farley and Frey, 1994.

All these values are "uncontrolled"; that is, we have not removed the effects of other variables, such as income and education. Since we know that ethnic groups differ in these other socioeconomic characteristics, we would expect the sorting of socioeconomic groups in space to translate into ethnic differences as well. Nevertheless, other studies have repeatedly shown that even upon controlling for these factors, residential segregation remains appreciable (Farley, 1977; Massey and Denton, 1993). One recent study using unique data from the 1980 Census demonstrated that even for persons of the same age, education, income level (and controlling also for nativity in the United States or abroad), ethnicity still has strong predictive power for the kind of neighborhood in which a household resided (White and Sassler, 1996).

It is useful to consider for a moment how this portrait of contemporary residential patterns appears against a broader historical backdrop. Our vernacular sociology is full of myths about what happened at earlier points in time to various ethnic groups, particularly those waves of European immigrants who entered through Ellis Island to make their way in America. One of those myths is that early immigrants were highly segregated (just as African American now are) and with the passage of time, socioeconomic advancement, and adaption to American culture, made their way in U.S. society and integrated residentially. How accurate is the myth?

Information from the 1910 census can be used to provide a window on the degree of ethnic segregation at a time immediately following one of the great waves of U.S. immigration (White, 1994). The new arrivals of the time—French Canadians, Poles, Jews (Yiddish speakers)—were extremely segregated: almost no member of these groups had a neighbor of any other ethnic group. Scores for other Eastern and Southern European origin groups were also quite high. Segregation of the Irish and German stock population was appreciable but much more modest (White, et al. 1994). This historical picture of the structure of European residential segregation is more consistent with the notion of a set of interconnected ethnic villages than a single polyethnic society, even among Americans of European ancestry. The "melting pot" had not yet been stirred.

The African American experience contrasts with that of the European groups. In 1910 Americans of African descent experienced segregation levels roughly in the middle of the "new" immigrant groups. But while Eurostock and Afrostock Americans experienced similar levels of segregation in 1910, most European stock groups (French Canadians, Italians, Poles) experienced a steady decline in segregation, while African Americans did not. Lieberson argues that both African Americans and the new European groups were subjected to discrimination, but it was more severe for the former. Furthermore, he emphasizes the place of potential economic competition in driving intergroup tensions and further discrimination (Lieberson, 1980). Those who have reviewed the historical record have argued that the Twentieth century was actually a period of *consolidation* of the American Black ghetto (Hershberg, 1981).

Most metropolitan areas in the United States did experience modest declines in Black–White residential segregation over the 1980s, however. What accounts for these declines? Farley and Frey find that one of the strongest predictors of segregation decline is the fraction of new construction among the housing stock. Thus, fast-growing areas, metropolitan regions with lots of shifting and sorting of their population (often driven by economic growth) are the ones in which segregation levels have declined (Farley and

Frey, 1994). These overall trends are so notable that Black–White segregation in the South is now on average less than segregation in the North.

Now consider *spatial assimilation*, a term we use to refer to making one's way into a residentially integrated environment. Most of the empirical research on this topic again takes native-born Whites (European stock, usually) as the reference group *with whom* one integrates, although this need not be the case. What traits predict integration, and how do *returns* to these traits differ across various ethnic groups? Again, the results are not completely uniform, but several clear patterns emerge.

As an example, examine the residential assimilation of Asian Americans contained in Figure 6.4. In a multivariate model controlling for a variety of socioeconomic, familial, and other characteristics, White, Biddlecom, and Guo found that education and income were the most powerful predictors of proximity to Anglos (White, Biddlecom, and Guo, 1993). Importantly, these socioeconomic traits strongly outweighed "immigrant status" (foreign birth, years in the United States) in the prediction. They found sizable differences within the Asian-origin population, however, with Chinese and Filipinos much less likely to reside near Whites, even after controlling for these other traits.

Figure 6.4
Asian Residential Assimilation
Segregation of Chinese and Koreans from Whites, 1990,
by Place of Birth and Socioeconomic Status

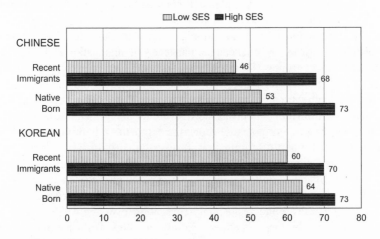

Source: White, Biddlecom & Guo, 1993

Similar results hold in other studies. In most cases, there are appreciable "returns" to socioeconomic status in producing proximity to Whites, but again, these results are not uniform across groups. African Americans received lower returns to their socioeconomic status (in terms of residential integration with whites) than comparable Asians and Latinos (Massey and Mullan, 1984). Logan and Alba, in a series of studies, continue to find group differences. Those with higher income tend to find their way into the suburbs and higher status neighborhoods. Nevertheless, groups differ in these returns, and some minorities achieve less integration or neighborhood status, even when their age, income, and education are comparable to European stock whites (Alba and Logan, 1991; Logan and Alba, 1993; White and Sassler, 1996).

While ethnic groups' preferences for living with coethnics may drive ethnic segregation, all ethnic groups presumably wish to translate personal socioeconomic gains into neighborhood status. The comparison of neighborhood status outcomes is especially telling, therefore. Recent work analyzing about 20 ethnic groups indicates that Americans of color (of comparable age, education, income, etc.) lived in lower status neighborhoods than Anglos. There are differences within the minority populations, too, with African Americans and Puerto Rican ancestry groups having outcomes inferior to those of comparable Americans of Cuban, Japanese, and Chinese ancestry (White and Sassler, 1996).

The persistence of ethnic residential segregation coupled with the economic stagnation of some older, industrial cities has fueled concern about the growth of an urban underclass, composed disproportionately of ethnic minorities (Wilson, 1987). Massey and Denton have drawn attention to "hypersegregation," a circumstance in which minority groups in cities are segregated along several dimensions: occupying different neighborhoods, spatially concentrated, and distant from nonminority neighborhoods. Relatedly, concern grows about a skills or spatial mismatch that leaves behind inner-city residents. Geography matters. Residents of inner-city areas appear to have experienced extra disadvantage over and above that predicted by labor force and social trends (Silver, White, and Iceland, 1993). This is especially so for minority youths, whose spatial isolation from job opportunities pushes up the ethnic disparity in unemployment rates (Ihlanfeldt, 1992).

How does one summarize all of this Census-based evidence on residential patterns:

1. Evidence points to declines in segregation over the Twentieth century. Appreciable differences remain among groups, however, so that by 1990 African Americans are the most segregated, with moderate segregation for Asian and Latino groups. Eurostock groups have low levels of segregation, but even here, there is variation depending on the timing of arrival, with the "old" Northern and Western European groups less segregated than Southern and Eastern European groups.

2. Members of most ethnic groups experience residential assimilation. That is, households translate their own educational and economic gains into residential integration with the Anglo population and higher status neighborhoods.

3. Notable group differences in residential outcome persist, even among persons of comparable age, family composition, education, and income. Americans of African heritage are especially disadvantaged in this regard.

In sum, the melting pot model, so enshrined in the American mythology, applies only selectively.

Mortgage Lending and Audit Studies

Census data have innumerable virtues, but they have several drawbacks. The Census leaves unmeasured many traits and behaviors relevant to issues of segregation, particularly those that encompass discrimination. Census data take a snapshot of results, and really do not tell us directly about how people search for housing and the obstacles they may face. The existence or persistence of residential segregation does not in itself prove discrimination. Can we assemble other evidence that might be more definitive? In this section we examine two sources of information on housing outcomes that are more closely tied to the operation of the housing market itself. First, we review studies of applications for home mortgages. Second, we turn to powerful studies of "audits," where matched individuals go in search of housing and experience discrimination (or the lack of it) directly.

Table 6.1
Mortgage Rejection Ratios in Selected Major Metropolitan Areas, 1991

City	Ratio
Chicago	3.08
Philadelphia	2.76
Atlanta	2.63
Detroit	2.61
St. Louis	2.56
Dallas	2.55
Houston	2.50
Boston	2.27
New York	1.89
Los Angeles	1.40
United States	1.91

Percent Blacks Applications Rejected/Percent Whites Applications Rejected
Source: Thomas, 1992.

Federal law requires lenders (banks, etc.) to report data on the character-istics of those who apply for mortgages. Studies of these data find that minor-ity group members are more likely to be rejected than non-Hispanic Whites when they apply for a home mortgage. Table 6.1 presents rejection ratios for the United States overall and for some major cities. The higher rejection ratios in the northern industrial cities such as Chicago and Boston are consistent with the higher levels of segregation found there. Nationally, Native Americans and Hispanics also have rejection rates that exceed those of Anglos, while Asians have a lower rejection ratio (Thomas, 1992).

Black–White mortgage rejection ratios did decline in most states between 1990 and 1991 and for most categories of size of mortgage sought[2]. Is this indicative of a corresponding decline, however slight, in discrimina-tion? Does the higher rejection ratio indicate more discrimination against African Americans than other minorities? Some of the banks with the highest rejection ratios claim active minority outreach programs that they believe added less qualified applicants to their pool.

These statistics do not control for all background characteristics of the applicants, however. In one recent study, the Federal Reserve Bank of Boston did try to take these other factors into account. Even in the presence of con-trols for income level, debt–income ratio, credit history, and other variables, Blacks were rejected at a rate 1.6 times that of Whites (Thomas, 1992; Munnel et al., 1996). Similar results have been obtained recently for the Milwaukee housing market (Squires and Kim, 1995). Moreover, minority home buyers are much less likely to seek conventional loans (using instead FHA and other government-backed loans, seller-financing, and the like), even after control-ling for age, income, and neighborhood characteristics of the unit. Whether this difference is due to purchaser preferences, inadvertent steering, or outright racial bias remains to be determined (Canner et al., 1991).

Multivariate studies, even of the kind mentioned here, can control for many traits but census and administrative data have inevitable weaknesses. They can-not measure all traits (personal and family characteristics, preferences) that influence housing search. One might argue, therefore, that these studies are not definitive. After all, minority group members may not seek housing amidst the majority. The existence of an ethnic mosaic may point to the exercise of prefer-ences, rather than proof of prejudice. Still, as this evidence accumulates, it demonstrates convincingly that the operation of the housing market is strongly influenced by the ethnic background of the home-seekers[3].

Think of how potentially powerful our analysis of the incidence of dis-crimination would be if we could conduct *randomized clinical trials*, as in medical research. New drugs and medical procedures can be tested where all things are controlled, except the procedure or drug under scrutiny. The analo-gy in the case of a residential segregation or discrimination study would be to randomly assign persons to an ethnic background and then examine what happened to them as mortgage applicants, renters, or other consumers. Obviously, since we cannot manipulate a person's ethnic background, social science is constrained from true random assignment in this area.

The alternative is to conduct an audit, mimicking a randomized trial and allowing only one social characteristic (ethnic background) to vary across environments. Systematic audit studies can be traced to the 1970s. Several dozen studies have been conducted by now. The audit is a powerful tool, but one that has a narrow application. The usual procedure is to send two "matched" testers to look for housing through the usual means, and "code" for any differential treatment. The testers—usually one from a majority group, and one from a minority group—are *assigned* characteristics to make them equivalent in the housing market. For example, mortgage applicants are given similar income and occupational profiles, marital and family status.

The differential treatment can include a variety of outcomes. It might include variation in the number of housing units shown, varying effort on the part of the agent to help with housing, and of course, steering of home-seekers to particular neighborhoods. In the view of many, audit studies provide incontrovertible evidence of discrimination (Fix et al., 1993; Yinger, 1995).

Table 6.2
Audit Tests for Discrimination in Housing:
Access to Information about Unit

Audit Setting	*Majority Favored (%)*	*Minority Favored (%)*
Rental		
Black versus White	15	5
Hispanic versus Anglo	12	6
Sales		
Black versus White	8	1
Hispanic versus Anglo	8	3

Source: Fix et al., 1993.

Table 6.2 is from another study (Fix et al., 1993) that examines both the owner and renter markets, and this time also examines outcomes for both African Americans and Latinos, focusing on the instance of unfavorable treatment in access to information about the housing unit. Note that majority group members *do* sometimes experience unfavorable treatment. (Some of this may be random fluctuation.) Nevertheless, the incidence of unfavorable treatment for Blacks and Latinos far exceeds that for equivalent Whites. A related study tested for the presence of steering (Turner and Wienk, 1993). In the vast majority of cases, no steering takes place: the Black and White auditors are treated alike. *But* in those 10% or 20% of cases where steering (differential treatment) is found, it was the Black home-seeker who was not shown homes in the White neighborhoods or was *not* shown homes in the higher income areas.

Yinger's values from the 1989 Housing Discrimination Study in 25 metropolitan areas indicate a "net" incidence of discrimination of nearly 20%, in Yinger's words, "About one-fifth of the time, blacks learn about fewer housing units than do comparable whites" [Yinger, 1995: 34–35]. The Hispanic–White net incidence was only slightly smaller. If one *cumulates* the fraction of adverse incidents as the housing search proceeds, the members of minority groups are substantially more disadvantaged (Massey and Denton, 1993: 104ff).

Our discussion of auditing has focused on racial and ethnic discrimination in housing. While there are some concerns about the design of these audit studies and the extent of the inferences one can make from them[4], they have clearly demonstrated their value, and audits have now been conducted to uncover age discrimination in employment and sex discrimination in consumer treatment.

The mortgage lending and audit studies provide strong evidence. Taken together, they tell us that the residential segregation values we observe for ethnic minority groups are not solely attributable to current differences in preferences and demographic background characteristics of persons searching in the housing market.

The Public Policy Response

After examining the racial discrimination that continues to characterize the U.S. housing market, an obvious next question is how the government chooses to respond. We ask, in particular, how strong is the commitment to defending principles of racial equality in housing? Looking at our government's prosecution of other violations provides a useful comparison. When someone engages in insider training, the penalties can be enormous, up to triple damages. Consider, for example, that in October 1993 Prudential Securities, Inc. agreed in a settlement to pay at least $371 million in restitution and fines to customers who suffered fraud (Eichenwald, 1993). This huge response is due, in part, to the importance we attach to the unfettered and open performance of the marketplace. Product liability suits offer another arena in which huge damages are awarded to plaintiffs allegedly harmed by the action of a manufacturer or marketer.

By extension, policy needs to reflect the substantial cost borne by members of society, both individually and collectively, both short-term and long-term, when discrimination is present. The dollar value of this discrimination in terms of the extra time, effort, and money needed to locate equivalent housing or higher prices paid for lower quality housing (or, relatedly, the loss in value arising from shortening a search or refraining from house-hunting) is substantial. John Yinger has estimated that these direct costs, a discrimination "tax" in his terminology, amount to about $3,000 every time a Black or Hispanic household searches for a house to buy (Yinger, 1995:102). The additional costs, ones that cannot be set down in dollars, are immeasurable[5].

Figure 6.5
Processing a Fair Housing Complaint, Post-1988

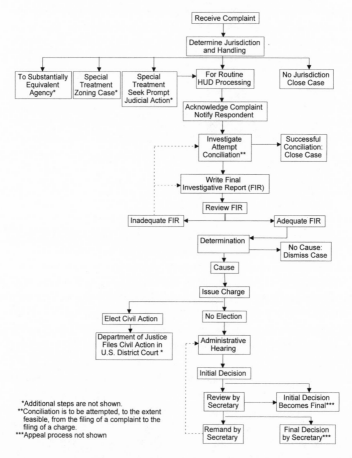

*Additional steps are not shown.
**Conciliation is to be attempted, to the extent feasible, from the filing of a complaint to the filing of a charge.
***Appeal process not shown

Source: The State of Fair Housing, 1989.

The response of the public sector to housing segregation and discrimination has varied over time. Prior to the civil rights era the government at all levels actually promoted segregation in many areas. Many authors, Massey and Denton (1993), Farley and Frey (1994) Metcalf (1988), Leigh (1991) and others have chronicled the pre-World War II efforts to use governmental means to restrict the housing options of ethnic minorities, primarily but not exclusively African Americans. Restrictive covenants, red-lining, and segregated public housing were just a few of the mechanisms through which discrimination operated.

The 1968 Fair Housing Act (PL90-284, 1 April 1968) was a watershed. It outlawed discrimination in the sale or rental of housing on the basis of race, color, religion, or national origin. The 1968 Act has been criticized for lacking teeth. Massey and Denton, for example, call its enforcement provisions, "inherently weak and ineffective" [Massey and Denton, 1993: 197]. The Act was the watered-down result of the "Dirksen compromise," orchestrated by Senator Everett Dirksen of Illinois to pass *some* fair housing legislation in the face of strong southern opposition to *any* civil rights provisions. The Act emphasized conciliatory redress, administrative activities, and clearly placed the burden of proof on the complainant. The federal role, outside of "pattern and practice" cases of systematic discrimination, was quite limited (Yinger, 1995:189). The Home Mortgage Disclosure Act (1975) and the Community Reinvestment Act (1977), by requiring the public release of information about loan and bank activity, may have provided further impetus to the effort to end housing discrimination. The 1988 amendments to the Fair Housing Act [PL100-430] added several new administrative procedures and enforcement provisions. Do these teeth bite?

The amendments provided new enforcement mechanisms and added disability and family status as bases for discrimination complaints. Currently, housing discrimination cases are processed in one on four ways. First, as before, an individual can bring private legal action based on the Fair Housing Act and the Civil Rights Act. A second method of enforcement, also present before 1988, operates through the U.S. Department of Justice (DOJ). The DOJ can initiate and prosecute cases of systemic discrimination, i.e., cases where a "pattern or practice" of discrimination is alleged. These cases are argued before a judge and jury and carry civil penalties of up to $100,000.

While the two methods of enforcement mentioned above were largely unchanged through the amendments, the remaining two are substantial departures from the government's previous ways of doing business. Under the 1988 amendments, an individual can bring a complaint to HUD (see Figure 6.5). The federal agency or an equivalent state or local office will attempt conciliation between the complainant and defendant. Whereas before the new legislation, complainants had no recourse when conciliation failed, now HUD itself could take up the case. If conciliation fails and probable cause is deemed to exist,

HUD's General Counsel can bring the case before an ALJ. Potential civil penalties range up to $50,000. Either party can still elect to take the case to a federal court as a civil action, but Congress intended to offer an alternative impartial method of hearing cases that would be more expeditious than a trial in U.S. District Court. In a second significant departure from the 1968 Fair Housing Act, HUD itself can initiate prosecution based on information from an individual complaint, financial regulatory agency, or HUD investigation. These cases are argued before an ALJ or, on election, in the Justice Department.

At the time Jimmy Carter took office, a HUD audit found that 27% of rental agents and 15% of real estate salespeople still openly discriminated against racial minorities. Furthermore, the study found, that a Black house hunter stood a 72% chance of encountering open discrimination upon visiting four rental agencies; the same house hunter would stand a 48% chance upon visiting four real estate agents in hopes of purchasing a house [Wienk et al. 1979: ES-2]. In the years following Carter's inauguration, levels of fair housing enforcement varied widely. It would be premature to pass final judgment on the efficacy of the 1988 amendments, but the data currently available suggest: (1) 1988 amendments have already brought some positive changes; and (2) there remains ample room for more strenuous enforcement.

Under both the Carter and Reagan Administrations, federal enforcement of fair housing provisions lacked consistency and stringency. Despite Carter's strong support for civil rights, enforcement of fair housing during his administration was weak.

A study on the federal fair housing enforcement effort undertaken by the United States Commission on Civil Rights reports that enforcement between January of 1975 and August of 1978—a time period beginning before Carter's term in office, and ending midway through Carter's term—was lax at best. HUD's enforcement levels were inconsistent throughout the Carter years. The total number of fair housing complaints, which the Office of Fair Housing and Equal Opportunity (the HUD section that enforces fair housing) brought to closure ranged from 2,774 in 1977 to 3,910 in 1978 (Table 6.3). HUD greatly reduced its backlog in 1978, earning compliments from the Commission on Civil Rights, but 1979 closure rates again dipped[6]. Another important measure of pre-1988 HUD efficacy is the number of complaints successfully conciliated. Complaints could be closed for many reasons, including insufficient cause, lack of evidence, HUD's inability to contact the complainant, or the complainant's decision to take the case to court using personal resources. Successful conciliations are taken to be those cases in which HUD has intervened and found a solution acceptable to the complainant. During the Carter Administration, HUD brought about 10% of total complaints to successful conciliation (Table 6.3). Of the pool of cases in which conciliation was actually attempted, HUD was successfully about half the time. Total yearly monetary

Table 6.3
HUD Fair Housing Enforcement Proceedings 1976–1991

	Complaints	% New Bases*	Closures	% Closed	Attempted Conciliations	Successful Conciliations	% Successful Conciliations	Total** Compensation
1976	3123		4049	130%	786	402	13%	$364,928
1977	6213		2774	89%	530	277	4%	$364,114
1978	3169		3910	123%	754	358	11%	
1979	3339		2912	87%	643	348	10%	
1980	3039		2890	95%	703	494	16%	$763,733
1981	2410		2710	112%	1142	829	34%	$893,092
1982	5112		4360	85%	1339	946	19%	$1,016,266
1983	4551							
1984	4533		4642	102%				$1,130,739
1985	4882		4112	84%				$1,020,818
1986	4157		4152	99%				$971,571
1987	4699		4125	88%				$752,739
1988	4422							
1989	7174	70%		50%***		1748		$2,324,206
1990	7675	43%		93%***		2614		$1,898,561
1991	9320	41%		108%***		2897		$2,469,591

* Many cases claim multiple bases

** In constant 1992 dollars (Consumer Price Index)

*** Does not include FHAP closures

All numbers include HUD and substantially equivalent state and local agencies unless otherwise noted.

Figures from 1979 through 1988 do not include the separate systemic discrimination program.

Complaints is number of new yearly complaints; Percent new bases is the number of complaints based at least in part on protected statuses added in 1988 (family status, handicap) divided by number of complaints; Percent closed is number of new complaints divided by closures; Percent success is successful conciliations divided by complaints. Sources: Special Analyses on Civil Rights; HUD Annual Report; Budget of the U.S.; The State of Fair Housing; Commission on Civil Rights: Shull, The President and Civil Rights Policy. Details available on request.

compensation increased markedly during Carter's term in office—from $368,114 in 1977 to $763,733 in 1980 (constant 1992 dollars) —but because conciliations also increased during that time period, average compensation did not show a similar increase[7].

The Department of Justice (DOJ) under the Carter Administration was more aggressive in its fair housing activity. The Department brought a substantial number of cases every year, and this number increased each year Carter was in office (Table 6.4), winning praise from the Commission on Civil Rights.

Table 6.4
Department of Justice Fair Housing Suits 1976–1991

	# of civil suits filed	*% new bases**
1976	n/a	
1977	18	
1978	19	
1979	26	
1980	n/a	
1981	0	
1982	2	
1983	5	
1984	17	
1985	18	
1986	n/a	
1987	n/a	
1988	n/a	
1989	30	57%
1990	55	80%
1991	97	68%

* Many cases claim multiple bases.

n/a = not available.

Percent new bases is number of suits filed based on statuses awarded protection in 1988 (handicap, familial status) divided by total suits.

Sources: Special Analyses (1977–1979); Metcalf (1981–1983); HUD Annual Report (1984–1985); The State of Fair Housing (1989–1991).

When Ronald Reagan assumed the presidency in 1980, he brought with him a sea change in government policy for everything from the budget to civil rights. Despite Reagan's redirection toward the New Federalism and his highly criticized civil rights record, closure rates were very similar to those recorded during the Carter years (Table 6.3). Data from Reagan's first two years in office show a high level of both conciliation attempts and successful conciliations in comparison to the Carter years. If these two years (data not available for later years) are an accurate indication of conciliation levels during

Reagan's term in office, it would seem that HUD was actually more effica-
cious and active during Reagan's term than during Carter's.

Table 6.5
Fair Housing Equal Opportunity (FHEO) Budget Outlays: 1976-1991

	Budget *
1976	
1977	
1978	
1979	
1980	
1981	$1,115,918
1982	$3,431,171
1983	$6,527,612
1984	$7,904,872
1985	$7,121,920
1986	$6,962,516
1987	$7,103,923
1988	$9,059,609
1989	$7,897,532
1990	$5,677,481
1991	$11,079,786

*In constant 1992 dollars (Consumer Price Index)

Source: Budget of the U.S.

The total monetary compensation in constant dollars awarded to complainants also increased from the Carter Administration to the Reagan
Administration (Table 6.3). The average yearly total monetary compensation
under Carter was $565,923 (for the two years in which data were available),
while under Reagan the yearly pre-amendment compensation average was
$964,204—a difference of around $400,000. Furthermore, during Reagan's
term in office, the budget for the Office of Fair Housing and Equal
Opportunity increased. The budget for the office in constant dollars increased
steadily during Reagan's time in office, from $1,115,918 in 1981 to
$7,897,532 in 1989 (Table 6.5). Enforcement within the Department of Justice
under Reagan contrasts sharply with both the HUD record under Reagan and
with the DOJ's record under Carter. In the first year Reagan was in office, the
Civil Rights division of the Department of Justice filed no suits whatsoever
(Table 6.4). The number of filings increased only slightly in the next two
years. But the Justice Department shifted philosophy also at this time, now
requiring proof of discriminatory intent before prosecuting a case. The average number of civil suits filed by the Department of Justice during the Reagan
Administration was 12—57% less than the average yearly number of suits

during Carter's term in office (for the years in which data are available), and furthermore, these suits have been regarded as being relatively unimportant (Metcalf 1988:18). For all the debate during his two terms we see that the record—a result of both the Reagan Administration's philosophy and the political compromises with Congress and the civil rights community—resulted in a more mixed record than might otherwise be anticipated.

George Bush began his term in office immediately before the March 12, 1989 implementation of the Fair Housing Amendments Act. Under the Bush Administration, fair housing enforcement showed a limited, but nonetheless, significant, increase. Interestingly, the primary changes in fair housing enforcement were improved conciliation rates and higher monetary awards, rather than recourse to the new enforcement options brought by the 1988 legislation.

The levels of complaints and compensation in 1989 reflect the changes of the 1988 Amendments. Number of complaints increased about 60% from 1988 to 1989, and continued to increase in 1990 and 1991 (Table 6.3). This sharp increase in complaints can be largely attributed to the addition of familial status and handicap as bases for housing discrimination complaints. In 1989 70% of post-Act complaints were based at least in part on newly protected bases.

Closure rates in 1989 did not increase proportionately to complaint rates. Only 50% of complaints were closed in 1989—the lowest closure rate of any year examined. The low closure rate in 1989 may be attributable to the difficulties of initiating an entirely new enforcement procedure, or perhaps a simple growth in new cases. Closure rates increase significantly in 1990 and 1991.

Closure rates measure administrative efficiency, but they do not indicate the level of relief complainants received, and the level of relief has increased since 1988. The 1988 Amendments required HUD to attempt conciliation to the degree feasible in all cases; furthermore, the Act now added the threat of a court case to push defendants to the bargaining table. Accordingly, the number of successful conciliations rose significantly after 1988—30% of complaints in the years 1989 through 1991 were successfully conciliated, compared to 14% of complaints between 1976 and 1982.

Under the 1988 Amendments, complaints that are not closed administratively move to the determination stage, in which HUD's Office of General Counsel determines whether there is reasonable cause to believe a discriminatory housing practice occurred or was about to occur. In 1989, only 91 (2%) complaints reached the determination stage. By 1991, this figure had increased to 1,183—13% of yearly complaints. Of the complaints that reached determination, 13% were judged to have reasonable cause. Either party in a suit can elect to have the case tried in a federal court, and between 1989 and 1991 a significant proportion of parties chose this option. The total number of cases tried in an Administrative Law Forum between 1989 and 1991 was 30— a surprisingly low number in relation to the over 7,000 complaints recorded each year by HUD, and the political fervor the establishment of ALJs sparked. Under a second new feature of the 1988 Amendments, HUD identified situations for Secretary-initiated investigation (15 in 1990; 25 in 1991), only a few of which actually came before an Administrative Law Judge.

The 1988 Amendments sparked a rise in *aggregate* monetary relief for complainants after three years of declining total compensation; however, *average* relief showed only a small increase after the amendments. HUD reports an average award of $1,945 per successful conciliation in post-Act 1989 as compared with an average of $1,385 in 1988 (US Dept. of HUD, State of Fair Housing 1989:17).

In 1992, Bill Clinton assumed the Oval Office proclaiming that he would bring change to America. Many anticipated that Clinton's presidency would be more supportive of a civil rights agenda than that of either of the previous two presidents: "civil-rights activists expect the Clinton administration to be much more vigilant than its Republican predecessors in enforcing anti-discrimination laws" (Roberts et al., 1993:45). Clinton's secretary of HUD, Henry Cisneros, pledged to increase enforcement of housing discrimination laws and in December 1998 HUD announced it would conduct a third national audit of housing discrimination (Goering and Squires, 1999). Despite the finding of gross mismanagement of HUD during the Reagan administration, under Clinton, funding increased for civil rights enforcement at HUD and many federal agencies (Goering and Squires, 1999). Still, complaints of housing discrimination, though they increased during the Clinton years, are much rarer than those of employment discrimination. Schill and Friedman (1999) note that though the number of housing cases filed rose during the 1990s, to about 10,000 per year, this number pales in comparison to the 80,000 employment claims. Furthermore, one of the principal innovations of the 1988 amendments, having one's case heard by an Administrative Law Judge instead of in federal court is used in only a minority of the cases, so the time it takes to settle cases has not decreased. Further, few cases are filed under the provision of no discrimination against families with children. Schill and Friedman concluded their study of the first decades of the 1988 amendments by pointing out that the data "about enforcement of complaints alleging violations of the Fair Housing Act raise almost as many questions as they answer...[but] they do suggest that they have important consequences." (1999:76).

While the legislative branch was developing the 1988 Amendments, and the executive branch was providing leadership to enforcement agencies and responding to legislative changes, the judicial branch was developing the case history. In the 1982 *Havens Realty Corp. v. Coleman,* the Supreme Court ruled that testers (auditors) have standing before the court to sue on the basis of discrimination and collect damages. Since the evolution of HUD activity included the enabling (and financial assistance for) conducting local audits, this decision opened up an entirely new avenue of enforcement. Even those testers who were only posing as apartment or home-seekers (and did not themselves intend to reside in the unit) could sue. While this strengthened the hand of some activists, other well-known court decisions may have weakened the hand of those who would bring court suits for discrimination. The *Wards Cove* case shifted the burden of proof in employment discrimination more toward the plaintiff. *Richmond v. Croson* struck down the Richmond, Virginia, minority "set-aside" program for city construction contracts.

Conclusion

What is the conclusion about the federal government's role in Fair Housing enforcement? We can say that legislative commitment has grown from 1968 to the present. As former HUD secretary Patricia Robert Harris testified in 1979 before a House subcommittee, the 1968 law was "less than half a loaf. It identified the problems, but supplied only the most pallid of solutions" (CQ Almanac 1980:373). The 1988 Amendments offered new and powerful means of addressing fair housing issues. When enforcement authority backs the conciliation process, conciliation is "highly effective in bringing respondents to the table, resolving complaints speedily, and providing access to the disputed housing" (Waldrop 1985–86:208). The numbers of successful conciliations after 1989 tend to support this claim. Percentage of complaints conciliated shows a significant increase after 1989—around a third of complaints were successfully conciliated after the amendments as opposed to about 20% before the amendments.

Still, the level of action has clearly varied over time and remains well below enforcement in other realms of government regulation. After many hard-won legal battles in the 1960s and 1970s, many in the Civil Rights community regarded the 1980s as a period of setbacks. The Civil Rights Act of 1990 emerged out of a debate about the relative permanence of some of the shifts that had taken place in the 1980s. Of course, this debate itself took place as the United States received one of the largest waves of new immigrants in its history.

A review of segregation trends suggests that the 20-year shift in the statutory and regulatory environment surrounding housing discrimination issues may have had some impact. After the plateau that was traced between 1960 and 1970, the following two decades did see noticeable (if not large) drops in segregation in major cities. Of course, other explanations compete for credit for the decline. A reduction in prejudice and hostility among White majority and the increasing income levels of minority group members can be cited as relevant.

Government action took place against a backdrop of growing public re-evaluation of the place of race and ethnicity in society. American society is still wrestling with how to redress past and present inequalities. Certainly the debate over Affirmative Action and its implementation, the controversy over employment verification of the immigrants, and the battle between President Bush and his opponents in Congress over new civil rights legislation stand testimony to a lack of consensus.

The debate continues. One only needs to scan the popular press or the op-ed pages of major American dailies. The very fact that the United States has many more "minority" group members than it once did has further complicated the picture. As the brochure for the conference at which this paper was first presented states, by the middle of the Twenty-first century, the United States may well become Majority–Minority. It is a peculiar turn of phrase, but it has been used for some time in California. Recall from the historical record, however, that the one-time "majority" of English stock Protestants gave way demographically to various minorities. Let us suggest a route for policy to consider, one that might be tolerated by persons from a variety of political persuasions.

First, consider the setting:

1. By all accounts ethnic prejudice has declined in America. By 1993 on the order of three-quarters of Whites agree with the principle of minority residential choice [National Opinion Research Center, 1994], up from about 40% three decades before.

2. Still, Whites express reluctance to support any government activity designed to affirmatively intervene to rearrange outcomes. The vast majority of Whites disagree with the proposition that equally qualified Blacks should be given preference over Whites. Furthermore, half of all of African Americans (a majority, in fact, of those expressing an opinion) also disagree with preferential treatment. (Kantrowitz, 1988).

3. Social science has demonstrated that segregation has declined, but that it is still present, and that the level of segregation varies measurably across ethnic groups. It is also not merely attributable to ethnic differences in socioeconomic status.

4. Audit studies have confirmed, that, despite some public opinion to the contrary, discrimination in housing is still very much a presence on the American scene.

Given this setting, we would like to argue that the United States consider a much more active program of monitoring residential patterns, testing for discrimination, and bringing actions through the courts and administrative agencies. With such a shift, administrative efficiency needs to increase. In 1990 nearly 3,000 complaints received by HUD were open for over 100 days.

Legislation that gives HUD the authority to issue "cease and desist" orders would provide additional incentive to bring parties to the conciliation process; it may also enable a complainant to occupy a disputed unit in a reasonable time.

What can social science do? In an increasingly diverse society, social science analysts can perform an important monitoring function. Census analyses are admitted snapshots, but reveal the results of the housing process for all 250 million Americans of dozens of ethnic backgrounds, across more than 40,000 urban neighborhoods in the United States. Such analyses can identify general patterns and trends, and they can point to problem spots. Audit studies can hone in on discrimination itself, drawing on the power of experimental design to identify how much discrimination exists, against whom, and through what mechanisms it operates.

Money has to talk here. If we can award over a third of a billion dollars to the 400,000 clients of one securities firm in one settlement, surely we can afford a commitment of equal value for the injury suffered by those millions of persons who experience discrimination, whether they trace their origins to Africa, Asia, Europe, or Latin America. Many of the tools are already in place. Using these tools would bring us closer to the preamble of Title VIII of the 1968 Fair Housing Act, which states that, "It is the policy of the United States to provide...fair housing throughout" the nation.

Notes

1. In this comparison, segregation is calculated with reference to the level of residential mixture with English Ancestry Whites (White, 1987). This is in keeping with much of past practice, which drew on the fact that English-origin settlers were numerically dominant in the early days of the nation and dominated its institutions. Segregation can be calculated for any pair of groups, however.

2. Mortgage level should correlate very highly with income level of the applicant(s), so this result suggests that declines in rejection ratios were broadly spread across income classes.

3. Debate becomes quite complex (Goering, 1996). A study of FHA mortgages found that African American borrowers are slightly more likely to default, but argues that discrimination in lending should have led to *lower* default rates, due to a stricter approval threshold for minority applicants (Berkovec et al., 1996), a finding that was quickly challenged (Yinger, 1996; Galster 1996).

4. Concerns include the ability of the auditors (testers) to truly represent themselves identically, the statistical approaches used in some studies, and the limited housing or geographic universes in which they have been applied (White, 1993).

5. An interesting perspective on this is found in the 1984 Congressional testimony of Clarence Thomas, then head of the Equal Employment Opportunity Commission. Remarking on the adequacy of redress under existing law, Thomas stated, "...the remedies under Title VII are feeble at best. Discrimination should merit a lot more than just being paid what you would have been paid had you gotten the job" [U.S. Congress, 1984]. Thomas stated elsewhere a preference for pursuing issues of discrimination at the level of the individual.

6. HUD closed 123% of complaints during 1978 yet only 87% during 1979. (Some complaints closed during one year were carried over from the previous year; hence "rates" may exceed 100%.) The variance between 1978 and 1979 could be a result of the Fair Housing and Equal Opportunity office dealing with less complex cases in 1978 in an effort to reduce the number of open complaints, leaving the more complex, harder to close cases for 1979.

7. Shull argues, further, that Congress gave Carter much less than he wanted for civil rights (Shull 1989:127). Housing appropriations decreased the most of all civil rights subissues, and housing was the area of least agreement between presidential requests and congressional appropriations (Shull 1989:126).

References

Alba, R. and J. Logan. 1991. "Variations on Two Themes: Racial and Ethnic Patterns in the Attainment of Suburban Residence." *Demography,* 28(August):431–453.

Berkovec, J., G.B. Canner, S.A. Gabriel, and T.H. Hannan. 1996. "Mortgage Discrimination and FHA Loan Performance." *Cityscape,* 2:9–24.

Canner, G.B., S.A. Gabriel, and J.M. Woolley. 1991. "Race, Default Risk, and Mortgage Lending: A Study of the FHA and Conventional Loan Markets." *Southern Economic Journal,* 58:249–262.

Congressional Quarterly Almanac. 1980. 96th Congress, 2nd Session. Vol. XXXVI. Washington, D.C.:CQ, Inc.

Eichenwald, Kurt. 1993. "Prudential Agrees to Pay Investors for Fraud Losses." *New York Times* p. A1, D2, Friday, October 22, 1993.

Farley, Reynolds. 1977. "Residential Segregation in Urbanized Areas of the United States in 1970: An Analysis of Social Class and Racial Differences." *Demography* 14(November):497-518.

Farley, R. and W. Frey. 1994. "Changes in the Segregation of Whites From Blacks During the 1980s: Small Steps toward a More Integrated Society." *American Sociological Review,* 59(February):23–45.

Fix, M. et al. 1993. *Clear and Convincing Evidence* Washington, DC: The Urban Institute.

Galster, G. 1996. "Comparing Loan Performance Between Races as a Test for Discrimination." *Cityscape,* 2:33–40.

Goering, J. 1996. "Guest Editor's Introduction." *Cityscape* [Special issue on Race and Default in Credit Markets] 2:1–8.

Goering, J. and G. Squires. 1999. "Guest Editors' Introduction". *Cityscape* [Special Issue Commemorating the 30th Anniversary of the Fair Housing Act]. 4:1-17.

Harrison, R. and D. Weinberg. 1992. "Segregation in U.S. Metropolitan Areas, 1990." Paper presented to the Population Association of America, April 1992.

Hershberg, T., ed. 1981. *Philadelphia* New York: Oxford.

Ihlanfeldt, K. 1992. *Job Accessibility and the Employment and School Enrollment of Teenagers.* Kalamazoo, MI: W.E. Upjohn Institute for Employment Research.

Kantrowitz, Barbara. 1988. "A Tenuous Bond from 9 to 5." *Newsweek.* Pp. 24-25, March 7, 1988.

Leigh, Wilhemina. 1991. "Civil Rights Legislation and the Housing Status of Black Americans: An Overview." *The Review of Black Political Economy* Winter/Spring 1991:5–25.

Lieberson, S. 1980. *A Piece of the Pie.* Berkeley: University of California.

Logan, J. and R. Alba. 1993. "Locational Returns to Human Capital: Minority Access to Suburban Community Resources." *Demography,* 30(May):243-268.

Martinez, Gebe. 1993. "HUD to Crack Down on Bias in Housing." *Los Angeles Times* 2/9/93:A5.

Massey, D. and N. Denton. 1993. *American Apartheid: Segregation and the Making of the Underclass.* Cambridge, MA: Harvard University Press.

Massey, D. and B. Mullan. 1984. "Processes of Hispanic and Black Spatial Assimilation". *American Journal of Sociology,* 89: 836–873.

Metcalf, G. 1988. *Fair Housing Comes of Age.* New York: Greenwood.

Munnell, A., G. Tootell, L. Browne and J. McEneaney. 1996. "Mortgage Lending in Boston: Interpreting HMDA Data." *American Economic Review.* 86(March):23-53.

National Opinion Research Center. 1994. Tabulations from the General Social Survey. (Personal Communication).

Roberts, Steven, et al. 1993. "Civil Rights after Guinier." *U.S. News and World Report* 6/14/93:45–47.

Schuman, Howard, Charlotte Steeh, Lawrence Bobo and Maria Krysan. 1997. *Racial Attitudes in America*. Cambridge, MA: Harvard University Press.

Schill, M. and S. Friedman. 1999. "The Fair Housing Amendments Act of 1988: The First Decade." *Cityscape* 4:57-78.

Shull, Steven. 1989. *The President and Civil Rights Policy.* New York: Greenwood.

Silver H., M. White, and J. Iceland. 1993. "Job Suburbanization and Black Disadvantage: A Dynamic County-Level Test of the Mismatch Hypothesis." Paper presented to the American Sociological Association, August 1993.

Squires, Gregory D. and Sunwoong Kim. 1995. "Does anybody who works here look like me: mortgage lending, race, and lender employment." *Social Science Quarterly* 76(December):823-838.

Thomas, Paulette. 1992. "Blacks Can Face a Host of Trying Conditions in Getting Mortgages." *Wall Street Journal* Pp. A1, A8-A9. November 30, 1992.

Turner, M.A. and R. Wienk. 1993. "The Persistence of Segregation in Urban Areas-Contributing Causes." Pp. 193-216 in *Housing Markets and Residential Mobility*, Kingsley and Turner, editors. Washington, D.C.: The Urban Institute Press.

United States Congress. 1984. *Testimony* of Clarence Thomas, Chairman, Equal Employment Opportunity Commission. Hearing before the Subcommittee on Employment Opportunities, 14 December 1984. H341-41.1, p. 16.

Waldrop, Alex. 1985–86. "Enforcement of the Fair Housing Act: What Role Should the Federal Government Play?" *Kentucky Law Journal,* 74:201–230.

White, M. 1987. *American Neighborhoods and Residential Differentiation.* New York: Russell Sage.

White, M., R. Dymowski and S. Wang 1994. "Ethnic Neighbors and Ethnic Myths: An Analysis of Segregation in 1910." Pp. 175-208 in S. Watkins, ed., *After Ellis Island*, New York: Russell Sage.

White, M. 1993. "Uncovering Discrimination: How Does Testing Compare with Other Tools?" Paper presented to the American Association for the Advancement of Science, Boston.

White, M., A. Biddlecom, and S. Guo, 1993. "Immigration, Naturalization, and Residential Assimilation among Asian Americans in 1980." *Social Forces,* 72(September):93–117.

White, M. J. and S. Sassler. 1996. "Residential Assimilation in 1980: Examining the Effects of Ethnicity Immigration and Naturalization." Paper presented to the Population Association of America, May 1996.

Wienk, Ronald E., Clifford E. Reid, John C. Simonson and Frederick J. Eggers. 1979. *Measuring Racial Discrimination in American Housing Markets: The*

Housing Market Practices Survey. Washington, D.C.: USDHUD, Office of Policy Development and Research.

Wilson, William J. 1987. *The Truly Disadvantaged*. Chicago: University of Chicago Press.

Yinger, J. 1995. *Closed Doors, Opportunities Lost*. New York: Russell Sage Foundation.

Yinger, J. 1996. "Why Default Rates Cannot Shed Light on Mortgage Discrimination," *Cityscape*, 2:25–32.

Federal Laws, Cases, and Regulations:

Havens Realty Corp, et al. v. Coleman et al., 455 U.S. 363 (1982)
Richmond v. J. A. Croson 488 U.S. 469 (1989)
Wards Cove Packing Co. v. Antonio 490 U.S. 642 (1989)
PL90-284 "Fair Housing Act of 1968"
PL100-430 "Fair Housing Amendments Act of 1988"

Chapter 7

Education and Employment in a Diverse Society: Generating Inequality through the School-to-Work Transition

V. Joseph Hotz and Marta Tienda

Introduction

The transition from school to work represents a defining feature of the early life course. An assumption pervading the literature on youth employment is that early labor market activity is desirable, both because it signals youth's awareness of adult activities and because these experiences may provide youth with valuable information about the likely consequences of premature school withdrawal (Shore, 1972; Meyer and Wise, 1982; Coleman, 1984; Hogan and Astone, 1986; Mortimer and Finch, 1992). However, this view has been contested by some analysts who find few lasting effects of early work experiences on future labor market outcomes (Ellwood, 1982; Becker and Hills, 1980; 1983) and by psychologists who find negligible developmental benefits associated with employment during the teen years (Greenberger and Steinberg, 1981; 1986; Steinberg et al., 1993).

The current controversy over the value of early work experience for young adult outcomes partly reflects the different methods researchers used to investigate these issues. Past studies differ in: (1) the criteria used to define a youth's first employment experience; (2) differential treatment of work experience acquired when youth were and were not enrolled in school; (3) the degree to which the analysis was differentiated among demographic groups; and (4) whether employment opportunities were expanding or contracting during the study periods. Each of these issues has implications for the conclusions drawn, especially the wisdom of policies that encourage youth to enter the workforce prior to departing school. We demonstrate that both the definition of a youth's initial employment experience and the definition of work episodes that occur during school enrollment are important for understanding the labor market stratification processes for minority youth and the potentially pivotal role of early labor market encounters.

185

With few exceptions, (Mortimer and Finch 1992; Lewin-Epstein, 1981; Levitan and Gallo, 1991; Ahituv et al., 1994; Tienda and Ahituv, 1996) the pervasiveness of work activity among adolescents who are enrolled in school has not been systematically documented. This is because most studies of the school-to-work transition ignore employment experiences that occur during periods of school enrollment, which tend to be irregular and sometimes ill-defined (Lynch, 1989; D'Amico and Maxwell, 1990; Gritz and MaCurdy, 1992)[1]. If adolescent work experience is as pervasive as suggested by several recent studies (i.e., Mortimer and Finch, 1992; Ahituv et al., 1994), then assessments about the benefits (or costs) associated with the work activity of young men and women based only on postschool experiences may yield distorted views of the returns to early employment and its consequences (see Schoenhals et al., 1998). Furthermore, developing a better understanding of how minority and non-minority youth responded to school and work incentives confronted during the 1980s can help elucidate race and ethnic labor market inequities into the Twenty-first century.

In this chapter we attempt to overcome several limitations of prior research on the timing and consequences of adolescent work experiences. We document the transition from school to work for a cohort of young men and women over a 10-year period. We also explore the sensitivity of conclusions about the timing of labor market entry to variation in the criteria used to define first jobs. Finally, guided by previous studies showing marked racial differences in the timing and sequencing of school departure and labor market entry of young men (e.g., Meyer and Wise, 1982; Ellwood, 1982; Coleman, 1984; Mare and Winship, 1984; Marini, 1984), we include Hispanics and women in our assessment of the variation in pathways from school to work (see Ahituv et al., 1994).

Our general objective is to document and compare differentials in the timing of labor force entry and school departure among youth, and to assess how teen labor market experiences influence the rate of entry to full-time employment. Our specific objectives include: (1) comparing the timing of school departures and initial contact with the labor market using alternative definitions of "first job" among Black, White, and Hispanic men and women; (2) documenting an individual's propensity to combine school and work by age, race, and Hispanic origin; and (3) assessing how early work experience influences the rate of transition to full-time employment.

The background section provides an abridged summary of the theoretical and substantive content of a growing scientific literature on youth employment. Following a description of the Data, Variables, and Methods, we present our descriptive results. We then report our Statistical Analyses, and summarize key results and outline issues warranting further research.

Background

Economic and sociological perspectives of the school-to-work transition, while differing in their emphases, have much in common. Both acknowledge the value of skill acquisition early in the life cycle; both suggest that perceptions and expectations formed during early work experiences influence decisions about school completion and job selection during young adulthood; and both recognize that labor market conditions affect an individual's ability to acquire early work experiences. More generally, economic and sociological models suggest that two decisions play a crucial role in how early labor market experiences influence subsequent labor market attainment, namely choices about how long to stay in school and when to begin to work full-time. Moreover, both of these theoretical perspectives stress the role that changes in labor market opportunities will have on the transition from school to work.

Regarding the choice-based aspects of school and work decisions, it is widely thought that many entry-level jobs may be "dead-end" jobs (Steinberg et al., 1993; Greenberger and Steinberg, 1986; Shore, 1972). However, experiences with such jobs may actually encourage students to prolong schooling by providing them with first-hand evidence of the poor job opportunities available to persons with limited education (Mortimer and Finch, 1992). Thus, having worked in dead-end jobs may produce a positive long-term labor outcome by prolonging schooling and increasing skill levels among youth before they enter full-time employment at later ages. For example, using the National Longitudinal Survey of 1972, Meyer and Wise (1982) found that having worked during high school increased the probability of working in the future, and was associated with higher wages (see also Manski and Wise, 1983: Chapter 3). However, their result was based only on respondents who had completed high school. This is a highly selective criterion to impose on some minority youth, Hispanics in particular.

Alternatively, experiences of fruitless job search or highly irregular employment at unrewarding jobs may reduce motivation to work and discourage school completion. Such outcomes may be especially likely among disadvantaged youth who cannot appreciate the connections between basic competencies and the tasks performed in entry-level jobs. These types of experiences reinforce profiles of school failure among adolescents and poor labor market outcomes among adults.

It is conceivable that minority youth are more likely than nonminority youth to experience negative feedback from entry into dead-end, low-paying jobs. Minority youth may not be able to envision the stepping-stone function of entry-level jobs, and they may recognize (quite realistically) that the absence of employment opportunities precludes them from attaining economic security and independence. Finally, minority youth may encounter alternatives that are more profitable than working in unskilled jobs (Sullivan, 1989; McLeod, 1995). These avenues for negative feedback are made more probable by the circumstances that characterize the life course experiences of such youth. For example, minority youth are more likely than White youth to reside in poor families. As a result, they may withdraw from school prematurely to undertake full-time employment (Tienda and Ahituv, 1996). Minority youth are also more likely to reside in neighborhoods where crime provides a profitable alternative to regular employment (Sullivan, 1989). But, as Mortimer and her associates have pointed out, noneconomic factors also influence adolescents' decisions about whether and when to work (Mortimer and Finch, 1992). Among the reasons for early work that are not motivated by economic necessity are the desires for some financial independence from parents or curiosity about the world of work (see Schoenhals et al., 1998).

The opportunities for securing employment also influence youth employment experiences. The late 1970s and early 1980s represented a period of slack labor demand in many localities in the United States. (Cyert and Mowery, 1987; Burtless, 1990; Levy and Michel, 1991). In his review of empirical research on youth joblessness, Rees (1986) noted that youth bear a disproportionate share of cyclical unemployment. For example, Lynch (1989) found significant effects of local demand conditions on re-employment probabilities for both men and women following the 1982 recession, but she did not carry the analysis through the recovery period that followed (Burtless, 1990). Presumably, the employment prospects of youth who first entered the labor market between 1979 and 1982 are bleaker than those of youth who entered during the late 1980s.

In fact, some scholars attribute the rising inequality among racial and ethnic groups to the reduction of unskilled and semi-skilled jobs during this period of massive industrial restructuring (Wilson, 1987; 1996; Kasarda, 1985; 1995). Slack labor markets imply that young adults who first entered the labor market during the early 1980s were more likely than cohorts who arrived in the labor market during expansionary periods to have poor initial employment experiences, but it is unclear whether these effects persist over time, if they exist at all (Ellwood, 1982; D'Amico and Maxwell, 1990; Hotz et al., 1995).

The idea that work experience acquired during adolescence has value that extends into adulthood is reasonable on its face. However, if employment during adolescence prematurely curtails the acquisition of basic skills, the net benefits of adolescent employment for young adults may be small or negative over the long run (Tienda and Ahituv, 1996; Hotz et al.,

1995). This reasoning implies that the potential benefits of early labor market entry should be contingent upon the circumstances of employment, especially the relative allocation of time between school and work, as well as the types of jobs held by enrolled youth (Mortimer and Finch, 1992; Schoenhals et al., 1998).

There are several theoretical reasons to expect early work experience to have long-term consequences on employment during young adulthood. From a sociological perspective, such links are suggested by socialization theory, which postulates that early work matters because it imparts to youth a realistic grasp of adult alternatives and shapes economic and social aspirations. "Socialization through work" implies that success in a job as an adolescent can facilitate the development of self-esteem, foster independence, broaden the base of appropriate role models, and provide feedback to youth who are in the process of forging their adult roles (Shore, 1972; Mortimer and Finch, 1992; Coleman, 1984).

From an economic perspective, the tenets of human capital theory, especially as formulated to account for labor market and income transitions over the life cycle, also emphasize the impact of prior work experience on subsequent labor market success. The theoretical models developed by Ben-Porath (1967), Ghez and Becker (1972), and Mincer (1962) all stress the value of work experience and on-the-job training in generating marketable skills that, in turn, increase workers' productivity in later years. However, human capital theories have been less successful at predicting what types of skills gained from early work have payoffs in later life.

Prior research has examined various aspects of the school-to-work transition, including: the timing of departures from school; the timing of entry to employment; the sequencing of school and military service with respect to full-time employment; and the significance of early labor-related events, including prolonged unemployment for adult work statuses and wages (Becker and Hills, 1980; 1983; Ellwood, 1982; Lynch, 1989; D'Amico and Maxwell, 1990). For example, the patterns of time allocation among schooling and work activities during adolescence is quite varied (Ahituv et al., 1994; Schoenhals et al., 1998). Some youth work throughout their high school years, while some do not hold a job until they complete their schooling. For others, the military serves as a gateway to the civilian labor market (Mare and Winship, 1984; Mare et al., 1984; Kilburn, 1994). Still others withdraw from school and are unable (or unwilling) to hold a job, opting instead, to participate in antisocial activities (McLeod, 1995; Sullivan, 1989)[2]. In general, minorities are more highly represented among the idle, while White youth seem to "jump-start" their labor market careers by acquiring valuable work experience as they increase their formal schooling (Ahituv et al., 1994).

With few exceptions, inferences about the school-to-work transition of minority and nonminority youth are based on Black–White racial comparisons. Although several recent studies about early work experiences have included Hispanics, generalized inferences about how and why Hispanics differ from other demographic groups have not been forthcoming (Lewin-Epstein, 1981; D'Amico and Maxwell, 1990; Gritz and MaCurdy, 1992)[3]. It is important to understand the nature of the adolescent work experiences of Hispanics for several reasons. First, relative to Blacks and Whites, Hispanic youth have been understudied, yet they represent one of the fastest growing segments of the U.S. population, and currently constitute a majority of the school-age population in many southwestern school districts. Second, Hispanics are racially diverse; hence, a consideration of the labor market experiences of White and non-White Hispanics could potentially generate new insights about how pigmentation produces and maintains labor market inequities among minority populations. Third, the labor market experiences of Hispanic adults challenge conventional explanations of labor market success. Hispanics achieve lower levels of schooling than Blacks, but in general they fare better than Blacks on such outcomes as participation rates, unemployment rates, and employment rates (Bean and Tienda, 1987; Tienda and Stier, 1991; 1996). These findings suggest that race may be directly related to employment outcomes, independent of educational achievement and skills.

That relatively few studies have focused on the *timing* of initial employment experiences partly reflects conceptual ambiguities in defining initial work experiences (Coleman, 1984; Mortimer and Finch, 1992; Schoenhals et al., 1998). Part-time employment, which often constitutes the exploratory phase of the youth employment experience, usually precedes the first episode of full-time employment (Shore, 1972; Rees, 1986; Meyer and Wise, 1982). Restricting the definition of first employment to that which occurs *after* school completion ignores the possibility that episodes of employment that are coterminous with school enrollment may reveal a commitment to work that carries into adult experiences (Lynch, 1989; Gritz and MaCurdy, 1992; Manski and Wise, 1983).

Accordingly, we document the incidence of youth employment during periods of school enrollment and examine the character of the school-to-work transition for Black, White and Hispanic men and women. Our general goal is to provide a comparative statistical portrait of the transition from school to work for White, Black, and Hispanic youth. Using an event-history approach, we focus on patterns of transitions, their rates of occurrence, and cumulative exposure to both the labor market and education during late adolescence and early adulthood. Our multivariate analysis documents the process of school departure and labor market entry as well as the linkages between early work experiences and full-time employment.

Data, Variables, and Methods

We use the National Longitudinal Survey of Youth (NLSY), a national probability sample of 11,406 individuals aged 14 to 21 as of January 1, 1979[4]. Several features of the NLSY make it especially well suited for our research objectives. First, Blacks and Hispanics were oversampled, permitting race and ethnic comparisons of various aspects of the transition to adulthood. Second, annual interviews solicited detailed information about respondents' schooling, training, and military experiences as well as detailed labor force histories. The latter is available on a weekly basis and includes comprehensive information about jobs held from the time respondents first appeared in the sample. Finally, the NLSY exhibits a low attrition rate, just over 10% over the 12-year period we analyze.

There are, however, many ways that the design of the NLSY limits the types of analyses we can perform. For example, many respondents aged 18 to 21 at the first interview (1979) had already completed or withdrawn from school and/or had multiple jobs. Although the NLSY obtained retrospective information about school and work behavior for the period prior to the first interview, gaps in this information diminish its usefulness, given our interest in identifying the first labor market encounter, the coincidence of employment and school enrollment, and the linkages between first work encounters and subsequent full-time employment. After conducting numerous sensitivity tests, we determined that incomplete information for the oldest respondents could distort our understanding of the school-to-work transition. To minimize the difficulties introduced by incomplete retrospective information, we restricted our analyses to individuals who were aged 13 to 16 as of 1978. For this age group, we observe the entire process of school departure and labor market entry. Our final sample of 2,889 young men includes 1,581 whites, 797 Blacks, and 511 Hispanics, and our sample of 2,478 young women includes 1,204 Whites, 763 Blacks, and 511 Hispanics.

Variable Definitions

Among the various definitions of first employment, the following are most common: first paid job; first full-time job; and first job after school completion. Each has its advantages and limitations but, in our judgment, the first job for pay demarcates the point of entry to the labor market. Because the definition of the first job is itself so varied in the existing literature, we use three definitions of first job along with two definitions of first school departure. (In the interest of parsimony, we use the most liberal and restrictive def-

initions of first job in our multivariate analyses.) Specific operational definitions of school departure and first job are as follows:

1. **School Departure.** We examine first departure from school for at least
6 consecutive months (liberal definition), or at least 12 consecutive months
(restrictive definition).

2. **First Job.** We use three definitions of first job which are based on two
criteria—weekly hours worked per job and the duration of the job. For each
job definition we know the industry sector, occupation, actual hours, and
wage rate. We can also determine respondents' education at the beginning of
each job held.

(a) The *liberal* definition of first job includes any job of any duration or
weekly hours. It comes closest to representing the first entry-level job.

(b) The *intermediate* definition of first job describes employment that
lasts for 6 months and at least 15 hours per week. It comes closest to the concept of steady work.

(c) The *restrictive* definition of first job represents a job that lasts for at
least a year on a full-time basis (i.e., 35 or more hours weekly), and represents the first full-time job.

Our race and ethnic categories are constructed with responses to several
subjective and objective items available in the NLSY. The race variable is based
on a subjective assessment of respondents' race by the interviewer (at the time of
the first interview). Interviewers were instructed to indicate whether respondents
were Black, White, or some other race. Based on 29 possible choices, ethnicity
reflects respondents' answer to the question, "What is your origin or descent?"[5]
To identify Hispanics, we used the ethnicity codes from the screener interview rather than respondents' self-report of Hispanic origin at the time of the
first interview. This decision was motivated by two factors. First, not only was
the screener item the basis for generating the oversample of Hispanics, but more
detailed questions about parents' origin were also solicited at this time, thereby
providing additional information with which to verify the responses.[6] Hispanics
can be of any race, but no studies of youth employment have empirically sorted
the race of Hispanics. Because information concerning race was obtained independently of that on ethnicity, we are able to distinguish between White and
non-White Hispanics. Our analyses exploit this feature of the NLSY in an
attempt to ascertain whether and how race matters for Hispanics.
Other independent variables used in our multivariate analyses include
respondent's age in 1978 (or age cohort) and measures of family background
such as fathers' and mothers' education, family income as of 1979, and
whether respondent lived with both parents at the first interview. A unique

feature of NLSY is that through the use of the Armed Services Vocational Aptitude Battery (ASVAB), it includes information about the differences in various mental aptitudes among survey respondents. This test, administered to individuals who apply to any branch of the Armed Forces, was also administered to all NLSY respondents in 1981. An individual's score on the Armed Forces Qualification Test, or AFQT, is the sum of the scores on four of the 10 subtests in the ASVAB: the Word Knowledge, Paragraph Comprehension, Arithmetic Reasoning, and Mathematics Knowledge subtests. The military interprets the AFQT score as a measure of general trainability and uses the scores to screen out individuals who are likely to have a low probability of successfully completing military training. Social scientists have used the AFQT as a general ability indicator, arguing that it performs like a scholastic aptitude test (See Cameron and Heckman, 1991; O'Neill, 1990).

In addition to these covariates whose values are fixed over time, we include in our analysis of wages and hours respondents' education and experience at the beginning of a job spell. To establish a link between early work experience and subsequent labor market status (timing, wages, and hours of first full-time job), we constructed a variable indicating whether respondents worked *before* their first school departure.

Methods

Our descriptive analysis of the process of school departure and labor market entry uses event history or life table methods to calculate the probability of exiting from school or entering the labor market (i.e., exiting joblessness). These techniques are well suited to handle problems of right censoring and attrition that characterize longitudinal data. Exit probabilities were derived from survival analyses computed separately for Black, White and Hispanic youth using alternative definitions of first job and school withdrawal. Subsequently, we computed proportional hazard models using time to the first event (i.e., first school departure and first labor market entry).

Descriptive Results

School Departure

Tables 7.1A and 7.1B summarize the patterns of school departure for young men and women by ethnicity. The entries for the liberal and restrictive definitions reflect the cumulative proportions of youth who exited school and remained out for 6 and 12 months, respectively. Several generalizations are warranted from these results. First, there are significant ethnic differences in patterns of school departure for both men and women, although for women, racial differences are trivial under the restrictive definition[7]. Hispanic youth leave school at a faster rate than either Blacks or Whites prior to age 18, especially between ages 16 and 17. Second, men exit school at a faster pace than women, although sex differences in school departure depend on ethnicity. Third, the median age of first school departure for the sample cohort is relatively invariant across sex and race/ethnic groups—hovering around 18.5 years for both definitions. However, differences in the mean age at first exit among demographic groups reflect race and ethnic differences in age-specific rates of high school noncompletion and patterns of post-secondary enrollment found in previous research (see Cameron and Heckman, 1991).

Table 7.1A

Cumulative Percent Leaving School Using Two Definitions of First Departure: Young Men Aged 13 to 16 in 1978 by Ethnicity (Life Table Estimates)

	Liberal Definition[a]			Restrictive Definition[b]		
Age	Whites	Blacks	Hispanics	Whites	Blacks	Hispanics
≤13	—	0.3	0.7	0.1	0.3	0.7
14	1.3	1.4	2.6	1.0	1.2	2.0
15	4.8	3.9	6.6	3.9	3.1	5.3
16	12.2	9.2	15.9	10.3	7.5	13.4
17	26.0	23.3	33.0	23.1	20.0	28.6
18	49.7	50.5	57.1	44.9	45.0	50.3
19	71.0	75.7	77.3	64.6	69.2	70.1
20	80.1	87.6	86.8	73.4	81.7	81.5
21	85.0	92.6	91.6	78.7	87.9	88.0
22	90.9	96.0	94.5	84.9	91.6	91.7
23	96.2	98.6	96.8	90.4	94.9	94.5
24	98.6	99.9	98.6	93.1	97.0	96.7
25+	100.0	100.0	100.0	—	98.3	—
Age at First Departure						
Mean	20.3	19.0	19.0	22.5	20.1	19.9
Median	18.6	18.4	18.3	18.7	18.6	18.4
[N][c]	[1265]	[797]	[511]	[1265]	[797]	[511]

Source: NLSY civilian sample

[a]Liberal Definition: Left school for 6 months or more.

[b]Restrictive Definition: Left school for 12 months or more.

[c][N] is unweighted population in the risk set.

Table 7.1B

**Cumulative Percent Leaving School Using Two Definitions
of First Departure: Young Women Aged 13 to 16 in 1978 by Ethnicity
(Life Table Estimates)**

Age	Liberal Definition[a]			Restrictive Definition[b]		
	Whites	Blacks	Hispanics	Whites	Blacks	Hispanics
≤13	—	—	—	—	—	—
14	0.3	0.4	0.8	0.3	0.2	0.6
15	1.2	1.9	3.5	1.1	0.9	3.3
16	5.3	6.1	12.0	4.6	4.0	10.5
17	19.4	19.4	28.6	17.1	14.8	24.0
18	46.0	46.9	52.9	41.3	38.6	45.6
19	67.6	71.5	73.9	60.4	61.9	66.5
20	76.1	82.4	83.3	68.3	74.5	77.3
21	82.3	88.0	87.6	74.5	82.0	82.7
22	90.0	92.7	90.7	81.9	87.6	86.2
23	95.0	95.9	92.9	87.7	91.5	88.5
24	96.2	97.0	94.1	90.4	93.7	89.8
25+	—	—	94.6	—	—	—
Age at First Departure						
Mean	20.3	20.0	20.3	22.4	21.3	21.9
Median	18.5	18.6	18.3	18.7	18.8	18.7
[N][c]	[1204]	[763]	[511]	[1204]	[763]	[511]

Source: NLSY civilian sample.

[a]Liberal Definition: Left school for 6 months or more.

[b]Restrictive Definition: Left school for 12 months or more.

[c][N] is unweighted population in the risk set.

Ethnic differences in school departure rates are negligible for youth less than 16 years old, but they widen after the legal age for school withdrawal. White men and women, for example, prolong schooling longer than their minority counterparts. Hispanics exhibit the highest incidence of school withdrawal at younger ages. Over twice as many Hispanic women left school before the legal age to quit, as compared to Black or White women. Premature school departure, however, was more prevalent among men than among women. Based on our restrictive definition of the age at first school leaving, approximately 10% of White men had left school (and remained out for at least a year) by age 16, compared to roughly 7% of Black and 13% of Hispanic men. For women, the comparable shares were 5%, 4%, and 10% for Whites, Blacks, and Hispanics, respectively.

Tables 7.1A and 7.1B also display interesting sex and ethnic differences in the rate at which youth prolong their schooling. Nearly 10% of White and Hispanic women remained in school beyond 24 years of age compared to 6%

of Black women. Whereas approximately three-fourths of minority women had left school and remained out for at least one year by their 20th birthday, only 68% of White women had done so. In contrast, a smaller proportion of young men remain in school into their twenties and, unlike the case of women, there is no difference between Blacks and Hispanics in the rate at which they remain in school at age 20 or 24.

These differences in patterns of school withdrawal by ethnicity are likely to have implications for the long-term employability of young men and women. Although premature school departure does not preclude further schooling later in life, there is strong evidence that Hispanic youth are less likely to return to school or to receive a general equivalency degree (Cameron and Heckman, 1991). On this basis, one might expect that Hispanic youth would encounter the greatest difficulties securing work. But, as the following results show, this is not the case. Furthermore, the experience of nonminority youth illustrates that prolonged schooling does not guarantee success in the labor market.

Labor Force Entry

Life table estimates of the *timing* of first jobs (reported in Tables 7.2A and 7.2B for men and women, respectively) also reveal considerable diversity along race and ethnic lines. While premature school departure renders Hispanics the most educationally disadvantaged group (Bean and Tienda, 1987: chapter 8), Black youth encounter the greatest difficulties entering the labor market. This generalization obtains for all definitions of first job[8]. More specifically, nearly half of Hispanic and White men had held an entry-level job by their 16th birthday, compared to 40 percent of Black men. By comparison, 40 percent of White women, 35 percent of Hispanic women, and barely over one-quarter of Black women had held a job before reaching their 16th birthday.

White and Hispanic men secure longer lasting jobs than Black youth, as indexed by our intermediate definition. For Black men, the median age at obtaining the first steady job is about 1 to 1.5 years later than for Whites and Hispanics—19 versus 18, respectively. Stated as a cumulative probability, by age 18, nearly three-fifths of White and half of Hispanic men had held a 15-hour per week job that lasted at least 6 months, compared to only 40% of Black youth. Sex differences in proportions who work appear to widen with age, particularly as the definition of first employment becomes more stringent. For women, the ethnic differences in the timing of first steady job were even more pronounced: 53% of White women, 41% of Hispanic women and 27% of Black women had worked at least part time for 6 months or more by their 18th birthday.

Table 7.2A
Cumulative Percent with Work Experience Using Three Definitions of First Job:
Young Men Aged 13 to 16 in 1978 by Ethnicity
(Life Table Estimates)

Age	Liberal[a]			Intermediate[b]			Restrictive[c]		
	Whites	Blacks	Hispanics	Whites	Blacks	Hispanics	Whites	Blacks	Hispanics
≤13	2.3	1.4	1.1	0.7	0.8	0.6	0.2	—	0.4
14	7.6	5.5	5.1	2.1	1.7	1.4	0.6	0.2	0.7
15	21.5	16.9	18.7	7.2	4.8	5.4	1.2	0.7	1.4
16	49.6	39.7	46.3	22.9	13.0	17.0	3.4	1.3	3.4
17	75.4	63.5	72.6	42.3	25.8	34.8	6.6	2.4	6.9
18	89.3	79.6	86.6	57.3	39.7	51.6	12.0	5.7	12.3
19	95.6	88.4	93.3	68.6	52.5	63.4	19.8	11.4	20.5
20	97.7	92.7	95.8	77.1	62.8	71.6	28.9	18.3	30.4
21	98.6	95.5	96.5	78.8	72.3	78.8	39.0	27.9	41.8
22	99.2	97.4	97.2	85.2	80.0	85.2	49.8	39.4	53.3
23	99.4	98.6	97.9	90.6	87.1	90.6	61.2	53.4	64.2
24	99.6	99.3	98.3	94.3	92.8	94.3	72.4	64.5	73.3
25+	99.7	99.6	—	96.2	95.4	96.2	79.4	70.9	79.7
Median	16.5	16.9	16.6	17.9	19.4	18.3	22.5	23.3	22.2
[N][d]	[1265]	[797]	[511]	[1581]	[797]	[511]	[1265]	[797]	[511]

Source: NLSY civilian sample.

[a] Liberal Definition: any duration and any hours.
[b] Intermediate Definition: 6 months duration and 15 hours or more per week.
[c] Restrictive Definition: 12 months duration and 35 hours or more per week.
[d] [N] is unweighted population in the risk set.

Table 7.2B

Cumulative Percent with Work Experience Using Three Definitions of First Job:
Young Women Aged 13 to 16 in 1978 by Ethnicity
(Life Table Estimates)

Age	Liberal[a]			Intermediate[b]			Restrictive[c]		
	Whites	Blacks	Hispanics	Whites	Blacks	Hispanics	Whites	Blacks	Hispanics
≤13	1.2	0.3	1.0	.01	—	0.4	—	—	0.2
14	5.8	2.2	3.7	1.0	0.5	1.1	0.2	0.1	—
15	16.0	10.4	13.0	4.1	2.2	3.5	0.6	—	0.4
16	40.3	27.4	34.9	16.7	6.8	12.2	1.1	0.5	1.2
17	68.2	48.7	59.2	35.8	15.9	25.3	3.5	1.6	3.9
18	85.0	67.0	77.0	53.3	26.9	40.6	10.0	3.9	8.8
19	93.0	79.8	88.2	66.2	39.4	54.8	18.4	8.2	15.5
20	96.0	87.2	93.7	74.9	52.2	64.5	26.1	14.0	24.0
21	97.2	91.4	96.2	81.4	62.1	72.7	34.3	20.3	33.0
22	97.9	94.2	97.4	87.3	70.7	79.8	45.0	29.5	42.2
23	98.3	95.5	97.9	92.1	79.3	84.9	57.2	41.3	50.8
24	98.6	96.6	98.4	94.4	86.2	88.7	66.1	51.9	57.4
25+	98.8	97.7	98.7	95.4	90.3	91.2	71.4	59.6	62.6
Median	16.8	17.5	17.0	18.2	20.3	19.1	22.9	24.3	23.2
[N][d]	[1204]	[763]	[511]	[1204]	[763]	[511]	[1204]	[763]	[511]

Source: NLSY civilian sample

[a] Liberal Definition: any duration and any hours.

[b] Intermediate Definition: 6 months duration and 15 hours or more per week.

[c] Restrictive Definition: 12 months duration and 35 hours or more per week.

[d] [N] is unweighted population in the risk set.

Figure 7.1a
Timing of Labor Market Entry:
Cumulative Proportions of Young Men Entering First Jobs
Based on Liberal and Restrictive Definitions of Employment

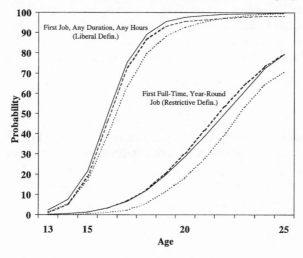

White _____

Black ....

Hispanic _ _ _ _

The fact that the labor market difficulties experienced by Black youth carry into their early adult lives is apparent from the timing of first full-time jobs. By age 20, roughly 30% of White and Hispanic men had obtained a full-time job that lasted a year or more, compared to less than 20% of Black men. Part of this difference reflects the higher military enlistment rates of Black men relative to Whites and Hispanics (Kilburn, 1994; Ahituv et al., 1994). Although lower shares of women than men had worked full time by their 20th birthday, ethnic differences in the age pattern of full-time employment for women paralleled that observed for men. The Black median age for full-time employment was about one year higher than the median age for White and Hispanic men and women. By age 25, 10% fewer Black men had held a full-time, year-round job compared to their White and Hispanic age counterparts. Approximately three-fifths of Black and Hispanic women had worked full-time before their 25th birthday, compared to over 70% of White women.

These racial differences in the rate of entry into first jobs are apparent in Figure 7.1 (7.1a and 7.1b for men and women, respectively) which displays the proportions of men and women making their first transitions into entry-level and full-time jobs. Two noteworthy features of these plots are: (1) the distinct differences in the steepness of the curves for entry versus full-time jobs; and (2) the consistently lower placement of the Black curves relative to the White and Hispanic curves. With respect to shape, the entry-level job curves rise sharply until about age 18, and flatten out thereafter. The survival function for full-time employment rises less steeply and fails to reach the height of the entry-level function by age 25, the last age respondents were observed in this sample.

Figure 7.1b
Timing of Labor Market Entry:
Cumulative Proportions of Young Women Entering First Jobs
Based on Liberal and Restrictive Definitions of Employment

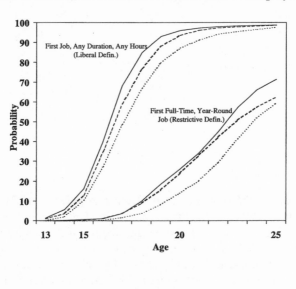

The *slower* rates at which Blacks enter the labor market are clearly discernible in both sets of curves. Hispanic–White disparities in the rate of labor market entry, while less pronounced than the Black–White disparities, are statistically significant in all but one instance, namely the Hispanic–White difference in the timing of full-time employment for men. In part, the delayed entry to the workforce experienced by Black youth, especially when compared to Hispanic youth, reflects their slower rates of school departure before age 18 (see Table 7.1)[9]. This finding is important for evaluating claims that work episodes that coincide with school enrollment produce positive employment effects during early adulthood (Meyer and Wise, 1982).

Combining School and Work

Tables 7.3A and 7.3B provide detail on racial differences in the propensity of youth to work during periods of school enrollment[10]. We first consider the evidence for young men presented in Table 7.3A. In general, Whites were more likely than minority youth to acquire work experience of any type while they are enrolled in school. Furthermore, ethnic and racial disparities in the propensity to combine school and work widen as the definition of jobs becomes more restrictive. For example, half of all White and Hispanic men who left school at age 16 had work experience according to our liberal criterion, compared to only 40% of Black men who left school at this age. A similar pattern obtains using the intermediate definition of first job, except that the White male advantage vis-à-vis minority youth is even greater. Specifically, 35% of White men who left school at age 16 reported having held a steady job prior to leaving school, compared, respectively, to 23% and 14% of Hispanic and Black men who first left school at age 16. About 9% of White youth who withdrew from school when they were 16 claimed they had held a full-time job for at least a year, but only 7% and 4% of Black and Hispanic youth, respectively, made this claim.

By age 19, the point at which half of all men had left school for 6 months or more, the vast majority (over 90%) reported some type of work experience. Approximately three-fifths of White and Hispanic men who left school at age 19 had held a steady job, while 19% and 15%, respectively, had already worked full-time. The work experience profile of Black men who withdraw from school at age 19 leaves them relatively disadvantaged vis-à-vis Whites and Hispanics, as less than half reported having held a steady job prior to leaving school. These results reinforce the profile of disadvantage that characterizes Black youth's transition from school to work. Although Blacks persist in school longer than Hispanic youth, they accumulate less work experience at specific ages.

Young women's tendency to combine school and work also showed greater racial and ethnic disparities, as the criteria used to define first jobs was made more restrictive. For example, among Hispanic women who left school at age 16, nearly half had held a job for pay, compared to 42% of White women and only 20% of Black women. A different pattern obtains using the

Table 7.3A
Percent with Work Experience by Age of First School Exit for at Least 6 Months Using Three Definitions of First Job: Young Men Aged 13 to 16 in 1978 by Ethnicity

Age	Liberal[a]			Intermediate[b]			Restrictive[c]		
	Whites	Blacks	Hispanics	Whites	Blacks	Hispanics	Whites	Blacks	Hispanics
14	21.4	13.3	12.5	0.0	0.0	0.0	0.0	0.0	0.0
15	37.5	22.7	22.7	9.4	0.0	9.1	0.0	0.0	5.9
16	54.3	40.4	49.4	35.2	13.7	22.8	9.0	6.7	4.1
17	78.2	65.6	81.4	50.8	31.9	43.8	13.3	5.3	15.9
18	89.1	76.9	85.2	61.8	38.1	48.1	13.2	4.3	7.3
19	92.9	91.2	94.2	66.5	46.5	58.8	18.7	8.5	15.1
20	97.1	94.6	93.5	74.6	64.2	70.4	21.8	13.9	36.4
21	98.5	96.0	94.7	74.6	73.9	61.1	15.4	20.0	0.0
22	100.0	96.2	100.0	72.8	57.7	100.0	18.4	5.6	11.1
23	100.0	100.0	100.0	88.6	100.0	87.5	27.3	28.6	16.7
24	100.0	50.0	100.0	100.0	0.0	100.0	33.3	0.0	100.0

Source: NLSY civilian sample.

[a] Liberal Definition: any duration and any hours.

[b] Intermediate Definition: 6 months duration and 15 hours or more per week.

[c] Restrictive Definition: 12 months duration and 35 hours or more per week.

[d] Age of first school exit at least 6 months; there were too few exits prior to age 13.

Table 7.3B
Percent with Work Experience by Age of First School Exit for at Least 6 Months Using Three Definitions of First Job: Young Women Aged 13 to 16 in 1978 by Ethnicity

Age	Liberal[a]			Intermediate[b]			Restrictive[c]		
	Whites	Blacks	Hispanics	Whites	Blacks	Hispanics	Whites	Blacks	Hispanics
14	0.0	0.0	0.0	0.0	0.0	0.0	0.0	0.0	0.0
15	6.2	11.8	23.8	0.0	0.0	0.0	0.0	0.0	0.0
16	41.8	20.0	48.4	16.5	4.4	12.9	1.3	0.0	4.8
17	68.9	43.7	63.4	42.6	16.2	27.7	7.7	2.1	3.0
18	84.1	63.8	77.6	55.9	26.4	46.9	7.8	3.8	10.5
19	92.3	74.4	86.1	58.0	29.9	44.4	14.7	2.6	6.9
20	95.4	88.0	96.2	61.5	50.0	46.2	12.3	10.0	11.5
21	100.0	88.6	94.4	73.1	57.1	61.1	11.5	8.6	5.6
22	97.0	100.0	91.7	72.7	64.7	66.7	12.1	14.7	16.7
23	100.0	100.0	100.0	62.5	53.8	87.5	6.2	23.1	25.0
24	100.0	100.0	100.0	80.0	100.0	100.0	40.0	0.0	50.0

Source: NLSY civilian sample.

[a] Liberal Definition: any duration and any hours.
[b] Intermediate Definition: 6 months duration and 15 hours or more per week.
[c] Restrictive Definition: 12 months duration and 35 hours or more per week.
[d] Age of first school exit at least 6 months; there were too few exits prior to age 13.

intermediate definition of first job in that the work experience advantage corresponds to White women: 16% of those who left school at age 16 had held steady jobs while enrolled in school compared to 13% of Hispanic and 4% of Black women. By age 19, the point at which over half of all women had left school for at least 6 months, only three-fourths of Black women compared to 86% of Hispanic and 92% of White women had worked for pay before leaving school. Among those who exited at age 19, over half of the White women and 44% of Hispanic women had held a steady job while enrolled in school. Less than one-third of Black women worked while enrolled in school before leaving school at age 19.

In sum, the results in Tables 7.3A and 7.3B confirm prior reports that substantial shares of youth *do* combine school and work during adolescence and young adulthood (Lewin-Epstein, 1981; Mortimer and Finch, 1992; Ahituv et al., 1994). Manski and Wise (1983) report similar results for college-age youth, but their sample is conditioned on having graduated from high school. Short-term, entry-level jobs are dominant at younger ages, but steady jobs and full-time jobs that last for a year or more are not uncommon among 18- and 19-year-olds, particularly for Hispanic and White youth.

A presumed advantage of early labor market entry is that youth accumulate work experience, which is associated with higher earnings and occupational status at later ages. However, if accumulation of experience occurs at the expense of educational attainment—that is, if employed youth withdraw from school at earlier ages—then the potential gains from early labor market experience may be totally offset during the early adult years, as earnings of more highly skilled workers surpass those of less educated workers (see Tienda and Ahituv, 1996). Therefore, it is worthwhile to entertain the hypothesis that the advantages of early entry to the labor market may be lost by the time youth reach early adulthood, a possibility that is addressed in the following section.

Multivariate Analyses

In this section we report the effects of personal and family background factors on the timing of first school withdrawal and first job entry based on liberal and restrictive definitions of both events. Tables 7.4A and 7.4B provide summary statistics for key background variables for men and women, respectively. The age distribution is quite similar among the three race and ethnic groups, but the youngest cohort is somewhat smaller than the other cohorts. AFQT scores differ appreciably along race and ethnic lines, with Black men scoring the lowest at 48 points, Whites the highest at 71 points, and Hispanic men between these extremes with 54 points. A similar pattern was obtained for women, except that women scored slightly higher than their male ethnic counterparts. By construction, the AFQT index ranges from 0 to 105, and average scores for the national population range from 74 to 48 for Whites and Blacks, respectively (Kilburn, 1994). As a general ability measure, the AFQT varies positively with age, therefore only age-adjusted effects are meaningful. Inclusion of age cohort in the multivariate models also controls for incomplete information in employment and education histories[11].

Table 7.4A
Background Characteristics of Respondents by Ethnicity
and Race: Young Men Aged 13 to 16 in 1978
(Means or Percents)

	Whites	Blacks	Hispanics
Cohort			
13	20.9	18.4	20.0
14	26.1	26.7	28.8
15	28.5	26.6	23.5
16	24.4	28.2	27.8
AFQT	70.9	47.6	54.5
(s.d.)	(20.0)	(18.5)	(20.4)
[N]	[1211]	[772]	[481]
Father's Education	12.4	10.4	8.5
(s.d.)	(3.3)	(3.3)	(4.7)
[N]	[1177]	[584]	[403]
Mother's Education	11.9	10.9	8.1
(s.d.)	(2.4)	(2.5)	(4.3)
[N]	[1208]	[722]	[463]
Live Both Parents at 14	86.8	55.7	71.2
[N]	[1262]	[796]	[510]
Family Income, 1978	22,004	10,974	12,964
(s.d.)	(13,599)	(8,084)	(9,893)
[N]	[1042]	[645]	[424]

Source: NLSY civilian sample.

As the statistics in Tables 7.4A and 7.4B make clear, Black youth resided in families with the lowest family incomes in 1978, but Hispanics reported the lowest parental education levels. Average White family incomes (from all sources) stood at approximately $22,000 in 1978, compared to roughly $11,000 and $13,000 for Blacks and Hispanics, respectively. Hispanic parents attained approximately 8.5 years of graded schooling, while Black parents averaged 10.5 to 11 years of schooling. Parents of White youth averaged 12 years of education[12]. Black youth were most likely, and White youth least likely, to have been reared in a parent-absent family. Just over half of young Black men and women reported living with both parents when they were 14 years old compared to approximately three-fourths of Hispanic youth and 86% of White youth.

Table 7.4B
Background Characteristics of Respondents by Ethnicity
and Race: Young Women Aged 13 to 16 in 1978
(Means or Percents)

		Whites	*Blacks*	*Hispanics*
Cohort				
	13	18.4	18.7	17.8
	14	25.5	26.6	29.2
	15	27.6	27.5	28.6
	16	28.5	27.1	24.5
AFQT		73.1	50.1	55.7
	(s.d.)	(17.0)	(16.7)	(18.4)
	[N]	[1149]	[745]	[488]
Father's Education		12.2	10.2	8.6
	(s.d.)	(3.2)	(3.5)	(4.5)
	[N]	[1114]	[560]	[430]
Mother's Education		11.9	10.7	8.0
	(s.d.)	(2.4)	(2.6)	(3.9)
	[N]	[1156]	[710]	[484]
Live Both Parents at 14		86.5	52.0	76.0
	[N]	[1203]	[759]	[509]
Family Income, 1978		22,523	11,453	13,305
	(s.d.)	(12,839)	(10,131)	(9,282)
	[N]	[959]	[654]	[431]

Source: NLSY civilian sample.

Waiting Times to School Departure

Tables 7.5A and 7.5B report the Cox regression analysis (Cox, 1972) of school departure for men and women. The slower school exit rates of Blacks relative to native Whites are surprising in light of the life table estimates showing racial differences in school exit rates that favored Whites. Although the race

Table 7.5A
Determinants of School Departure Rates Using
Two Definitions of Exit: Young Men Aged 13 to 16 in 1978
(Asymptotic Standard Errors)

	Liberal[a]		Restrictive[b]	
	(1)	(2)	(1)	(2)
Cohort				
14	-.003	-.013	.102	.097
	(.061)	(.062)	(.064)	(.065)
15	.108	.093	.244	.232
	(.061)	(.062)	(.064)	(.064)
16	.036	.014	.214	.197
	(.063)	(.063)	(.065)	(.065)
Ethnicity/Race				
Hispanic-White	-.073	-.217	-.076	-.274
	(.068)	(.073)	(.070)	(.076)
Hispanic-Non-White	-.077	-.078	.003	-.200
	(.095)	(.099)	(.097)	(.100)
Black	-.305	-.401	-.367	-.487
	(.055)	(.059)	(.056)	(.060)
If Foreign Born	-.213	-.254	-.257	-.303
	(.096)	(.097)	(.098)	(.099)
AFQT	-.022	-.019	-.026	-.022
	(.001)	(.001)	(.001)	(.001)
Mother's Ed.[c]		-.013		-.012
		(.009)		(.009)
Father's Ed.[c]		-.021		-.035
		(.007)		(.008)
Family Income[c]		-.007		-.009
		(.002)		(.002)
If Live at Home, 1979		-.159		-.115
		(.094)		(.096)
If Live in Female-Headed Household at 14		.090		.071
		(.060)		(.060)
Log Likelihood	-16152.6	-16089.6	-15403.3	-15332.1
[N]	[2464]	[2459]	[2464]	[2459]

Source: NLSY Civilian Sample.w

[a] Liberal Definition: Left school for 6 months or more.

[b] Restrictive Definition: Left school for 12 months or more.

[c] We have included dummy variables for observations with missing responses on these items.

Table 7.5B
Determinants of School Departure Rates Using
Two Definitions of Exit: Young Women Aged 13 to 16 in 1978
(Asymptotic Standard Errors)

	Liberal[a]		Restrictive[b]	
	(1)	(2)	(1)	(2)
Cohort				
14	.056	.039	.039	.017
	(.064)	(.065)	(.067)	(.068)
15	.028	.026	.068	.057
	(.063)	(.064)	(.066)	(.067)
16	-.214	-.194	-.077	-.064
	(.065)	(.065)	(.067)	(.068)
Ethnicity/Race				
Hispanic-White	-.085	-.264	-.177	-.385
	(.068)	(.073)	(.071)	(.077)
Hispanic-Non-White	-.098	-.003	.045	-.070
	(.102)	(.104)	(.103)	(.106)
Black	-.208	-.305	-.315	-.408
	(.056)	(.059)	(.057)	(.061)
If Foreign Born	-.434	-.473	-.452	-.494
	(.096)	(.097)	(.099)	(.100)
AFQT	-.013	-.011	-.017	-.015
	(.001)	(.001)	(.001)	(.001)
Mother's Ed.[c]		-.019		-.024
		(.009)		(.009)
Father's Ed.[c]		-.020		-.022
		(.008)		(.008)
Family Income[c]		-.008		-.006
		(.002)		(.002)
If Live at Home, 1979		-.420		-.378
		(.092)		(.093)
If Live in Female-Headed Household at 14		.008		.046
		(.059)		(.060)
Log Likelihood	-15522.8	-15427.3	-14814.4	-14720.3
[N]	[2375]	[2368]	[2375]	[2368]

Source: NLSY Civilian Sample.
[a]Liberal Definition: Left school for 6 months or more.
[b] Restrictive Definition: Left school for 12 months or more.
[c]We have included dummy variables for observations with missing responses on these items.

Table 7.6A
Determinants of Transitions to Employment Using
Two Definitions of First Job: Young Men Aged 13 to 16 in 1978
(Asymptotic Standard Errors)

	Liberal[a]		Restrictive[b]		
	(1)	(2)	(1)	(2)	(3)
Cohort					
14	-.029	.032	-.063	-.064	-.068
	(.060)	(.060)	(.072)	(.072)	(.072)
15	-.248	-.247	-.121	-.123	-.107
	(.060)	(.060)	(.072)	(.072)	(.072)
16	-.517	-.515	-.130	-.135	-.113
	(.061)	(.061)	(.073)	(.073)	(.073)
Ethnicity/Race					
Hispanic-White	-.068	-.029	-.054	-.017	.000
	(.067)	(.070)	(.076)	(.081)	(.081)
Hispanic-Non-White	-.162	-.129	-.199	-.235	-.183
	(.096)	(.100)	(.113)	(.118)	(.117)
Black	-.270	-.286	-.317	-.288	-.308
	(.052)	(.055)	(.062)	(.066)	(.066)
If Foreign Born	-.063	-.038	.154	.129	.096
	(.094)	(.094)	(.108)	(.109)	(.109)
AFQT	.004	.002	-.001	-.001	-.002
	(.001)	(.001)	(.001)	(.001)	(.001)
Mother's Ed.[c]		.012		-.008	-.010
		(.009)		(.010)	(.010)
Father's Ed.[c]		.006		-.019	-.021
		(.007)		(.009)	(.009)
Family Income[c]		.001		.005	.004
		(.002)		(.002)	(.002)
If Live at Home, 1979		-.063		.131	.113
		(.094)		(.115)	(.115)
If Live in Female-Headed Household at 14		..056		-.007	.007
		(.057)		(.068)	(.068)
If Work before School Departure	—	—			.275
					(.070)
Log Likelihood	-16553.5	-16510.3	-12818.6	-12778.9	-12757.5
[N]	[2464]	[2459]	[2464]	[2459]	[2027]

Source: NLSY Civilian Sample.

[a] Liberal Definition: any duration and any hours.

[b] Restrictive Definition: 12 months or more duration and 35 or more hours per week.

[c] We have included dummy variables for observations with missing responses on these items.

[d] Endogenous to liberal model; not included.

Table 7.6B
Determinants of Transitions to Employment Using
Two Definitions of First Job: Young Women Aged 13 to 16 in 1978
(Asymptotic Standard Errors)

	Liberal[a]		Restrictive[b]		
	(1)	(2)	(1)	(2)	(3)
Cohort					
14	-.195	-.188	-.017	-.015	-.010
	(.063)	(.064)	(.083)	(.084	(.084)
15	-.249	-.220	-.054	-.059	-.061
	(.063)	(.063)	(.082)	(.083)	(.083)
16	-.485	-.443	-.027	-.051	-.058
	(.063)	(.064)	(.081)	(.081)	(.082)
Ethnicity/Race					
Hispanic-White	-.122	-.066	.051	.047	.023
	(.067)	(.070)	(.083)	(.089)	(.089)
Hispanic-Non-White	-.041	-.100	-.239	-.203	-.231
	(.098)	(.100)	(.135)	(.138)	(.139)
Black	-.274	-.299	-.133	-.117	-.116
	(.056)	(.059)	(.070)	(.074)	(.074)
If Foreign Born	-.021	-.021	.034	.038	.019
	(.092)	(.093)	(.114)	(.115)	(.115)
AFQT	.009	.008	.011	.010	.008
	(.001)	(.001)	(.001)	(.002)	(.002)
Mother's Ed.[c]		.030		-.003	-.001
		(.009)		(.012)	(.012)
Father's Ed.[c]		-.011		-.002	-.004
		(.008)		(.010)	(.010)
Family Income[c]		.003		.003	.003
		(.002)		(.003)	(.003)
If Live at Home, 1979		.332		.261	.246
		(.085)		(.113)	(.113)
If Live in Female-Headed Household at 14		.139		-.074	.087
		(.058)		(.075)	(.075)
If Work before School Departure	—	—			.364
					(.075)
Log Likelihood	-15573.9	-15501.3	10616.3	10580.9	10568.3
[N]	[2375]	[2368]	[2375]	[2368]	[2368]

[a] Liberal Definition: any duration and any hours.
[b] Restrictive Definition: 12 months or more duration and 35 or more hours per week.
[c] We have included dummy variables for observations with missing responses on these items.
[d] Endogenous to liberal model; not included.

and ethnic differences are contrary to those produced by the life table analysis reported in Table 7.1, they have a straightforward explanation. For both men and women, the *gross* effects of race and ethnic origin are positive, indicating that Blacks and Hispanics exit from school at a *faster* rate than their White counterparts. These are the basic results reported in Table 7.1. However, controlling for developed ability differences that are correlated with school retention *reverses* the race and ethnic effects on school departure by our liberal criterion, and completely eliminates them for Hispanic men and women. A parallel story obtains for the restrictive definition of school departure after ability differences are taken into account, except that White Hispanic women exhibit a significantly slower pace of school departure compared to White non-Hispanic women with similar AFQT scores. No comparable school retention effect emerges for Hispanic men whose AFQT scores are identical to those of Whites.

Adjustment for differences in family background among Blacks, Whites, and Hispanics accentuates racial and ethnic variation in school departure patterns. This is particularly apparent when a restrictive criterion (i.e., nonenrollment for at least 12 months) is used to define school exits. These results show that both Hispanic and Black youth leave school at significantly lower rates than those of Whites with similar family backgrounds and developed ability. Also, Black and Hispanic women leave school for at least a year at a rate two-thirds as fast as White women with comparable ability and similar family backgrounds.

Substantively, the results reported in Tables 7.5A and 7.5B indicate that once ability differences and family background are taken into account, white men exit school at rates 49% to 64% faster than Black men, and about 24% faster than Hispanic men. Among women, adjustments for differences in ability and family background imply that White women's school exit rates are 36% to 50% higher than those of Black women (using liberal and restrictive criteria for school departure), and 23% to 47% higher than those of White Hispanic women. These results imply that minority youth are more likely to graduate from high school and pursue post-secondary schooling than Whites with comparable AFQT scores and similar family backgrounds.

Higher AFQT scores prolong schooling by lowering exit rates between 1.5% and 2% for each raw score point. By any standard, this is a sizable effect. Thus, it appears that racial and ethnic disparities in school departure rates are largely mediated by differences in developed job aptitudes, as measured by AFQT scores. The AFQT result is robust, as it persists after introducing controls for family background (model 2) and irrespective of whether a liberal or restrictive criterion is used to define school departures. Of the family background variables, mother's education exerts little influence on the time of men's school departure, but father's education and higher family incomes slow men's exit rates in both the liberal and restrictive specifications. Results for women are generally similar except that mother's education also increases school retention for them.

Interestingly, once socioeconomic background is taken into account, the absence of a parent per se does not accelerate school departures. However, living at home significantly increases school retention rates relative to living on one's own.

Finally, the significant age cohort effects for men in the restrictive specification indicate that incomplete information for the oldest respondents may distort the estimated effects, but given the consistency of results across the two specifications of the dependent variable, these distortions are not likely to be large[13].

Age at First Job

Tables 7.6A and 7.6B summarize the key results of the analysis of labor force entry. Our dependent variable is age at the occurrence of the first job for pay (based on our liberal criterion of any duration and any weekly hours), or the first full-time job that lasted at least one year. Negative coefficients indicate a slower rate of entry to employment.

The life table analyses summarized in Tables 7.2A and 7.2B indicated that Black men experience significantly slower transition rates to employment compared to Whites, irrespective of the criteria used to define first job. This conclusion is not altered by controlling for differences in AFQT scores. Substantively, this implies that Black men with AFQT scores comparable to those of Whites make a significantly *slower* transition to employment, irrespective of the criteria used to specify first employment. Stated differently, among Black and White men who are statistically equivalent in terms of their AFQT scores and family background, Black men's odds of securing employment are only 0.75 the odds of White men. However, there are essentially no differences between Hispanic and White men in the rate of entry to either beginning or full-time jobs once differences in AFQT scores and family background characteristics are standardized statistically.

Among women, adjusting for differences in AFQT scores similarly did not eliminate racial differences in the rate of attaining their first job. For example, Black women, like their male counterparts, experienced slower transitions into first jobs compared to White or Hispanic women of similar ability. However, *no* differences in the rate at which White and Hispanic women achieved their first jobs were evident once adjustments were made for differences in the AFQT scores and family backgrounds. Racial differences in women's transition to employment did not carry over to entry into full-time jobs. Rather, the transition to full-time employment was identical among Black, White, and Hispanic women with equivalent AFQT scores and family backgrounds. For women, differences in scholastic achievement and family background account for the observed racial and ethnic disparities in how quickly they enter the labor force in the life table estimates. This is an important difference vis-à-vis men, for whom racial (but not ethnic) differences persist even after taking into account variation in individual and family characteristics.

The direct influence of family background and individual test scores on the transition to work are substantively interesting not only because they circumscribe the effects of race, but also because they may provide critical insights for understanding the mechanisms that maintain inequities among minority and nonminority youth. Higher AFQT scores are associated with accelerated labor force entry for *both* men and women, and also women's transition to full-time employment. However, high AFQT scores slow men's rate of entry into full-time employment by prolonging school enrollment or encouraging military enlistment (Mare and Winship, 1984; Ahituv et al., 1994; Kilburn, 1994). The mechanisms producing this complex sex and race interaction and the effects of AFQT scores on entry to employment are not immediately apparent, and warrant further investigation.

Family background has an inconsequential effect on the rate at which young men secure entry-level employment, probably because most young men participate in the labor market during adolescence, irrespective of their economic status (Schoenhals et al., 1998). Apparently this is less so for young women. Maternal education accelerates the rate at which young women enter the workforce. Role modeling and socialization are two mechanisms that can produce the gender-specific effect of mother's education inasmuch as well-educated mothers are both more likely to work outside the home than their less educated counterparts, and also are more likely to impart values approving of female employment to their daughters. Young women who lived at home in 1979 were 39% more likely to find an entry-level job than their counterparts who lived on their own. The odds that young women would hold an entry-level job were higher for those reared in parent-absent families compared to those reared in two-parent families. This result appears to capture the work-inducing effect of economic need because the family structure effect is net of family income.

Results for the transition to full-time employment also reveal appreciable sex differences. Beyond the trivial effects of race and ethnic origin, only AFQT scores and two background variables accelerated young women's entry to full-time employment, namely living at home (versus on one's own) in 1979 and having acquired work experience before leaving school. Specifically, the odds of obtaining a full-time job were 28% higher for women who lived at home in 1979 versus those who lived on their own. Equally striking are the linkages between early work experience and the transition to full-time work for young women. The latter imply that the odds of full-time employment were 44% higher among women who reported having worked before leaving school compared to those who did not. This finding suggests that there are links between early work experiences and subsequent labor force outcomes.

Although family background does not influence men's transition to an entry-level job, we show substantial effects for full-time employment. Specifically, father's education delayed young men's entry to first full-time employment by prolonging school enrollment (see Table 7.6A), while family income accelerated the rate of transition to full-time employment. One factor that is particularly important for understanding the links between adolescent and young adult employment is work activity that takes place during high school enrollment. The experience of having worked *before* leaving school significantly increased the rate of entry to full-time jobs. Substantively, this coefficient indicates that the odds of securing a full-time job were 32% higher for men who acquired labor market experience prior to leaving school relative to those who did not acquire such experience.

Conclusion

To recapitulate, the issues motivating our empirical research concern racial and ethnic differences in: (1) the timing of school departure and labor market entry; (2) the nature of the first labor market encounter; and (3) the consequences of adolescent labor market experience for employment outcomes during early adulthood. Our analysis of school departure and labor market entry indicates considerable overlap between these two activities, with racial and ethnic differences in each clearly apparent.

Although racial differences in the timing of labor market entry have been examined extensively, no prior study has considered racial differences in the school-to-work transition among Hispanics. Our findings showing that race and ethnic variation in the transition to employment can be reversed or eliminated after adjusting for differences in AFQT scores and family background is both provocative and problematic. If the AFQT measure is truly an index of scholastic and/or job-related aptitudes, then prior studies that failed to consider this influence on school departures and employment transitions may have misrepresented the significance of race (Heckman, 1995). Until we can answer this question satisfactorily, our findings about racial and ethnic differences must be regarded as tentative. However, our results underscore the urgency of scrutinizing the AFQT index and investigating how the use of this performance measure might be adapted to employment decisions in the civilian sector (see Heckman, 1995). The significance of race for Hispanics also deserves further scrutiny. It is important, in particular, to determine whether our non-White effects basically serve as proxies for national origin distinctions between Puerto Ricans and other Hispanics.

Several conclusions follow from the results presented above. The first and most important concerns the substantial race and ethnic differences in the rates at which young men and women leave school and enter the labor force. Among men we observed pronounced race and ethnic differences in the probability of getting a job. Black men experience the greatest difficulty entering the labor market. These results emphasize the need to support research directed toward understanding the mechanisms and barriers that limit young Black men's access to the labor market.

A second conclusion concerns the need to promote further data research to extend our knowledge of the school-to-work transition. Despite the great analytical potential of the NLSY for investigating various aspects of the school-to-work transition, our initial investigation has also made us aware of numerous limitations of these data. Respondents currently in the NLSY sample are now in their late 20s to early 30s, and well beyond the transitional phase of their life course. Given the dramatic changes in the racial and ethnic composition of the U.S. population during the 1980s and 1990s that were driven by immigration and differential fertility, and the changes in labor market opportunities during the same time period (Kasarda, 1995), collection of data about today's youth seems a necessary adjunct for policy formulation about tomorrow's workers.

Fortunately, the new youth cohort has begun with younger children—kids in pre-adolescence—rather than the large age spectrum used by the NLSY. This is warranted to adequately portray the process of school departure. Legal restrictions on school departure notwithstanding, many youth, particularly minorities, leave school permanently *before* they are entitled to do so legally. And, these are the kids most in need of attention by policy makers. Unfortunately, the new youth cohort does not include an oversample of Asian men and women. Virtually nothing is known about the school-to-work transition of this rapidly growing and highly diverse minority population (but see Schoenhals et al., 1998).

Third, we recommend additional research on the use of the Armed Forces Qualifying Test as a measure of scholastic aptitude, labor market readiness, skills, or other performance indicators. The military has used the AFQT and the components of the ASVAB battery of tests to predict the successful completion of initial military training and an enlistee's aptitude for various jobs (or occupations) within the armed forces. Social scientists have also found that the AFQT is a good predictor of various aspects of a youth's civilian labor force and schooling outcomes. It may be that there are lessons to be learned from the military with respect to developing indicators of aptitudes of "trainability," which may be able to improve the matching of workers to job specialties in the civilian sector. This potential benefit appears to warrant further research on the development and refinement of such indicators.

Notes

1. Jeylan Mortimer and her associates have developed a program of research that focuses on the school and work experiences of adolescents (see review in Mortimer and Finch, 1992). Ellen Greenberger and Lawrence Steinberg (1981; 1986) also have focused on the overlap of school and work during adolescence. In the main, both teams have focused on the developmental aspects of early work experience, although Mortimer's team has also considered the increased complexity of the job tasks assumed by adolescents.

2. Status attainment research does not view the temporal ordering of schooling and work as problematic, and basically asserts a sequence. Longitudinal studies have questioned this assumption (Rindfuss et al., 1987).

3. Most recent studies that included Hispanics are concerned with evaluating the returns to early experience rather than documenting more general race and ethnic differences in the transition from school to work.

4. The NLSY gathered data on 1,290 additional youth respondents who were in the military at the time of the 1979 interview. We restrict our focus to the civilian sample, excluding the oversamples of disadvantaged white youth, but including the oversamples of minority youth. This decision was based on extensive diagnostic analyses that revealed significant differences between the White random and nonrandom samples, but relatively minor differences between the Hispanic and Black oversamples.

5. Respondents were allowed to identify up to four groups, but were asked to indicate to which group they felt closest. We used this response to classify those individuals who reported more than one ethnic group. The Black and White groups are not of Hispanic origin.

6. We can identify four different groups based on the respondent's answer to the origin question: (1) Chicano, Mexican, or Mexican American; (2) Puerto Rican; (3) Cuban, Other Hispanic, or Other Spanish; and (4) respondent does not identify with a Hispanic group in the "origin" question, but is identified as Hispanic by the screening interview. Unfortunately more fine-grained analyses of Hispanic subgroups were not possible because the age restriction reduced sample sizes by approximately one-half.

7. We computed a log-rank test to determine whether the race and ethnic differences in exit rates were statistically significant. Unless otherwise noted, only statistically significant differences are reported.

8. Based on a log-rank test, we reject the hypothesis that the age-specific proportions securing jobs was identical among race and ethnic groups for both men and women. The only exception is the White–Hispanic difference in the timing of first full-time employment. However, for men, the Black–White and Black–Hispanic contrasts for full-time jobs were significantly different.

9. Our estimates of work experience prior to school departure are slightly

conservative for respondents who were 15 or 16 years of age in 1978, but more precise for the two younger age groups. This results because respondents who had already left school at the time of the first interview were queried in more general terms about their prior work experience—i.e., they were asked about jobs of 20 hours or more that lasted two or more months.

10. Percents reported in Tables 7.3A and 7.3B refer to work experience prior to the beginning of the age interval at which school departures occurred.

11. There is no optimal solution for left censoring, particularly when the truncated history is selective. Although left censoring in employment and education histories is not great in these cohorts, it does exist. Controls for age cohort help monitor this problem, but they do not provide a completely satisfactory solution.

12. Because of nontrivial amounts of missing data on the parental education and family income variables, we included dummy variables for the missing cases. This was deemed preferable to losing observations and potentially introducing selection bias through nonresponse.

13. We estimated a model that included year dummies to determine whether cohort effects might be due to period effects and discerned no significant pattern in the results. More importantly, the effects of age cohort were not washed out.

References

Ahituv, Avner, Marta Tienda, Lixin Xu and V. Joseph Hotz. 1994. "Initial Labor Market Experiences of Minority and Nonminority Men." *1994 Proceedings of the Industrial and Labor Relations Research Association*. Madison, WI: ILLR. pp. 17-25.

Bean, Frank D. and Marta Tienda. 1987. *The Hispanic Experience in the United States*. New York: Russell Sage Foundation.

Becker, Brian E. and Stephen M. Hills. 1980. "Teenage Unemployment: Some Evidence of the Long-Run Effects on Wages." *The Journal of Human Resources*, 15(3):354–372.

Becker, Brian E. and Stephen M. Hills. 1983. "The Long Run Effects of Job Changes and Unemployment Among Male Teenagers." *The Journal of Human Resources*, 17(2):197–211.

Ben-Porath Yoram. 1967. "The Production of Human Capital and the Life Cycle of Earnings." *Journal of Political Economy*, 75:352–365.

Burtless, Gary, ed. 1990. *A Future of Lousy Jobs: The Changing Structure of U.S. Wages*. Washington, DC: The Brookings Institution.

Cameron, Stephen V. and James Heckman. 1991."The Role of Family, Labor Markets and Public Policy in Accounting for Minority Schooling Attainment." Department of Economics, University of Chicago: Unpublished manuscript.

Coleman, James S. 1984."The Transition from School to Work." *Research in Social Stratification and Mobility*, 3:27–59.

Cox, D.R. 1972. "Regression Models and Life Tables (with discussion), *Journal of Royal Statistical Society*, B, 34:187–220.

Cyert, Richard M. and David C. Mowery eds. 1987. *Technology and Employment: Innovation and Growth in the U.S. Economy*. Washington, DC: National Academy Press.

D'Amico, Ronald and Nan L. Maxwell. 1990. "Employment during the School-to-Work Transition: An Explanation of Black–White Wage Differentials and Bifurcation of Black Income." Paper presented at 1990 Annual Meeting of the Population Association of America, Toronto.

Ellwood, David. 1982. "Teenage Unemployment: Permanent Scars or Temporary Blemishes." In Richard B. Freeman and David A. Wise, eds., *The Youth Labor Market Problem: Its Nature, Causes and Consequences*. Chicago: University of Chicago Press pp. 349-390.

Ghez, Gilbert R. and Gary Becker. 1972. *Allocation of Time and Goods over the Life Cycle*. New York: Columbia University Press.

Greenberger, Ellen and Laurence Steinberg. 1981. "The Workplace as a Context for the Socialization of Youth." *Journal of Youth and Adolescence*, 10(3):185–210.

Greenberger, Ellen and Laurence Steinberg, 1986. *When Teenagers Work: The Psychological and Social Costs of Adolescent Employment*. New York: Basic Books.

Gritz, R. Mark and Thomas MaCurdy. 1992. "Participation in Low Wage Labor Markets by Young Men." Final Report to the U.S. Department of Labor. DOL\BLS\ #E-9-J-0046.

Heckman, James J. 1995. "Lessons from the Bell Curve." *Journal of Political Economy*, 103:1091–1120.

Hogan, Dennis and Nan Marie Astone. 1986. "Transition to Adulthood." *Annual Review of Sociology*, 12:109–130.

Hotz, V. Joseph, Lixin Yu, Marta Tienda, and Avner Ahituv. 1995. "Returns to Work Experience in the Transition from School to Work for Young Men in the U.S.: An Analysis of the 1980s." Chicago: Unpublished manuscript, NORC.

Kasarda, John D. 1995. "Industrial Restructuring and the Changing Location of Jobs." In Reynolds Farley, ed., *State of the Union*, Vol. I. New York: Russell Sage pp. 215–267.

Kilburn, Rebeca. 1994. "Minority Representation in the U.S. Military." Unpublished Ph.D. Dissertation, University of Chicago.

Levitan, Sar A. and Frank Gallo. 1991. "Preparing Americans for Work," *Looking Ahead*, 13,18–25.

Levy, Frank S. 1987. *Dollars and Dreams*. New York. Russell Sage Foundation.

Levy, Frank S. and Richard C. Michel. 1991. *The Economic Future of American Families: Income and Wealth Trends*. Washington, DC: The Urban Institute.

Lewin-Epstein, Noah. 1981. *Youth Employment During High School: An Analysis of High School and Beyond*. Washington, DC: National Center for Education Statistics.

Lynch, Lisa M. 1989. "The Youth Labor Market in the Eighties: Determinants of Re-employment Probabilities for Young Men and Women." *Review of Economics and Statistics*, 71 (February):37–45.

McLeod, Jay. 1995. *Ain't No Makin' It*. Boulder: Westview Press.

Manski, Charles and David A. Wise. 1983. *College Choice in America*. Cambridge MA: Harvard University Press.

Mare, Robert and Christopher Winship. 1984. The Paradox of Lessening Racial Inequality and Joblessness Among Black Youth: Enrollment, Enlistment, and Employment, 1964–1981." *American Sociological Review*, 49:39–55.

Mare, Robert, Christopher Winship, and Warren Kubitschek. 1984. "The Transition from Youth to Adult: Understanding the Age Pattern of Employment." *American Journal of Sociology*, 90(2):326–351.

Marini, Margaret Mooney. 1984. "The Order of Events in the Transition to Adulthood." *Sociology of Education*, 57(April):63–84.

Meyer, Robert H. and David A. Wise. 1982. "High School Preparation and Early Labor Force Experience." In Richard B. Freeman and David A. Wise, eds. *The Youth Labor Market Problem: Its Nature, Causes and Consequences*. Chicago: University of Chicago Press pp. 277–339.

Mincer, Jacob. 1962. "On-the-Job Training: Costs, Returns and Some Implications," *Journal of Political Economy*, 70:50–79.

Mortimer, Jeylan T. and Michael D. Finch. 1992. "Work experience in Adolescence." Unpublished Report prepared for Public/Private Ventures. Philadelphia: Public/Private Ventures.

O'Neill, June. 1990. "The Role of Human Capital in Earnings Differences Between Black Men and White Women." *Journal of Economic Perspectives*, 4:25–45.

Rees, Albert. 1986. "An Essay on Youth Joblessness." *Journal of Economic Literature*, 24:613–628.

Rindfuss, Ronald R., C. Gray Swicegood, and Rachel A. Rosenfeld. 1987. "Disorder in the Life Course: How Common and Does It Matter?" *American Sociological Review*, 52(December):785–801.

Schoenhals, Mark, Marta Tienda and Barbara Schneider. 1998. "Educational Consequences of Adolescent Employment." *Social Forces*, 77:725-764

Shore, Milton F. 1972. "Youth and Jobs: Educational, Vocational, and Mental Health Aspects." *Journal of Youth and Adolescents*, 1(4):315–323.

Steinberg, Laurence, Suzanne Fegley, and Sanford M. Dornbush. 1993. "Negative Impact of Part-Time Work on Adolescent Adjustment: Evidence from a Longitudinal Study." *Developmental Psychology*, 29(2):171–180.

Sullivan, Mercer. 1989. *Getting Paid: Youth Crime and Work in the Inner City*. Ithaca: Cornell University Press.

Tienda, Marta and Haya Stier. 1991. "Joblessness and Shiftlessness: Labor Force Activity in Chicago's Inner City." In Christopher Jencks and Paul Peterson, eds., *The Urban Underclass*. Washington, DC: Brookings Institute pp. 135–154.

Tienda, Marta and Avner Ahituv. 1996. "Ethnic Differences in School Departure: Does Youth Employment Promote or Undermine Educational Achievement?" In Garth Mangum and Stephen Mangum, eds., *Of Heart and Mind: Social Policy Essays in Honor of Sar Levitan*. Kalamazoo, MI: Upjohn Institute, pp. 93–110.

Wilson, William J. 1987. *The Truly Disadvantaged*. Chicago: University of Chicago Press.

Wilson, William J. 1996. *When Work Disappears*. New York: Knopf.

Chapter 8

Ethnic and Racial Intermarriage in the United States: Old and New Regimes

Gillian Stevens and Michael K. Tyler

Introduction

In 1964, Gordon outlined seven different processes of ethnic and racial assimilation: cultural, structural, marital, identificational, attitude receptional, behavior receptional, and civic (Gordon, 1964). He considered marital assimilation—ethnic and racial intermarriage—to lead inevitably to identificational assimilation, i.e., the loss of the group's separate identity. Still considered a "litmus test" of assimilation (Alba, 1995), intermarriage is a complex social and demographic phenomenon. For example, the recognition of a couple as being "intermarried" rests on socially constructed definitions of ethnicity and race, which vary across context and time. Social and demographic factors affect the likelihood of intergroup contact and so affect the likelihood that men and women of different ethnic and racial groups meet and form intimate relationships. The likelihood of men and women involved in intimate relationships formally marrying rather than, say, cohabiting, also affects the prevalence of intermarriage.

In this chapter we discuss some of the demographic and sociological explanations predicting levels and patterns of intermarriage and then describe old and new patterns of intermarriage in the United States. We then speculate about future trends in intermarriage and the role of intermarriage in the assimilation of ethnic and racial groups in the new century.

Personal Preferences and Demographic Factors in Marriage Patterns

Intermarriage is an almost infallible indicator of assimilation for several reasons. High rates of intermarriage signal the disappearance of strong impediments to long-term intimate interracial and interethnic relationships among adults (Alba, 1995). At the same time, the individuals involved in an inter-marriage have, or develop, kinship ties and social networks within two ethnic or racial groups (Johnson, 1985; Waters, 1990). The children of these mar-riages, who acquire elements of both parents' ancestries, embody the lack of distance between the two ancestry groups. The putative ancestry of the chil-dren can also be ambiguous because of their intimate kinship ties to two eth-nic groups, the possible muting of any distinct physical markers of member-ship in one or the other ethnic groups, and the incomplete or dual socializa-tion into the distinct mores and cultures of one or both groups.

Why does ethnic and racial intermarriage occur? It is easiest to begin answering this question by considering the other side of the coin: ethnic and racial homogamy, in which individuals marry others of the same ethnic or racial group. Ethnic and racial homogamy is one example of the single most commonly observed pattern in assortative mating—marriage between part-ners of matching or similar characteristics. There are two major explanations for homogamy. The first emphasizes individuals' preferences in mate selec-tion, and the second emphasizes how social and demographic considerations constrain individuals' choices of marital partners.

The role of preferences in mate selection has been investigated in the social psychological research focusing on interpersonal processes. The "matching hypothesis" states, for example, that people prefer spouses with characteristics similar to or matching their own (Berscheid et al. 1971). There is a wide variety of empirical support for preferences for marriage partners with similar or matching characteristics. For example, Americans are more likely to marry peo-ple of similar or matching levels of physical attractiveness (Stevens et al., 1990), education (Mare, 1990), social class, religious affiliation (Glenn, 1982), and even eye color (Pearson, 1900 cited in Warren, 1966). Researchers investigating ethnic and racial intermarriage thus often presume, all else being equal, that individuals prefer to have a spouse of the same or "matching" race or ethnicity rather than a spouse of a different race or ethnicity.

How strong the preferences are for a marital partner of the same race and ethnicity (or any other characteristic) is another question. The main hypothe-sis in the literature on assortative marriage patterns is that preferences for a marital partner of the same race or ethnicity are weakened by processes of acculturation and structural assimilation. Individual-level signs of accultura-tion and structural assimilation include native-born versus foreign-born nativi-ty, mixed versus single ethnic ancestry, knowing only English versus profi-ciency in a non-English language, and higher educational, economic, and occupational statuses. Empirical research shows that the probability of ethnic intermarriage varies with these signs of acculturation. For example, native-born Americans are more likely to intermarry than foreign-born Americans (e.g., Kitano et al., 1984), Americans of mixed ancestry are more likely to intermarry than those of a single ancestry (e.g., Alba and Golden, 1986), Americans who spoke a non-English language in childhood are less likely to intermarry than those who learned only English (e.g., Stevens and Swicegood, 1987), and Americans of higher educational attainment (e.g., Lieberson and Waters 1988) and higher occupational statuses (e.g., Schoen and Cohen, 1980) are more likely to marry outside of their racial or ethnic group than those with lower attainments.

Demographic factors, which can operate independently of personal preferences, also influence the prevalence of homogamy versus intermarriage. For example, the relative sizes of the racial and ethnic groups can strongly affect the prevalence of homogamy versus intermarriage. All else being equal, the likelihood of in-group marriage is lower among members of smaller groups and higher among members of larger groups. Relative group size also affects levels of homogamy in another way. If the ethnic and racial groups are about equivalent in size, then the overall levels of ethnic and racial intermarriage are highest.

A second demographic factor that affects the prevalence of homogamy is the sex ratio within an ethnic or racial group. An uneven sex ratio forces some members of the more common sex to marry outside the group. The sex ratio at birth is about 105 males to 100 females for most ethnic and racial groups. (The American Black population, with a sex ratio at birth that is about even, is a known exception.) Mortality rates during *infancy* and *childhood* usually slightly favor women and so the sex ratio is usually about even among young adults in most groups. However, sex ratios during the typical marrying ages can vary because of sex-specific patterns of migration. Migration streams from specific countries are sometimes dominated by one or the other sex (Donato, 1990). For example, the Chinese immigrants recruited to build the U.S. railroads in the mid-1800s were almost exclusively men, and the Irish brought in as domestic servants during the late 1800s were mostly women. The more extreme the sex ratio among migrants, the more likely the migrants of the more common sex are to contract ethnic intermarriages. And sometimes the act of migrating is prompted by intermarriage. The American military bases in Korea, Japan, the Philippines, and Germany, for example, have resulted in large number of women migrating to the United States as wives of American servicemen (Jasso and Rosenzweig, 1990) and in most cases the wife's ancestry differs from her husband's.

High levels of ethnic residential and social segregation within the United States can affect the range of personal contacts between members of the same or different ethnic or racial groups (Kerkhoff, 1964:289). The main assumption is that people cannot meet and perhaps marry unless they interact in the same context. If the people living in or interacting in various geographic, spatially, or socially-defined contexts have similar ethnic and racial characteristics, because of self-selection or because of some other sorting mechanism, homogamy will result even if people do not strongly prefer to have spouses with characteristics similar to their own (Bozon and Héran 1989). Because the geographic and social landscape of the United States is a patchwork of socially-defined groups, this line of research consistently shows that levels of geographic segregation and geographic concentration among ethnic groups strongly predict the levels of ethnic homogamy (e.g., Stevens and Swicegood, 1987).

Demographers' studies of mate selection thus typically assume that individuals' abilities and opportunities to find and marry a partner of the preferred, i.e., the same or matching, ethnic or racial ancestry are affected by demographic or structural factors. If these demographic factors explain the observed prevalence of in-group marriage versus intermarriage, then preferences for in-group marriage are presumed to be weak. If, however, observed levels of racial and ethnic homogamy are higher than expected on the basis of demographic factors, then preferences for in-group marriage are presumed to be strong.

Homogamy versus Intermarriage in the United States

There are a variety of ways to measure the degree of intermarriage versus homogamy. Measures based on census or survey data, which show the relative frequencies of in-group marriages and intermarriages, include all extant marriages, some of which may have been contracted long ago but exclude marriages dissolved by death or divorce. Measures based on incidence data, such as vital statistics data, marriage licenses, or marriage license applications, are quicker to show new trends than analyses based on census or survey data because all recent marriages are included, even those of short duration, which are less likely to be caught by cross-sectional surveys or censuses. On the other hand, incidence data are often limited in scope and in amount of detail. Not all states, for example, gather detailed information about the race and ethnicity of their newly married couples (Alba and Golden, 1986). In this chapter we rely on U.S. census data (Ruggles and Sobek, 1995; U.S. Bureau of the Census 1966; 1972; 1985; 1994) because they allow the description of the prevalence of in-marriage versus intermarriage for detailed racial and ethnic groups for the entire nation.

In Table 8.1, we show measures of ethnic and racial in-marriage and intermarriage for married women reporting one of the twenty-five racial and ethnic ancestries listed in the table stub. This table was modeled on Table 6.1 in *From Many Strands* by Stanley Lieberson and Mary C. Waters (1988) but is based on 1990 rather than 1980 U.S. Census data and refers to all married

Table 8.1

Odds of Ethnic and Racial In-Marriage versus Intermarriage for Married Women in the United States, 1990

Women's Racial or Ethnic Ancestry Group	Percent Women Inter-married	Husbands of Ancestry as Percent of Total Husbands	Odds of Marriage to Husband of Ancestry Group for:		Odds Ratio
			Group Member	Other	
Belgian	25.2	0.2	0.337	.002	148.2
Czech	28.8	1.0	0.405	.009	46.0
Danish	28.7	1.0	0.402	.010	41.8
Dutch	37.7	3.7	0.604	.035	17.5
English	52.2	21.1	1.092	.220	5.0
Finnish	24.8	0.4	0.329	.003	104.4
French	35.3	5.2	0.546	.051	10.7
German	55.6	35.0	1.252	.449	2.8
Hungarian	28.7	0.9	0.402	.008	47.5
Irish	47.4	20.5	0.900	.224	4.0
Italian	44.4	7.9	0.799	.060	13.3
Norwegian	34.1	2.2	0.517	.020	26.0
Polish	38.1	5.2	0.616	.044	13.9
Portuguese	46.0	0.6	0.851	.003	246.3
Scottish	35.1	7.1	0.541	.070	7.8
Swedish	29.4	2.7	0.416	.026	15.8
Swiss	32.4	1.0	0.479	.009	53.0
USSR (former)	43.1	3.0	0.756	.023	33.4
Welsh	30.6	1.5	0.441	.015	29.4
Yugoslavian	33.0	2.0	0.492	.016	30.1
Black	97.6	7.8	40.347	.004	9,454.3
Hispanic	80.0	7.6	4.003	.013	311.7
Asian/Pacific Islander	75.7	3.0	3.113	.003	1,034.1
American Indian	38.6	0.7	0.629	.003	187.2
Other	85.3	3.2	5.823	.005	1,275.7

women rather than to American-born women in their first marriages. "Percent women in-married" refers to the percentage of women of the specified racial or ethnic group whose husbands report the same or overlapping racial or ethnic affiliation. (The 1980 and 1990 U.S. Censuses allowed respondents to choose several ancestries. A respondent could, for example, report both English and French.) For example, 52.2% of the women reporting English ancestry have husbands who also report English ancestry. "Husbands of Ancestry as Percent of Total Husbands" refers to the percentage of all husbands who report the specified racial or ethnic affiliation. Thus, 21.1% of all husbands report "English" as an ethnic ancestry. The "Odds of Marriage to Husband of Ancestry Group for Group Member" is the ratio of the percentage of women in-married to the percentage of women not in-married. For women of English ancestry, the ratio equals 1.092 (= 52.2/100-52.2). The "Odds of Marriage to Husband of Ancestry Group for Other" is the parallel ratio for women who are not of the specified ethnicity or race. Thus, for women who are not of English ancestry, the odds of marriage to a husband of English descent versus marriage to a husband of some other descent equals 0.220. The odds ratio is the ratio of the two odds. Thus, the odds of women of English ancestry having a husband of English ancestry are about 5.0 (=1.092/0.220) times the odds of women of non-English descent having a husband of English ancestry.

European Ancestry Groups and Intermarriage

The results reported in Table 8.1 fall into two main sets: those referring to a European ancestry and those referring to some other ancestry. The first set, which includes twenty different European ancestry groups, is presented in detail to show the end product of almost a century of ethnic assimilation and adaptation among European ethnic ancestry groups.

Deanna Pagnini and Philip Morgan's analysis of marriage patterns around 1910 in the United States provides a historical benchmark for evaluating patterns of assortative marriage among European ethnic groups. Their results showed high levels of in-group marriage among all European ancestry groups, and caste-like levels among the Eastern and Southern European ancestry groups. Among women of German ancestry, for example, 94% had German husbands, while 98% of Italian wives had Italian husbands (Pagnini and Morgan, 1990: Table 8.4). The results presented in Table 8.1 show that in 1990, about three generations after Pagnini and Morgan's benchmark study, intermarriage among women of European ancestry is very common. Most women of European ancestry have husbands of a different ancestry. Only among the two largest European ancestry groups, English and German, are there even simple majorities of wives with husbands of the same or overlapping ancestry.

Nevertheless, these percentages, although low, *still* overemphasize the appearance of in-group marriage, particularly among the older European ancestry groups. Several generations of intermarriage mean that many Americans in 1990 have complex ethnic backgrounds and so have several options in deciding which components of their ancestry background to report. A large percentage of Americans reported more than one ancestry in the 1990 U.S. Census, and a woman is considered "in-married" in Table 8.1 even if her husband reported an ancestral background that only partly overlapped hers. Furthermore, two of the three groups reporting the highest levels of in-group marriage are German and Irish. More Americans reported German or Irish than would be expected on the basis of natural increase and previous intermarriage (Hout and Goldstein, 1994). Given the attractiveness of "German" and "Irish" in the reporting of Americans' ancestral affiliations, it seems plausible that many of these marriages appear homogamous only because one spouse's reporting of "German" or "Irish" nudged the other spouse to do the same.

Overall, the prevalence of in-marriage is low among the European ancestry groups, even among the largest groups. However, once the effect of relative group size is taken into account by calculating the odds ratios, women in some of the smaller groups appear to have a higher propensity for in-group marriage, in particular, women of Portuguese, Belgian, and Finnish ancestry. The higher odds of in-marriage within these groups can be explained by their relatively high levels of residential and geographic segregation. Americans of Portuguese ancestry, for example, are strongly clustered in the state of Massachusetts. Still, less than half of the women of these ancestries have husbands whose ancestry matches or overlaps with theirs. For women reporting European ancestry, intermarriage is now, by and large, the expected outcome. If high levels of intermarriage herald the disappearance of ethnic distinctions, then the results in Table 8.1 suggest that the historically strong ethnic distinctions among European groups are now largely irrelevant in marriage preferences.

The results presented in Table 8.1, and versions of it based on other data (e.g., Alba and Golden, 1986; Alba and Kessler 1979; Kalmijn, 1993a; Lieberson and Waters, 1988; Stevens and Swicegood, 1987), provide support for theories of ethnic assimilation in which intermarriage is both the inevitable product of, and an accomplice in, ethnic group assimilation. In general, predictions of intermarriage among Europeans have followed expectations with respect to the impact of demographic factors such as group size and segregation, and individual characteristics such as generational status, non-English language usage, and educational, occupational, and economic attainments.

The results shown in the second panel of Table 8.1, however, seem to be telling another story, or perhaps, a much earlier chapter of the same story.

These numbers refer to the four non-White racial and ethnic categories previously used by federal agencies (U.S. Office of Management and Budget, 1977); we added one more category, "Other," so that the categories would be exhaustive. These categories are awkward because they obscure ethnic and racial variation within the groupings. The category, "Hispanic," for example, encompasses several distinct cultures, while the distinctions among the Asian and Pacific Islander groups include differences in language as well as in culture and countries of origin. Nor do the categories allow the description of multiracial ancestry. These and other issues led the U.S. Office of Management and Budget to recently revise Directive 15, "Race and Ethnic Standards for Federal Statistics and Administrative Reporting," which had specified racial and ethnic definitions for most federal purposes (Edmonston et al., 1996). Nevertheless, until the new standards are implemented, the best alternative is to use the racial and ethnic categories outlined in Directive 15. Although these categories conceal ethnic and racial intermarriage occurring within them, the boundaries between these categories appear to be more distinct than those drawn within them when describing marriage patterns (Gilbertson et al., 1996; Kitano et al., 1984; Padilla 1984; U.S. Bureau of the Census, 1994).

The results in the second panel of Table 8.1 show, with the exception of respondents reporting American Indian ancestry, that large majorities of women share a racial or ethnic ancestry with their husbands. Over three-quarters of Asian and Pacific Islander women, four-fifths of Hispanic women, and 97% of Black women have husbands of the same racial ancestry. The corresponding odds of in-group marriage are all above 1.0 (again with the exception of American Indian), and the relative odds of in-group marriage are of a different order of magnitude for Black and Asian or Pacific Islander women than for women of most European ancestries. The odds of a Black woman having a Black husband are over 9,000 times the odds of a non-Black woman having a Black husband while the odds of, for example, a Dutch woman having a Dutch husband are only about 17 times those of a non-Dutch woman having a Dutch husband. Because these results for women classified by race differ so sharply from those for women reporting a European ethnic ancestry, we turn to a more explicit investigation of recent trends in the patterns and prevalence of racial intermarriage and in-marriage.

Black Americans and Intermarriage

Above, we argued that the high levels, and in some cases the caste-like levels, of homogamy observed among the European ancestry groups shortly after the turn of the Twentieth century have sunk so low that in most cases only a minority of European women in 1990 can be considered "in-married," even under very generous definitions of in-group marriage. At the turn of the century, intermarriage between Blacks and Whites was even rarer than intermarriage involving men and women of the various European ancestries (Roberts, 1994). The very low historic rates of the Black–White intermarriage resulted from strong racial prejudice, strong patterns of residential and school segregation, and a long history of racial economic and social inequality.

Table 8.2
Percentages of Married Men and Women with Spouses
of Same Race or Spanish Origin, 1960-1990

Race or Spanish Ancestry		*Percentages of Married Men and Women with Spouses of Same Racial Ancestry*			
		1960	*1970*	*1980*	*1990*
White	Women	99.8	99.7	99.0	98.6
	Men	99.8	99.6	98.9	98.3
Black	Women	99.1	99.2	98.8	97.6
	Men	99.0	98.6	96.4	94.1
Asian	Women	81.1	76.4	72.2	75.7
	Men	86.1	85.4	85.2	88.7
American Indian	Women	75.8	61.0	46.3	38.6
	Men	82.5	64.2	47.6	41.5
Other	Women	56.6	54.9	81.3	85.3
	Men	69.4	62.7	83.8	84.4
Spanish Origin	Women	—	82.3	81.3	80.0
	Men	—	82.5	82.2	81.9

Notes: Data for men and women of Spanish origin in 1960 are not available. Men and women of Spanish origin could be of any race.

By 1960, however, about 1% of Black men and women had spouses of other races (see Table 8.2). In absolute numbers, the 1% represented about 59,000 couples, with most of these couples, about 51,000, comprised of a Black and a White spouse. There was only a small increase in the numbers of Black/non-Black couples in the 1960s, but during the 1970s the number of Black–White couples almost doubled, from 65,000 to 121,000, and during the 1980s the number increased to well over 200,000 couples or to about 0.41% of all married couples in the United States in 1990. This increase in the prevalence of interracial marriages follows an increase in the number of newly contracted interracial marriages (Kalmijn, 1993b).

This upward trend in the numbers of racially-mixed marriages is accompanied by the emergence of a sex-specific pattern. In 1960, the percentages of married Black men and married Black women in racially homogamous marriages were about equal, 99.0 and 99.1 respectively (Table 8.2). In 1970, the percentage of married Black men in racially homogamous marriages slipped slightly to 98.6% while the percentage of married Black women remained stable. Although the percentages of married Black men and married Black women in racially homogamous marriages both decreased during the 1970s and 1980s, the percentage of married Black men with Black spouses fell faster. By 1990, over twice as many married Black men had non-Black wives than vice versa, 5.9% versus 2.4%.

The asymmetry in the percentages of married Black men and women in racially-mixed marriages is difficult to understand because the low sex ratio among the adult American Black population exerts demographic pressure on Black women, not Black men, to choose non-Black partners. One explanation for the asymmetry relies on the hypothesis of an "exchange" in the selection of marriage partners. Women's emphasis on men's economic characteristics and men's emphasis on women's noneconomic characteristics presumably encourage non-Black women to marry Black men with higher levels of education resulting in an "exchange" of the Black men's higher levels of education with the women's higher racial status (Schoen and Wooldredge, 1989). But why this pattern emerged only in the last 20 years is unclear — although the underenumeration of Black men in the 1960 U.S. Census may be part of the explanation.

Possible explanations for the general increase in intermarriages involving Black men or Black women include the removal of the remaining state-specific legal bans on racial intermarriage, decreases in racial prejudice, decreases in residential and school segregation, growing racial equality along economic and other social dimensions, and growing demographic pressures. None of these possibilities, however, fully accounts for the upward trend in Black/non-Black marriages.

Demographic factors, for example, do not explain the increase in interracial marriages among Black men and women. Although the percentage of Blacks who intermarry is negatively correlated with the percentage of the population that is Black across 33 states (Kalmijn, 1993b: Figure 2), measures of the "marriage market" exert little influence on the probability of racial intermarriage (e.g., Lichter et al., 1995; Schoen and Kluegel, 1988). Thus, preferences for racial in-marriage and barriers against racially mixed marriages appear to outweigh demographic constraints. In addition, the decreases in racial prejudice have been modest; decreases in racial residential segregation have been slow to occur (Farley and Frey, 1994); and the progress towards racial social and economic equality has been uneven (Farley, 1984). Finally, in many Black–White intermarriages, one or both partners are foreign-born (Tucker and Mitchell-Kernan, 1990) and so less likely to have been socialized in a context still marred by racism.

Hispanics and Intermarriage

Table 8.2 shows the trends in marriages involving Spanish-origin spouses. Although the absolute number of marriages involving at least one Spanish-origin partner has more than doubled between 1970 and 1990, the percentage of homogamous marriages has remained fairly stable, drifting downwards by only about 2% over the two decades. Unlike intermarriage among Blacks, demographic and structural factors appear to strongly influence the prevalence of inter-marriages among Hispanics. Research shows, for example, that demographic opportunities for intergroup contact, the extent of socioeconomic differentiation within the Mexican American population, and the extent of Spanish language maintenance strongly predicted the prevalence of Mexican American/Anglo marriages in 53 metropolitan areas—although sex ratio, group size, and structural assimilation did not (Anderson and Saenz, 1994). Individual-level indicators of assimilation, e.g., generational status and occupation, also strongly predict inter-marriage versus in-group marriage. Foreign-born Mexicans and those of lower occupational statuses are much more likely to marry a spouse of similar ancestry than native-born Hispanics and those of higher occupational statuses (Fitzpatrick and Gurak, 1979; Schoen and Cohen, 1980).

The relative stability over the last 20 years in the percentages of homogamous marriages among Hispanics probably reflects the balancing of opposite trends: the influence of the continuing acculturation and structural assimilation among native-born generations and the continued immigration of foreign-born Hispanics. Although there are some disquieting findings about the socioeconomic and educational mobility of later-generation Hispanics (e.g., Wojtkiewicz and Donato, 1995), the research on marriage patterns suggests that intermarriage does vary with indicators of assimilation, i.e., generational status, and educational and occupational mobility. The fairly high level of in-marriage among the general Hispanic population thus appears to be maintained by the continued arrival of foreign-born Hispanics, many of whom are poorly educated and speak only Spanish.

Asians and Intermarriage

Table 8.2 shows the percentages of homogamous marriages for Asian (Japanese, Chinese, or Filipino) men and women from 1960 to 1990. The percentages of Asian women in homogamous marriages are lower than for Asian men. The differential reflects, in part, the in-migration of Asian "war brides," almost all of whom are married to non-Asian men (Saenz et al., 1994). The differential may also reflect complex sex-specific patterns of exchange and socioeconomic selectivity (Hwang et al., 1995). Other research also shows that the probabilities of Asian men and women marrying non-Asian women and men vary in expected fashion with individual-level indicators of assimilation and acculturation such as generational status (Kitano et al., 1984; Sung, 1990), and length of residence among foreign-born Asians (Hwang et al., 1994). Structural factors, such as the numbers of Asians in specific geographic locations, also appear to influence the prevalence of intermarriage.

North American Indians and Intermarriage

The probability of American Indian men and women being involved in homogamous marriages in 1960 was roughly on par with the probabilities of in-group marriage for Asian men and women, but by 1990 fewer than half of American Indian men and women had spouses of American Indian descent. One trend driving down homogamy among American Indian men and women is urbanization. In the United States, the identity of American Indians has revolved around tribal or subtribal affiliations rather than the designation "American Indian" per se. Urbanization alters the ties between community and Indian tribes, the traditional basis of Indian identity, and so facilitates intermarriage (Sandefur, 1986).

The sharp increases in the percentages of American Indian men and women who are racially intermarried, particularly between 1960 and 1980, also track the sharp increases across the decades in the number of people who identify themselves as American Indian (Nagel, 1995; Passel, 1976; Passel and Berman, 1986). The increases in the numbers of people claiming American Indian ancestry are largest in areas in which American Indians have not traditionally lived and are not attributable to migration or fertility (Passel and Berman, 1986). Some scholars have therefore argued that many of the people claiming American Indian ancestry in the 1970 and later Censuses are of mixed ancestry and are emphasizing their Indian heritage in response to the rise in ethnic activism and in "Red Power" activism in particular (Nagel, 1995). Because, in general, Americans with complex ancestries are more likely to intermarry than others, the upsurge in intermarriage over the last several decades among American Indians may reflect a complex set of relations involving the percentages of this population with bi-cultural heritage, and a lower propensity for intermarriage within this subpopulation.

Table 8.3
Trends in Intra- and Inter-Racial Marriages in the United States: 1960-1990

Race of Spouses	1960	1970	1980	1990
	Numbers in 1,000s			
White/White	37,072	40,578	43,568	44,749
Black/Black	3,033	3,344	3,418	3,334
Asian/Asian	148	230	398	1,191
American Indian/American Indian	63	77	119	123
Other/Other	18	46	1,013	1,246
Total Intra-racial	40,334	44,275	48,516	50,642
White/non-White	142	298	906	1394
Black/non-Black	59	76	168	290
Asian/non-Asian	58	111	222	534
American Indian/non-Amer. Indian	34	92	270	369
Other inter-racial	22	65	429	444
Total Inter-racial	157	322	997	1,516
Total Marriages	40,720	44,597	49,514	52,159
	Percentages			
White/White	91.56	90.99	87.99	85.79
Black / Black	7.49	7.50	6.90	6.39
Asian / Asian	0.37	0.52	0.80	2.28
American Indian / American Indian	0.16	0.17	0.24	0.24
Other / Other	0.04	0.10	2.05	2.39
Total Intra-racial	99.61	99.28	97.98	97.09
White / non-White	0.35	0.67	1.83	2.67
Black / non-Black	0.15	0.17	0.34	0.56
Asian / non-Asian	0.14	0.25	0.45	1.02
American Indian / non-Amer. Indian	0.08	0.21	0.55	0.71
Other inter-racial	0.05	0.15	0.87	0.85
Total Inter-racial	0.39	0.72	2.01	2.91
Total Marriages	100%	100%	100%	100%

Note: Summing the numbers of inter-racial marriages yields double the given total because each inter-racial marriage appears in the panel twice. A White/Black marriage, for example, appears once in the line "White / non-White" and once in the line "Black / non-Black."

Overall Trends in Racial and Ethnic Homogamy and Intermarriage

Table 8.3 summarizes the trends in intra- and inter-racial marriages between 1960 and 1990 from a slightly different perspective. Rather than focusing on the percentages of married men and women of each racial or ethnic ancestry who have spouses of similar or different ancestries, this table focuses on marriages. The first panel, for example, shows the numbers of intraracial or in-group marriages for five racial and ethnic categories: White, Black, Asian, American Indian, and Other. The second panel shows the numbers of interracial marriages. Each interracial marriage appears twice in this panel—a Black/White marriage, for example, appears in the line for "White/non-White" and in the line for "Black/non-Black." Hence, summing the numbers (or percentages) of interracial marriages across the five categories yields double the given totals of interracial marriages. The bottom panel of Table 8.3 provides the corresponding percentages of all marriages in the United States classified by the racial ancestry of the spouses.

The numbers and percentages provided in Table 8.3 are exhaustive in the sense that they include all extant American marriages appearing in the Census. However, the racial and ethnic categories cut across the category of "Hispanic" or Spanish origin because individuals of Spanish or Hispanic origin could be of any race. Table 8.4 thus provides the parallel information for marriages in 1970 to 1990 involving Spanish origin or Hispanic spouses.

Table 8.4
Trends in Marriages Involving a Spanish Origin Spouse in
the United States: 1970 - 1990

Race of Spouses	1970	1980	1990
		Numbers in 1,000s	
Spanish origin/Spanish origin	1,368	2,087	2,823
Spanish origin/non-Spanish origin	584	931	1,328
Total	1,952	3,018	4,151
		Percentages	
Spanish origin/Spanish origin	3.07	4.21	5.41
Spanish origin/non-Spanish origin	1.31	1.88	2.55
Percent of U.S. Marriages	4.38%	6.22%	8.19%

Spouses of Spanish origin can be of any race. Data not available for 1960.

Overall, the numbers of intraracial marriages grew from about 40 million in 1960 to almost 51 million in 1990, an increase that reflects the general growth of the U.S. population and more specifically the growth in the numbers of married couples of each race. However, the percentages of homogamous marriages for each of the racial ancestry categories across decadal year show the impact of the shifting ethnic and racial composition of the U.S. population. The percentage of racially homogamous White marriages, which largely consist of European ancestry spouses, decreased from about 92% of all marriages in 1960 to about 86% in 1990. During the same time period, the percentages of intraracial marriages involving Asians, American Indians (Table 8.3), and Americans of Spanish or Hispanic origin increased (Table 8.4). In spite of the increased racial diversity among racially homogamous marriages, the percentage of all marriages that are racially homogamous has remained relatively stable and quite high, dropping only from 99.6% in 1960 to 97.1% in 1990.

The overall percentages of interracial marriages show, of course, the opposing trend across the 30 year time span. The percentage of interracial marriages increased from .4% to 2.9%. Although the increase in Black/non-Black marriages, most of which were Black–White marriages, seems to have garnered much of the attention, much of the general increase in the overall percentage in interracial marriages was contributed by the growth in the number of Asian/non-Asian and American Indian/non-American Indian marriages.

Although it is possible to focus on the nine-fold increase in the absolute number of interracial marriages, from 157,000 to 1,516,000, over the last 30 years, it is important to keep in mind that the absolute number of racially homogamous marriages also increased during the same time period. The percentage of marriages in the United States that are racially homogamous has thus remained relatively stable and at a very high level. In spite of the increase in the number of interracial marriages, fewer than 3% of U.S. marriages in 1990 were interracial.

Summary and Discussion

Ethnic and racial intermarriage is often considered to be the single most important, and final, process in the assimilation of racial and ethnic groups. In the "old" intermarriage regime in the United States, this appears to have been the case. The cumulative effect of increasing rates of intermarriage among Americans of the various European White ethnic ancestries has successfully blurred the historically salient barriers among Americans of European descent. Within this population, "intermarriage" is now the norm and ethnicity largely irrelevant in marital choices.

Many of the European ancestry groups were, however, once thought to be racially distinct and unassimilable. Why did intermarriage among Americans of European ancestry become so common? There were several demographic factors involved. The major waves of immigration before and after the turn of the century were comprised of immigrants from numerous countries of origin. Sex ratios among arrivals from some countries were sometimes far from even.

The ethnic diversity among the immigrants and the uneven sex ratios both heightened the odds of intermarriage. The hiatus in immigration from the 1930s until the 1960s also meant that the proportion of children with complex ancestries—one of the main outcomes of intermarriages—was able to accelerate across generations without having to compete with a continuing influx of new immigrants with clearly defined ancestries. The hiatus in immigration also meant that the European ethnic ancestry groups aged as cultural groups in the American context, and so definitive cultural distinctions such as unique languages largely disappeared. In addition, during much of the first two-thirds of the Twentieth century, high levels of social and economic mobility dispersed immigrants and their descendants across the full educational and economic distributions (see Massey p. 77).

Now, however, the intermarriage regime is different. First, intermarriage across racial lines remains relatively rare and the upward trend in racial intermarriage is slow. In 1960, the percentage of marriages that were interracial was a minuscule 0.4%. By 1990, a full generation later, only 2.9% of the nation's 52 million married couples consisted of spouses from two of the five major racial categories. Although the percentages of homogamous marriages involving White Americans dropped, the percentages of homogamous marriages involving Americans of Asian, of Hispanic, and of "Other" racial descent increased. As a result, although racial diversity *among* homogamous marriages has increased, the overall proportion of all marriages in the United States that are racially homogamous has remained high.

Second, there are good reasons to expect that the upward trend in racial intermarriage will remain slow. The United States has become a country of perpetual immigration (Massey, 1995). Not only are foreign-born Asians and Hispanics more likely to marry homogamously than native-born Asian and Hispanic Americans, the geographic clustering of the new immigrants (Frey, 1995) further heightens the odds of in-group marriage. High levels of immigration also help maintain culturally distinct markers such as non-English language usage among native-born as well as foreign-born group members (Stevens, 1992).

The absolute numbers of intermarriages between Black and non-Black Americans have, however, increased since 1960. Yet, the dramatic multiplication of the number of racial intermarriages involving Black men or Black women, particularly Black men, rests on such a low base that as of 1990, the vast majority of married Black men and married Black women had Black spouses. The persistence of the social and demographic factors that discourage intermarriage, e.g., socioeconomic disparities between Black Americans and others, and the segregation of Black Americans (Massey and Denton, 1993), does not portend a precipitous increase in intermarriage between Blacks and others anytime soon.

The numbers and percentages of American Indian interracial marriages have also increased, markedly so. However, this increase accompanies a transformation in the tendency of Americans to identify themselves as "American Indian." This transformation means that the interpretation of the trend in intermarriage, and the impact of the trend on, for example, the children's racial identification, is difficult to anticipate.

Third, the possible role of intermarriage as an assimilative force is being sapped by general changes in marriage behavior over the last century. Since about 1960, marriage has become rarer and shorter-lasting. The percentage of Americans who remain unmarried has increased. Age at marriage has increased among those who marry. Divorce rates increased throughout much of the century and have stabilized at a high level. Overall, Americans are spending a lower proportion of their adult lives in marriage. This "retreat from marriage" (Schoen and Weinick, 1993b) means that one of the main outcomes of intermarriage, a formally committed and intimate association between spouses of differing races with all that it implies about a deeper appreciation and tolerance of racial differences, is experienced for shorter periods of times within the partners' life spans. The retreat from marriage, which has been accompanied by a growth in nonmarital childbearing (Parnell et al., 1994) and a growth in single-parent households, means that fewer children are being raised and socialized in racially complex households than would otherwise be the case.

Sharp racial differences in the "retreat from marriage" (Lichter et al., 1991; Oropesa et al., 1994) are further sapping the potential of racial intermarriage as an assimilative force. The retreat from marriage is particularly apparent among Blacks (Bennett et al., 1989; Tucker and Mitchell-Kernan, 1995). Black men and women express less desire for marriage than Whites (South, 1993), are less likely to marry than Whites (Schoen and Kluegel, 1988), and among those who marry, Blacks marry at later ages than Whites (Koball, 1998). As the institution of marriage becomes less important in Americans' lives, and in Black American's lives in particular, the widening gap between the marriage behavior of the races further depresses the potential for racial intermarriage.

The old and new regimes of racial and ethnic marriage patterns in the United States are thus very different. The earlier regime of intermarriage started with caste-like levels of ethnic homogamy among Americans of various European descents but within three generations, intermarriage became the norm. The current marriage regime, on the other hand, is marked by high and fairly stable levels of in-group marriage within the major ethnic and racial divisions of White, Black, Asian, and Hispanic, and there are few reasons to expect intermarriage rates across these divisions to accelerate quickly. The continuing arrival of foreign-born Asians and Hispanics will help maintain fairly high levels of homogamy within Asian and Hispanic groups. Although interracial marriages involving Black Americans have become more common, the vast majority of married Black Americans still have Black spouses. Finally, the "retreat from marriage" suggests that as fewer Americans, particularly Black Americans, marry, intermarriage may be losing its power to propel the assimilation of racial and ethnic groups.

The relative dearth of interracial marriages does not necessarily mean, however, that interracial relationships are not occurring or that the numbers of interracial children are not increasing. Cohabitation, for example, may be providing an alternative to marriage (McLanahan and Casper, 1995). There appears to be less homogamy among cohabitating couples than among formally married couples with respect to important dimensions such as age (Schoen and Weinick, 1993a). Perhaps the less formal nature of cohabitating relationships as compared to legal marriages means that relatively more cohabitating relationships are interracial. Whether interracial cohabitating relationships should be considered alongside interracial marriages as part of the process or product of the assimilation of ethnic and racial groups remains to be seen.

References

Alba, Richard D. 1995. "Assimilation's Quiet Tide." *The Public Interest, 119*: 3–18.

Alba, Richard D. and Reid Golden. 1986. "Patterns of Ethnic Marriage in the United States." *Social Forces,* 65:202–223.

Alba, Richard D. and Ronald C. Kessler, 1979. "Patterns of Interethnic Marriage Among American Catholics." Social Forces, 57:1124-40.

Anderson, Robert N. and Rogelio Saenz. 1994. "Structural Determinants of Mexican American Intermarriage, 1975–1980." *Social Science Quarterly,* 75:414–430.

Bennett, Neil, David E. Bloom, and Patricia H. Craig. 1989. "The Divergence of Black and White Marriage Patterns." *American Journal of Sociology,* 95:695–712.

Berscheid, E., K. K. Dion, E. Walster, and G. Walster. 1971. "Physical Attractiveness and Dating Choice: A Test of the Matching Hypothesis." *Journal of Experimental Social Psychology,* 7:173–189.

Bozon, M. and F. Héran. 1989. "Finding a Spouse. A Survey of How French Couples Meet." *Population,* 44:91–120.

Donato, Katharine M. 1990. "Recent Trends in U.S. Immigration: Why Some

Countries Send Women and Others Send Men." Presented at the Annual Meetings of the Population Association of America, Toronto, Canada.

Edmonston, Barry, Joshua Goldstein, and Juanita Tamayo Lott, eds. 1996. *Spotlight on Heterogeneity. The Federal Standards for Racial and Ethnic Classification. Summary of a Workshop*. Washington, DC: National Academy Press.

Farley, Reynolds. 1984. *Blacks and Whites. Narrowing the Gap?* Cambridge, MA: Harvard University Press.

Farley, Reynolds and William H. Frey. 1994. "Changes in the Segregation of Whites from Blacks." *American Sociological Review*, 59:23–45.

Fitzpatrick, Joseph P. and Douglas Gurak. 1979. *Hispanic Intermarriage in New York City: 1975*. New York City: Fordham University Hispanic Research Center.

Frey, William H. 1995. "The New Geography of Population Shifts." In Reynolds Farley, ed., *State of the Union. America in the 1990s*, Vol. II: Social Trends. New York: Russell Sage Foundation, pp. 271–336.

Gilbertson, Greta A., Joseph P. Fitzpatrick, and Lijun Yang. 1996. "Hispanic Intermarriage in New York City: New Evidence from 1991." *International Migration Review*, 30:445–459.

Glenn, Norval. 1982. "Interreligious Marriage in the United States: Patterns and Recent Trends." *Journal of Marriage and the Family*, 44:555–566.

Gordon, Milton M. 1964. *Assimilation in American Life*. New York: Oxford University Press.

Hout, Michael and Joshua R. Goldstein. 1994. "How 4.5 Million Irish Immigrants Became 40 Million Irish Americans: Demographic and Subjective Aspects of the Ethnic Composition of White Americans." *American Sociological Review*, 59:64–82.

Hwang, Sean Shong, Rogelio Saenz, and Benigno E. Aguirre. 1994. "Structural and Individual Determinants of Outmarriage among Chinese- , Filipino- , and Japanese-Americans in California." *Sociological Inquiry*, 64:396–414.

Hwang, Sean Shong, Rogelio Saenz, and Benigno E. Aguirre. 1995. "The SES Selectivity of Interracially Married Asians." *International Migration Review*, 24:469–491.

Jasso, Guillermina and Mark R. Rosenzweig. 1990. *The New Chosen People: Immigrants to the United States*. New York: Russell Sage.

Johnson, Colleen L. 1985. *Growing Up and Growing Old in Italian American Families*. New Brunswick, NJ: Rutgers University Press.

Kalmijn, Matthijs. 1993a. "Spouse Selection among the Children of European Immigrants: A Study of Marriage Cohorts in the 1960 Census." *International Migration Review*, 27:51–79.

Kalmijn, Matthijs. 1993b. "Trends in Black–White Intermarriage." *Social Forces,* 72:119–146.

Kerkhoff, A. C. 1964. "Patterns of Homogamy and the Field of Eligibles." *Social Forces,* 42:289–297.

Kitano, Harry H. L., Wai-Tsang Yeung, Lynn Chai, and Herbert Hatanaka. 1984. "Asian-American Interracial Marriage." *Journal of Marriage and the Family,* 46:179–190.

Koball, Heather. 1998. "Have African American Men Become Less Committed to Marriage? Explaining the Twentieth Century Racial Cross-Over in Men's Marriage Timing." *Demography,* 35:251–258.

Lichter, Daniel L., R. L. Anderson, and Mark D. Hayward. 1995. "Marriage Markets and Marital Choice." *Journal of Family, Issues* 16:412–431.

Lichter, Daniel T., Felicia B. LeClere, and Diane K. McLaughlin. 1991. "Local Marriage Markets and the Marital Behavior of Black and White Women." *American Journal of Sociology,* 96:843–867.

Lieberson, Stanley and Mary C. Waters. 1988. *From Many Strands: Ethnic and Racial Groups in Contemporary America.* New York: Russell Sage Foundation.

Mare, Robert D. 1990. "Five Decades of Educational Assortative Mating." *American Sociological Review,* 56:15–32.

Massey, Douglas S. 1995. "The New Immigration and Ethnicity in the United States." *Population and Development Review,* 21:631–652.

Massey, Douglas S. and Nancy A. Denton. 1993. *American Apartheid: Segregation and the Making of the Underclass.* Cambridge, MA: Harvard University Press.

McLanahan, Sara and Lynne Casper. 1995. "Growing Diversity and Inequality in the American Family." In Reynolds Farley, ed., *State of the Union. America in the 1990s*, Vol. II: Social Trends. New York: Russell Sage Foundation, pp. 1–46.

Nagel, Joane. 1995. "American Indian Ethnic Renewal: Politics and the Resurgence of Identity." *American Sociological Review,* 60:947–965.

Oropesa, R. S., Daniel T. Lichter, and Robert N. Anderson.1994. "Marriage Markets and the Paradox of Mexican American Nuptiality." *Journal of Marriage and the Family,* 56:889–907.

Padilla, Felix M. 1984. "On the Nature of Latino Ethnicity." *Social Science Quarterly,* 65:651–664.

Pagnini, Deanna L. and S. Philip Morgan. 1990. "Intermarriage and Social Distance among U.S. Immigrants at the Turn of the Century." *American Journal of Sociology,* 96:405–432.

Parnell, Allan M., Gray Swicegood, and Gillian Stevens. 1994. "Nonmarital Pregnancy and Nuptiality in the United States." *Social Forces,* 73:263–288.

Passel, Jeffrey S. 1976. "Provisional Evaluation of The 1970 Census Count of American Indians." *Demography,* 13:397–409.

Passel, Jeffrey S. and Patricia A. Berman. 1986. "Quality of 1980 Census Data for American Indians." *Social Biology,* 33:163–82.

Roberts, Robert E. T. 1994. "Black–White Intermarriage in the United States." In Walter R. Johnson and D. Michael Warren, ed., *Inside the Mixed Marriage. Accounts of Changing Attitudes, Patterns, and Perceptions of Cross-Cultural and Interracial Marriages*, Lanham, MD: University Press of America, pp. 25–80.

Ruggles, Stevens and Matthew Sobek. 1995. *Integrated Public Use Microdata Series: Version 1.0. [MRDF].* Minneapolis: Social History Research Laboratory, University of Minnesota.

Saenz, Rogelio, Sean Shong Hwang, and Benigno E. Aguirre. 1994. "In Search of Asian War Brides." *Demography,* 31:549–559.

Sandefur, Gary D. 1986. "American Indian Intermarriage." *Social Science Research,* 15:347–371.

Schoen, Robert and Lawrence Cohen. 1980. "Ethnic Endogamy among Mexican American Grooms: A Reanalysis of Generational and Occupational Effects." *American Journal of Sociology,* 86:359–366.

Schoen, Robert and James R. Kluegel. 1988. "The Widening Gap in Black and White Marriage Rates: The Impact of Population Composition and Differential Marriage Propensities." *American Sociological Review,* 53:893–907.

Schoen, Robert and Robin M. Weinick. 1993a. "Partner Choice in Marriages and Cohabitations." *Journal of Marriage and the Family,* 55:408–411.

Schoen, Robert and Robin M. Weinick. 1993b. "The Slowing Metabolism Of Marriage: Figures from 1988 U.S. Marital Status Life Tables." *Demography,* 30:737–746.

Schoen, Robert and John Wooldredge. 1989. "Marriage Choices in North Carolina and Virginia, 1969–71 and 1979–81." *Journal of Marriage and the Family,* 51:465–481.

South, Scott J. 1993. "Racial and Ethnic Differences in the Desire to Marry." *Journal of Marriage and the Family,* 55:357–370.

Stevens, Gillian. 1992. "The Social and Demographic Context of Language Use in the United States." *American Sociological Review,* 57:171–185.

Stevens, Gillian, Dawn Owens, and Eric C. Schaefer. 1990. "Physical Attractiveness and Education in Marriage Choices." *Social Psychology Quarterly,* 53:62–70.

Stevens, Gillian and Gray Swicegood. 1987. "The Linguistic Context of Ethnic Endogamy." *American Sociological Review,* 52:73–82.

Sung, Betty Lee. 1990. "Chinese American Intermarriage." *Journal of Comparative Family Studies,* 21:337–352.

Tucker, M. Belinda and Claudia Mitchell-Kernan. 1990. "New Trends in Black American Interracial Marriage: The Social Structural Context." *Journal of Marriage and the Family,* 52:209–218.

Tucker, M. Belinda and Claudia Mitchell-Kernan, eds. 1995. *The Decline in Marriage Among African Americans.* New York: Russell Sage Foundation.

U. S. Bureau of the Census. 1966. *1960 Census of Population.* Subject Reports, Marital Status. Washington, DC: U.S. Government Printing Office.

U. S. Bureau of the Census. 1972. *1970 Census of Population.* Vol. II. Subject Reports, Marital Status. PC(2)-4C. Washington, DC: U.S. Government Printing Office.

U. S. Bureau of the Census. 1985. *1980 Census of Population.* Vol. II. Subject Reports, Marital Status. Final Report PC92-4E. Washington, DC: U.S. Government Printing Office.

U. S. Bureau of the Census. 1994. *The Hispanic Population in the United States: March 1993.* Current Population Studies. Washington, DC: U.S. Government Printing Office.

U.S. Office of Management and Budget. 1977. "Statistical Directive No. 15: Race and Ethnic Standards for Federal Agencies and Administrative Reporting." *Federal Register* 43: 19269–19270.

Warren, Bruce L. 1966. "A Multiple Variable Approach to the Assortative Mating Phenomenon." *Eugenics Quarterly,* 13:285–290.

Waters, Mary C. 1990. *Ethnic Options: Choosing Identities in America.* Berkeley: University of California Press.

Wojtkiewicz, Roger A. and Katharine M. Donato. 1995. "Hispanic Educational Attainment: The Effects of Family Background and Nativity." *Social Forces,* 74:559–574.

Chapter 9

Sixty-five Plus in the U.S.A.

Cynthia M. Taeuber

Diversity and growth—those are two words that describe America's elderly population. We tend to say "the elderly" as if they were all the same. But they are not. In 1990, there were over 31 million elderly Americans, people aged 65 or older. By 2000 the elderly numbered 35 million. The experience of aging is different for different groups. Elderly men and women tend to have quite different life circumstances, for example. Some older people, especially oldest old single women, tend to have significant health and financial problems. Others, especially married couples, tend to be more economically secure and healthy. "The elderly," like other age groups, are mixed in their needs, abilities, and resources.

Growth is another aspect of the elderly population. America has been a nation of youth. In colonial times, half the population was under age 16. Most never reached old age. Now, America is an aging society. In 1990 and 2000, less than one in four Americans were under age 16. Half were 33 or older. The elderly population is growing, especially the oldest old, the term commonly used for those aged 80 or 85 and over (U.S. Bureau of the Census, 1990).[1]

Numerical Growth

The United States has been riding a demographic roller coaster since World War II. In the 1930s the United States had a baby bust, in the 1950s a baby boom, in the 1970s a baby bust, and in the 1980s a baby boomlet (also called the baby boom echo) (Figure 9.1). The absolute sizes and relative difference in the age groups relate to the kinds of activities and the needs of our population.

Figure 9.1 U.S. Population Pyramids 1990a, 2010b, 2050b
(Population in millions).

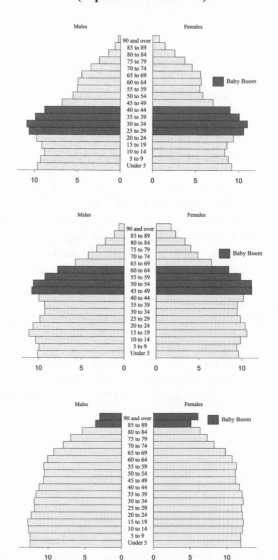

aU.S. Bureau of the Census 1990 Census of Population and Housing. Series CPH 74 "Modified and Actual Age, Sex, Race and Hispanic Origin Data."
bU.S. Bureau of the Census, Jennifer C. Day, "Population Projections of the United States: 1992 to 2050," Current Population Reports, P25-1092, U.S. Government Printing Office, Washington, DC, 1992 (middle series projections).

In 1990 and 2000, we had about as many children age 10 and under as we had persons aged 60 or older. The baby boom, those born from 1946 to 1964 (aged 26 to 44 in 1990), has moved into middle age. They are one-third of the American population. They have mostly finished with schooling now, are in the labor force, and are raising families. The baby bust is completing high school and are entering college and the labor force (born 1965 to 1975). One in eight Americans is 65 years or older. That's just under 35 million people. Figure 9.1 tells us about the demographic forces that bear on individual and public-policy choices.

Most babies will survive to their elder years, but there are differences in life expectancy. Based on the mortality experience of 1990, life expectancy at birth was 79 years for White women, but it is only 67 years for Black men. Back in 1900, average life expectancy was about 49 years[2]. As life expectancy has increased, issues about the quality of life of older people face us. With increasing life expectancy, we can expect to see more long-term chronic illness, disability, and dependency. As a result, it is increasingly likely that more people in their 50s and 60s will have surviving frail relatives who will need care.

The growth of the oldest old population is stunning. One in 31 (Day, 1992) Americans was 80 years or older in 2000; by 2050, at least 1 in 12 could be 80 years or older[3]. Three million Americans were 85 years or older in 1990 and 4.2 million in 2000. One million were 90 or older compared to almost 1.5 million a decade later. Over 50,000 people reported in the 2000 Census that they were aged 100 years or older, nearly triple the number in 1980. In 1990, four in five centenarians were women. Four in five were White. The oldest old are projected to be the fastest growing part of the elderly population well into the next century. We will experience steady but undramatic growth of the total elderly population from 1990 to 2010. It is the year 2011 when the first of the baby boom reaches age 65 (Figure 9.1). Under middle-series projections, in 2010, we assume reduced mortality of men in their 50s, 60s, and 70s. As a result, we'll probably see more elderly married couples unless divorce rates increase for this age group.

After 2010, growth of the elderly population will be more dramatic as the baby boom becomes the grandparent boom. From 2010 to 2030, the elderly population could grow almost five times faster than the total population.

After 2030, we will see the final phase of the gerontological explosion. The baby boom will be aged 65 to 84 from 2030 to 2050. In 2050, the baby boom will be the great-grandparent boom, 85 years and over (Figure 9.1). The young old population will decrease as the baby bust enters this age group.

The discussion above provides a quick glimpse of the future. Now we will look at the 1990 situation in more detail, with comparisons to 2000 where possible. America's most populous states are also the ones with the most elderly (Figure 9.2). In both 1990 and 2000, nine states had more than one million

Figure 9.2
Total Population Aged 65 Years and Over: 1990

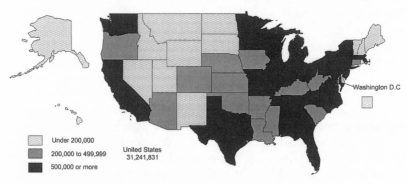

Washington D.C

Under 200,000

200,000 to 499,999

500,000 or more

United States
31,241,831

Source: U.S. Bureau of the Census, 1990 Census of Population and Housing.

Figure 9.3
Percent Change in Population Aged 65 Years and Over: 1980 to 1990

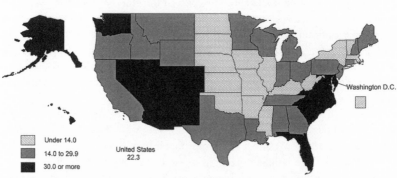

Washington D.C.

Under 14.0

14.0 to 29.9

30.0 or more

United States
22.3

Source: U.S. Bureau of the Census, 1980 and 1990 Censuses of Population: for 1980, "General Population Characteristics," PC80-1-B1, Table 67; for 1990, Summary Tape File 1A.

Figure 9.4
Total Population Aged 65 Years and Over: 1990

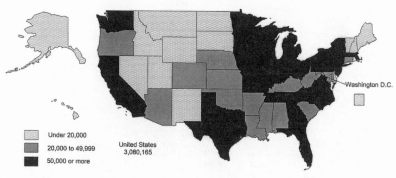

Under 20,000

20,000 to 49,999

50,000 or more

United States
3,080,165

Washington D.C.

Source: U.S. Bureau of the Census, 1990 Census of Population and Housing.

Figure 9.5
Percentage of Persons Aged 65 Years and Over Living Alone

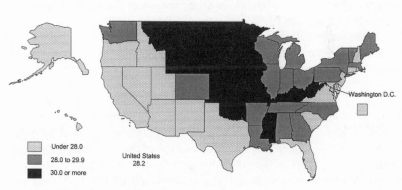

Under 28.0

28.0 to 29.9

30.0 or more

United States
28.2

Washington D.C.

Source: U.S. Bureau of the Census, 1990 Census of Population and Housing.

Figure 9.6
Percent of Elderly in Nursing Homes by Age Group: 1990

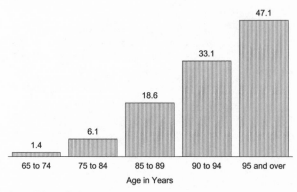

Source: U.S. Bureau of the Census.

elderly. Florida had both a large number and the highest proportion with 18% of their population 65 years or older. Midwestern farm states had a higher proportion of elderly than most other states because of out-migration of young persons.

Of course, the elderly population has been increasing since Colonial times. What is new is the rapid pace of aging. Since 1900, the total American population has tripled. The elderly population increased by a factor of ten, from 3 million in 1900 to 31 million in 1990 and 35 million in 2000. The elderly population increased by 22% over the decade of the 1980s (Figure 9.3) and another 12% in the 1990s.

Those states with a large number of elderly also had large numbers of persons 85 years or older (Figure 9.4). Eight states had more than 100,000 oldest old. In most states, about 1% was aged 85 years or older. The Midwestern farm states had about 2%.

Elderly women are more likely than elderly men to live alone. The District of Columbia had the highest proportion of elderly living alone (35%) in 1990 (Figure 9.5). The farm states of the Midwest, as well as a few Southern and Western States, had 30% to 31% of their elderly living alone. Hawaii, with only 17% of the elderly living alone, had the Nation's lowest proportion. The Midwestern farm states also have a high percentage of their total populations living in nursing homes, which may be related to out-migration of the younger population.

In 1990 and 2000, nearly 1.6 million elderly people lived in nursing homes in the United States though the percent of those 65 and over who lived in nursing homes declined from 5.1 to 4.5. Nearly half of these, 740,000 persons in 1990 and 773,000 in 2000, were aged 85 and over. The likelihood of living in a nursing home increases with age (Figure 9.6). In 1990 less than 2% of the 65- to 74-year-old population lived in nursing homes in 1990, compared with about 6% of those aged 75 to 84. It is after age 85 that the proportions are more significant with about 1 in 5 (18.6%) persons aged 85 to 89 living in nursing homes as did just under half (47.1%) of persons aged 95 or older. Still, these proportions are lower than what may assume to be the case for the population at such advanced ages. Women were about four-fifths of persons aged 85 and over living in nursing homes.

Figure 9.7
Parent Suport Ratio
Persons 85 and over per 100 persons aged 50 to 64 years old

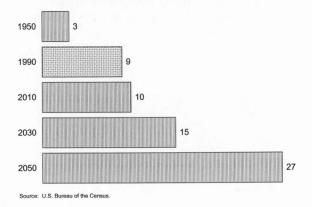

Source: U.S. Bureau of the Census.

Familial Support

In the future, we can expect the four-generation family to become more common. More children will know their grandparents and even their great-grandparents. There is no historical precedent for this.

It is increasingly likely that more and more people, especially those in their 50s and 60s will have surviving parents, aunts, and uncles. In 1950, there were 3 people aged 85 or older per 100 people aged 50 to 64 years (Figure 9.7). In 1990, there were 9 oldest old per 100 people aged 50 to 64 years. By the middle of the next century, there would be about 27 per 100 in the United States. Not only has the number of oldest old increased, but the number needing care has also increased. Care is now given for more years than was usual in the 1950s. Already, the problem of parent care is affecting workers, especially women who provide most of the care for elderly relatives. A Census Bureau study using 1986 data from the Survey of Income and Program

Participation found that about 4.4 million elderly persons needed assistance with one or more everyday activities, such as dressing, eating, personal hygiene, preparing meals, and getting around outside the house (Hapine et al., 1990)[4]. There is a strong relationship between age and the need for personal assistance with everyday activities. About half of the oldest old, those 85 and older, are frail and need assistance (Figure 9.8). More people in their 50s and 60s will be facing the physical difficulties of helping the frail oldest old move about. Within each age category, women were more likely to need assistance than men. Additionally, women have more years of expected dependency than men (Katz et al., 1983).

Figure 9.8
Percent of Elderly Needing Assistance
WIth Everyday Activities by Age Group: 1986

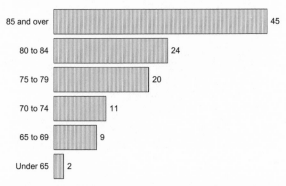

Source: U.S. Bureau of the Census, "The Need for Personal Assistance with Everyday Activities: Recipients and Caregivers,"
Current Population Reports, Series P-70, No. 19, U.S. Government Printing Office, Washington DC, 1990, Table B.

The elderly of the future may be quite different in this respect from the elderly of today. Data from the research of Kenneth Manton and his colleagues at Duke University (Manton et al., 1993a & b). suggest limitations to activities from disabilities may have decreased significantly in the decade of the 1980s, even among the oldest old. It appears this is partially a result of increased use of mechanical aids, improved medical technology (such as cataract operations and methods of rehabilitation of victims of strokes), and better health behaviors. As we learn more about health behaviors and implement what we learn, it could make a difference in the future. It appears increased educational attainment is the driving force behind the apparent improvements, and the use of mechanical aids may be a multiplier.

Family support is not a one-way street. Grandparents often provide regular financial and babysitting support to their adult children and grandchildren.

In 1987, American grandparents provided primary babysitting care for nearly 2 million children. Grandparents have taken their adult children and more than 3 million grandchildren to live in their homes.

Diversity of the Elderly Population

The 33 million Americans who are 65 years or older differ in their social and economic characteristics. In an increasingly interdependent and aging world, the United States is remarkable for the diversity of its older population. We will need more understanding of our differences and similarities. It is never easy to arrive at a shared vision where there are strong differences, but that is our challenge. The pace and direction of demographic changes will create compelling social, economic, and ethical choices for individuals, families, and governments in the next century.

Race and Ethnicity

Figure 9.9
Percent White Non-Hispanic of the Total Population
65 and Over: 1980-2050

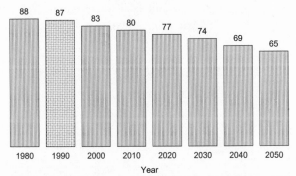

Source: U.S. Bureau of the Census, 1980 from 1980 Census of Population; 1990 from "U.S. Population Estimates by Age, Sex, Race, and Hispanic Origin: 1980 to 1991," Current Population Reports, P25-1095; 2000 to 2050 from Jennifer C. Day, "Projections of the United States, by Age, Sex, Race, and Hispanic Origin: 1992 to 2050," Current Population Reports, P25-1092, U.S. Government Printing Office, Washington, DC, 1992 (middle series projections).

Today's elderly population is predominately White (Figure 9.9). We can expect to see more racial diversity and more persons of Hispanic origin within America's elderly population in the coming years than we saw in 1990. In 1990, 87% of elderly persons were non-Hispanic Whites. That could decrease to 65% by the middle of the next century. Additionally, we expect an increasingly larger proportion of the elderly population to be Hispanic (may be of any race) as immigrants age.

Figure 9.10
Percentage of the Population that is 65 Years and Over,
By Race and Hispanic Origin: 1990

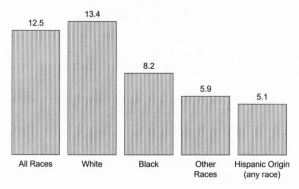

Source: U.S. Bureau of the Census, 1990 Census of Population Housing, Series CPH-L-74.

Figure 9.11
Elderly Hispanics, by Age and Type of Origin: March 1992
(in thousands)

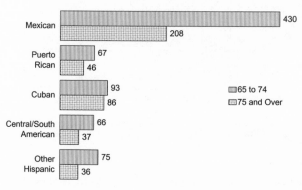

Note: Hispanics may be of any race.

Source: U.S. Bureau of the Census, Data consistent with "The Hispanic Population in the United States: March 1992",
Current Population Reports, P20-465RV, U.S. Government Printing Office, Washington, D.C., 1993

Nationally, Whites have the highest proportion elderly (Figure 9.10). One in 8 Whites were 65 years or older in 1990. By contrast, only 8% of Blacks and 5% of Hispanics were elderly. The demographic processes of fertility and mortality are important to understanding these percentages. Given the race/ethnic fertility differentials discussed earlier (Swicegood and Morgan, page 99), the White population is older on average than the Black and Hispanic populations. To the extent that persons of color die at younger ages than Whites (Rogers, page 129), then Whites will have a better chance of becoming as elderly or the oldest old. The Hispanic population is diverse itself. More than half of the Hispanic elderly population is of Mexican origin (Figure 9.11). Among the origin types, Cubans, on average, are the most aged. Six percent of the total Cuban population was 75 years or older in 1990.

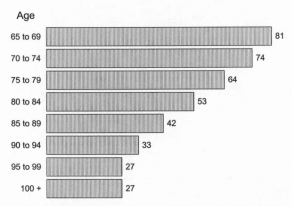

Source: U.S. Bureau of the Census, 1990 Census of Population and Housing, Series CPH-L-74, "Modified and Actual Age, Sex, Race, and Hispanic Origin Data."

Gender Differences

Figure 9.12
Number of Men Per 100 Women, by Age: 1990

Elderly women outnumbered elderly men by about 3:2 in 1990 and 2000. The difference increases with age (Figure 9.12). Elderly men are more likely than women to be living in a family. After age 75, most men are married, but most women are widowed and living alone. The death of a husband often marks the point of economic reversals for the surviving wife. In the future, we can expect to see a larger proportion of women, especially Black women, who have never married, as the never-married women in the population age.

Another reason for the overrepresentation of women is the higher death rates at younger ages for men, particularly Black men.

Figure 9.13
Income of Elderly Householders Living Alone, by Age and Sex: 1990

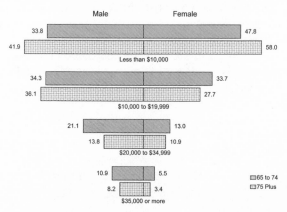

Source: C. DeNavas and E. Welniak, U.S. Bureau of the Census, "Money Income of Households, Families, and Persons in the United States: 1990," Current Population Reports, Series P-60, No. 174, U.S. Government Printing Office, Washington, DC, July 1991, Table 8.

Income and Poverty

The income picture for the elderly population is mixed. Overall, the economic position of the elderly has improved since the 1970s (Littmann, 1991). The elderly have substantially greater assets on average than the nonelderly, especially when the value of their homes are considered (Eargle, 1990). At the same time, the elderly, along with children, are the least likely to get out of poverty (Short and Littmann, 1991). Not everyone within the elderly population shared equally in the income gains that occurred overall since the 1970s. The elderly who live alone are more likely than elderly married couples to have low incomes. Most of the elderly living alone are women who are generally less economically secure than elderly men (Figure 9.13). Three in four elderly poor are women. Nearly 3 in 5 women 75 years and over had incomes of less than $10,000 in 1990.

Other subgroups also differ. Married couples, especially White married couples, have lower poverty rates than elderly living alone (most elderly unrelated individuals live alone) (Figure 9.14). Poverty is lowest for elderly White men aged 65 to 74 years, less than 5%. Black and Hispanic women have higher poverty rates than White women aged 65 to 74. The economic situation for elderly Black women who are poor has been especially intractable in that their poverty rates have not improved over the decade (Radner, 1991; Ryscavage, 1991). Among the elderly 75 years and older, the poverty rate in 1990 for Black women was 44% compared with 17% for White women and 8% of White men. The vast majority of these women are widowed and live alone.

The nation had 3.8 million elderly with incomes below the poverty level in 1989 and an estimated 3.4 million in 2000 (Dalaker, 2001). The largest states tend to have the largest number of poor elderly. Four states had more than 200,000 poor elderly. They were Texas, New York, Florida, and California. Alaska had the smallest number of poor elderly.

Figure 9.14

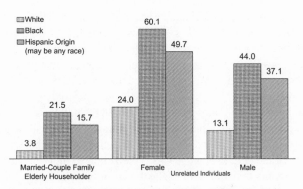

Source: U.S. Bureau of the Census, Mark Littman, "Poverty in the United States: 1990," Current Population Reports, Series P-60, No. 175, U.S. Government Printing Office, Washington, D.C., 1991, Table 5.

**Elderly Poor Persons in 1990, by Household Relationship,
Race and Hispanic Origin**

Nationally, nearly 13% of elderly were poor. In nine states, all Southern, more than one in five elderly were poor. Mississippi had 29% poor elderly, the highest proportion among the states. Louisiana and Alabama each had 24 percent poor. California, Alaska, and Connecticut had 7% to 8% poor elderly, the lowest levels in the nation.

Education

Educational attainment within the elderly population is increasing significantly. Sixty-three percent of persons aged 65 to 69 had completed at least a high school education in 1990 compared with only 46% of persons 75 years and over. Four in 10 persons aged 75 and older had an 8th grade education or less. Eleven percent of all elderly had completed four or more years of college (Kominski, 1991).

The encouraging news is the proportion of the elderly population with at least a high school education will increase significantly in coming years because younger age groups tend to have completed more years of schooling. More than 8 in 10 people aged 25 to 64 years old have at least a high school education. The better educated tend to be better off economically and stay healthier longer.

Conclusion

This chapter describes the characteristics of elderly in 1990 and makes some comparisons to data from the 2000 census. One lesson we are learning is that the life one leads as a younger person affects one's prospects in older age. As such, it is wrong to assume the older population of tomorrow will look the same as today's elderly. We can look at the characteristics of younger cohorts to predict change.

A key we have focused on is that the United States will have a much larger, even more diverse, older population in the future. This growth is a virtual certainty, not only in the United States but also throughout the world. The coming growth of the elderly is remarkable. We will need more understanding of our differences and our similarities. The directions we choose, the decisions we make, all will directly affect the quality and vitality of our lives for many decades. As individuals, and as a society, we will face a challenge to anticipate the changes in needs and desires of a diverse, aging population.

Notes

1. Throughout this chapter, counts of persons by age, sex, race, and Hispanic origin for the total United States are from the modified series. Counts for individual states are from Summary Tape File 1-A for 1990 and Summary File 1 for 2000. Characteristics from the 1990 Census in this chapter are from the Summary Tape Files.

2. National Center for Health Statistics.

3. Unless stated otherwise, the projections used in this chapter are from the middle series. The middle series does not anticipate significant changes in any of the components of population from recent trends.

4. The questions on need for personal assistance were whether a noninstitutionalized person required the help of another person, because of a health condition which had lasted three months or longer, to: (1) take care of personal needs such as dressing, eating or personal hygiene; (2) get around outside the household; (3) do light housework; (4) prepare meals; and (5) keep track of bills and money. These are referred to as "everyday activities" and are somewhat different than the lists of activities included in the measures, Activities of Daily Living (ADLs) and Instrumental Activities of Daily Living (IADLs).

References

Day, Jennifer, 1992. U.S. Bureau of the Census, "Population Projections of the United States, by Age, Sex, Race, and Hispanic Origin: 1992 to 2050," *Current Population Reports*, P25-1092, U.S. Government Printing Office, Washington, DC.

Dalaker, Joseph. 2001. "Poverty in the United States: 2000." *Current Population Reports*, P60-214, U.S. Government Printing Office, Washington, DC.

Eargle, Judith, 1990. U.S. Bureau of the Census, "Household Wealth and Asset Ownership: 1988," *Current Population Reports*, Series P-70, no. 22, U.S. Government Printing Office, Washington, DC.

Harpine, Cynthia, John McNeil, and Enrique Lamas, U.S. Bureau of the Census. 1990. "The Need for Personal Assistance with Everyday Activities: Recipients and Caregivers," *Current Population Reports*, Series P-70, no. 19, U.S. Government Printing Office, Washington, DC, June.

Katz, Sidney, et al., 1983. "Active Life Expectancy," *The New England Journal of Medicine*, November 17, pp. 1218–1224.

Kominski, Robert, 1991. U.S. Bureau of the Census, "Educational Attainment in the United States: March 1989 and 1988," *Current Population Reports*, Series P-20, no. 451, U.S. Government Printing Office, Washington, DC.

Littmann, Mark, 1991. U.S. Bureau of the Census, "Poverty in the United States: 1990," *Current Population Reports*, Series P-60, no. 175, U.S. Government Printing Office, Washington, DC, August.

Manton, Kenneth G., Larry S. Corder, and Eric Stallard. 1993a. "Estimates of Change in Chronic Disability and Institutional Incidence and Prevalence Rates in the U.S. Elderly Population from the 1982, 1984, and 1989 National Long-Term Care Survey," *Journal of Gerontology*, 1993, vol. 48, no. 4, pp. S153–S166.

———. 1993b. "Changes in the Use of Personal Assistance and Special Equipment from 1982 to 1988: Results from the 1982 and 1989 NLTCS," *The Gerontologist*, 1993, vol. 33, no. 2, pp. 168–176.

Radner, Daniel B. 1991. "Changes in the Income of Age Groups, 1984–1989," *Social Security Bulletin*, vol. 54, no. 12 (December), pp. 2–18.

Ryscavage, Paul. 1991. "Trends in Income and Wealth of the Elderly in the 1980s," paper presented to the American Society on Aging in New Orleans, March 18, 1991.

Short, Kathleen and Mark Littman, U.S. Bureau of the Census. 1990. "Transitions in Income and Poverty Status: 1985–1986," *Current Population Reports*, Series P-70, no. 18, U.S. Government Printing Office, Washington, DC, June 1990; also Series P-70, no. 24, U.S. Government Printing Office, Washington, DC, August 1991.

U.S. Bureau of the Census. 1990. Census of Population, Series CPH-L-74, *Modified and Actual Age, Sex, Race, and Hispanic Origin Data*.

Part IV

Implications and Conclusions

Chapter 10

Rethinking American Diversity: Conceptual and Theoretical Challenges for Racial and Ethnic Demography

Hayward Derrick Horton

Introduction

The increasing racial and ethnic diversity in the United States raises many issues for demographers and for society in general. Racial and ethnic identification, accurate enumeration, and cultural adaptation are clearly important topics that demographers have been addressing over the last two decades. However, one issue that has not been fully addressed is racism in the context of population and structural change. Accordingly, the purpose of this chapter is to discuss the implications of increasing diversity on the nature and magnitude of American racism in the Twenty-first century. Specifically, the following questions are addressed: (1) What is the relationship between increasing population diversity and racism in the United States? (2) What are the conceptual and theoretical implications of the incorporation of racism as a concept of analysis for future studies of racial and ethnic demography? and (3) What are the policy implications of this change in population composition for American racism?

The preceding chapters have highlighted many of the key issues that concern demographers. Without question, the changes in the definitions of racial categories, and the problems associated with intermarriage, self-identity, and immigration patterns are highly pertinent. Differentials in fertility and mortality by race are expected to continue well into the Twenty-first century. Racial segregation in housing and differences among the elderly by race are likewise expected to be problematic for many years to come.

However, all of these issues bring to mind a discussion that occurred in my undergraduate social demography course. At the end of a lecture on the dramatic increase in America's minority populations, a White student frantically raised his hand. He asked me a question that until that time had never been asked in any course that I had taught: *How many White people were there in the United States?* Sensing his dismay, I allayed his fears. I told him that there were approximately 200 million Whites in America; and, that Whites are likely to be the majority for the foreseeable future. The student let out a loud sigh that brought a roar of laughter from the entire class.

Interestingly enough, the student did not ask *why* Whites will continue to be the majority. If he had, I would have said that this majority status is likely to be maintained irrespective of whether Whites are a numerical minority (which in itself is highly unlikely) because of the racism that is inherent to the American social structure. This is because the White population controls the wealth, status, and power in America. Accordingly, this chapter addresses racism in the context of population and structural change in the United States.

The Social Demography of American Racism

Racism Defined

As noted in the preceding chapters, race is a social construction. Thus, the meaning of race varies across time and space. Similarly, the term racism has so many common and political uses that it is often confused with race, racial prejudice, and racial inequality. Sociologists who use the term are quite specific in its meaning however: *racism is a multilevel and multidimensional system of dominant group oppression which scapegoats the race of one or more subordinate groups* (van den Berghe, 1967; Blauner, 1972; Wilson, 1973; Feagin and Vera, 1995; Bonilla-Silva, 1997). One of the ironic implications of the systemic nature of racism is that in contemporary America, most members of the dominant population are not racist. Yet, they benefit from a system that differentially rewards and punishes society's members based upon race (Ture and Hamilton, 1992).

Applying the concept of racism to the study of racial and ethnic demography necessitates the usage of two accompanying terms: *population control* and *population power*. In this context, population control is not limited to the attempts to obtain or maintain an optimal population size (Bouvier, 1992; Cohen, 1995). Population *control* also means deliberate efforts by the dominant population to limit the size, inhibit or force the geographic mobility of, and/or deny citizenship to one or more subordinate or foreign populations. Population *power* refers to the ability to exercise population control, and to change the social structure so as to maintain the advantages of the dominant population[1]. It is important to note that population control and population power are not inherently racist concepts. It is the *why* and the *how* of the usage of the aforementioned that link them to racism. In short, the concept of racism becomes meaningful within the context of racial and ethnic demography via the application of population control and population power[2].

An Example of Racism, Population Control, and Population Power

Lieberson's classic, *A Piece of the Pie,* describes an excellent example of racism, population control and population power in the United States (Lieberson, 1980). The purpose of this study was to compare the experience of Blacks with White immigrants from 1880 to 1980. Specifically, Lieberson (1980) sought to empirically determine if the level of discrimination experienced by Blacks exceeded that faced by White immigrants. He in fact was able to document that this was the case. However, Lieberson also revealed the nature and extent of the reaction of American society to the unprecedented European immigration that occurred between the late 1800s and the early 1920s.

This immigration coincided with the transformation of the American industrial economy from an agrarian to an industrial base. In addition, this population settled into the places to which the political and economic power of the nation was shifting—the cities. In short, these immigrants were perceived to be a threat to the dominant population of that era (Lieberson, 1980).

Moreover, Lieberson (1980) provides overwhelming evidence of how the concept of race varies from one time and context to the next because the Southern, Central, and Eastern Europeans (hereafter, SCEs) who were coming to America in such great numbers *were not considered White*. It is important to note that this belief was not one held solely by the lay person. To the contrary, Lieberson documents how even the intelligentsia, sociologists included, provided "scientific" evidence that this "*race*" was genetically, culturally and socially inferior to "Whites." In this case, being White meant Northern or Western European (hereafter, NW).

In addition, Lieberson (1980) documents that the immigration quota system that was established in the 1920s limited and controlled the size of the SCE population. This was done for the sole purpose of maintaining the NW dominance in American society. In short, the SCEs faced *racism* rather than simply xenophobia or ethnocentrism.

Finally, Lieberson (1980) notes the process by which these people who were considered *sub-human* were eventually admitted to the family of the White race. This occurred when there was a dramatic influx of Blacks to the North in the form of the Great Migration. SCEs were pronounced White and joined the NWs in practicing racism against Blacks. Thus, despite their supposed inferiority, SCEs were embraced when there was a perceived greater "external" threat.

This example provides an understanding of the relationship between population and structural change and racism. Moreover, it provides an excellent parallel to contemporary America. Once again, American society is experiencing dramatic levels of immigration at a time of a transformation in its industrial base. What is needed at this point is a theoretical or conceptual framework that will facilitate an understanding of contemporary American diversity and the racism related thereto.

The Population and Structural Change Thesis

The population and structural change thesis argues that changes in the relative size of the minority population *interact* with changes in the social structure to exacerbate the level and nature of racial inequality in society (Horton, 1995). In the case of contemporary America, the dramatic increases in minority populations are occurring simultaneously with the transformation of the American economy from a manufacturing to a service/information industrial base. As was the case with the advent of the industrial revolution, workers have been, and will continue to be, displaced during the current transition (Bluestone and Harrison, 1982; Horton, 1995). Wilson (1987) cites *social dislocation* as a major reason for the high levels of un- and underemployment among Black blue-collar workers. However, the position held here is that social dislocation goes beyond the working class, Black or White, and is at best a partial explanation for racial inequality. In short, the changes in the American industrial economy are occurring at a time when the size of the *minority middle class* has likewise increased (Horton, 1995).

This means that for the first time in America's history, the middle class of the dominant population has to compete with its counterparts among America's minority populations (Bennett, 1987). In short, being White and college educated is no longer a guarantee to a "good" job.[3] Hence, it is in this context that racism in contemporary times emerges. The dominant population uses its power to maintain its position in the social structure. One manner of doing so is to change the "rules of the game" so as to benefit members of the dominant population (Franklin and Moss, Jr., 1994). Examples of these rule changes are the attacks on Affirmative Action and the passage of Proposition 209 in California. It is no coincidence that these attacks on provisions to protect minority rights have first occurred in the state that arguably is experiencing the most dramatic change in its economy and racial/ethnic composition. Moreover, it is the middle-class segment of the dominant population that is making the most strident cries of "reverse discrimination" and "quotas are unfair" (Blackwell, 1991). This flies in the face of the fact that until the establishment of Civil Rights laws in the mid-1960s, there was a *quota* of nearly 100% dominant population members for the good jobs in the United States (Wilson, 1980). Minorities were relegated to lower-status jobs or quasi-professional positions in service to their respective populations[4]. In short, population and structural changes function as triggering mechanisms for the use of population power and control to resurrect or fortify a racist social system.

Sociological Consequences of Racism in the Context of Population and Structural Change

The consequences of racism at any time are many (Feagin, et al., 1996). However, they are multiplied more so when society is undergoing dramatic population *and* structural change (Horton and Burgess, 1992). Here, only three will be addressed because they have likewise been discussed in prior chapters of this volume. They are: the meaning of Whiteness; what it means to be Black in America; and the immigration question.

THE MEANING OF WHITENESS. In reality it is almost artificial to discuss white identity in America separate from the meaning of being Black. Just as wealth and poverty are inextricably linked, so are Whites and Blacks. These two populations have become the bi-polar standards for wealth, status, and power in America. Other groups determine and measure their place(s) in the social structure based upon their proximity to, or distance from, these poles in the racial order (Bonilla-Silva, 1997). Nevertheless, for purposes of theoretical analysis, a separation of these two populations is useful.

Population and structural change have altered the meaning of "White" in American society. In part, this is a direct result of the presence of Latinos and their dramatic growth in American society. Since Latinos can, technically, be of any race, a distinction was made between race and Hispanic status in the last decennial Census. What has resulted is the practice of reporting two categories of Whites, one being a non-Hispanic category[5]. However, even before this practice, there has been the tendency to code persons from North Africa (e.g., Egypt, Libya) and the Middle East as White (U.S. Bureau of the Census, 1992).

Nevertheless, there is a significant discrepancy between census theory and racial practice in America (Anderson, 1988). Persons who are identifiably of North African or of Middle Eastern descent are not considered White by the general White population[6]. A recent example will help demonstrate the point that, to non-Europeans, *Whiteness* is a status that, at best, should be considered on loan. At the time of the Oklahoma City bombing in 1995, there was an immediate assumption that this crime was perpetrated by Arab terrorists.

Thus, Arab Americans were immediately suspect. One particularly Arab American professional was detained, harassed, and humiliated by FBI agents because he boarded a plane in Oklahoma City and had a connecting flight in London[7]. Similar suspicions of Iranian Americans arose during the Iranian hostage crisis in 1979 and numerous incidents occurred in connection with the World Trade Center/Pentagon attacks.

In short, instead of being White, these persons actually have a designation as "anything but Black." When the primary focus of the dominant population was the control of Blacks, other minority populations enjoyed an "honorary White status." As long as their numbers were few, then these non-European "Whites" could be tolerated. However, increasingly European Americans, the true dominant population in this society, exercise power and control over these non-Europeans in such a manner that brings into question the utility of the honorary White designation. Ironically, Europeans and descendants thereof, be they tourists, visitors, or illegal aliens, are never considered foreigners. Thus, by virtue of being "true" Whites, these foreigners achieve a level of acceptance in American society that eludes even the "honorary Whites," who were born in the United States[8].

THE MEANING OF BLACKNESS. Like White racial identity, population and structural change in the context of racism are changing the meaning of Blackness in America as well. Black ethnicity is a topic that has been addressed for some time. Economist Thomas Sowell (1980) argued that there are three distinct groups of Blacks: the descendants of slaves, free Blacks, and West Indians. Moreover, he maintains that a disproportionate number of Black leaders have come from the latter two groups.

However, the greatest change in Black identity may stem from two other contemporary trends. The first is the practice of many Blacks to refer to themselves as *"African Americans."* This trend was started by a national Black elite (politicians and intelligentsia) who apparently felt there was a need to emphasize the cultural ties of Blacks in America with Africa. It should be noted that most Blacks, not being part of the Black middle class (and certainly not the national Black elite), continue to use the term *Black*. In fact, even many educated Blacks use the terms interchangeably. Ironically, this trend has had just the opposite effect. Many West Indians, who can identify with being Black, do *not* identify with the term African American. It is probably safe to assume that Blacks who are naturalized citizens from Africa likewise would not identify with this label. For instance, a Nigerian would probably consider herself as a *Nigerian American* instead. Thus, what has happened, for all practical purposes, is the *ethnicitization of a race* (Horton, 1992a). In short, like other hyphenated Americans blacks may now have a name that is capitalized. However, it is fair to say that it minimizes the significance of the Black experience in America (Franklin and Moss, Jr., 1994). Blacks were, and continue to be, oppressed in this society because of their color, not their culture (Massey and Denton 1993; Feagin and Vera, 1995). The new group designation fails to appreciate this fact.

The second trend that is changing Black identity is the increase in the population of Black-White parentage. It is important to note that most Blacks have some White ancestry (Bennett, 1987; Spickard, 1989). Such was the nature of slavery that many White men, and more than a few White women, took sexual advantage of Black women and men (Blassingame, 1979). However, in contemporary times these couplings are generally of mutual consent (Spickard, 1989). Usually of the Black male–white female variety, the children of these unions are increasingly wanting to be designated as mixed as opposed to simply Black. This is not surprising. In this society, as in most others, it is the mothers who have the primary responsibility of passing on the cultural identity (Billingsley, 1992). It would follow that the White mothers would want their mixed offspring to be designated as "anything but Black" due to the social disadvantages of Black status. This is supported by the fact that there doesn't appear to be the same level of concern in the cases when the parentage is that of White with other groups. Moreover, there is some evidence that this "anything but Black" sentiment is held with other groups as well[9].

It is maintained here that this rise in the number of mixed persons who wish not to be identified with being Black is *not* indicative of a more tolerant society. Just as the mulattos of the slavery era, these *neo-mulattos* are attempting to distance themselves from a category of people that appear to be permanently the object of racism in America (Feagin and Vera, 1995). However, the growth in this population does speak to the changing role of White women. They have benefited significantly from the Civil Rights movement. In short, the increase in the number of White women with Black mates is a testament to the increase in their own power in this society.

But similar arguments have been made for decades relative to the Black population (DuBois, 1899; Frazier, 1957; Horton, 1992a). However, more often than not, the determinant of differentiation has been social class. DuBois (1899) noted these class differences at the turn of the century. Frazier (1957) wrote a scathing critique of the Black middle class because of their mimicry of White upper-class society and their disdain for Blacks in the working and lower classes. However, in contemporary times, the sociologist who has gained the greatest notoriety on the issue of class differentiation within the Black population is Wilson (1980; 1987; 1996). It should be noted that the race versus class issue has been debated for nearly two decades and certainly will not be continued here (Willie, 1979; Horton, 1992b; Thomas and Horton, 1992; Horton, 1995). However, what has gotten less attention is the impact of the race–class *interaction* relative to Black ethnicity (Butler, 1991; Horton, 1992a).

In short, it has been over three decades since the passing of the historic 1964 Civil Rights legislation. For nearly three decades, class differences within the Black population have persisted in the context of social isolation and social dislocation (Wilson, 1987). Three decades is sufficient time for class differences to evolve into ethnic differences within the Black population (Horton, 1992a). This *ethnic divide* is likely to be one of the greatest challenges to both demographers and society as well. For the former, it may involve rethinking the implications of two segments of a population that are so different on sociodemographic indicators as to be considered separate populations altogether. For the latter, it may mean having to deal with an increasingly disadvantaged population without the benefit of the class of individuals who traditionally provided the leadership for both the Black underclass and society itself in addressing the problems thereof.

THE IMMIGRATION QUESTION. As noted in an earlier chapter in this volume, much of the increase in American diversity is due to the dramatic levels of immigration of Asians and Latinos. When one considers the sheer numbers of immigrants, let alone the rates of increase, it is clear that the United States will likely be a *very different place* in the Twenty-first century. However, the consideration of the impact of racism in the context of population and structural change might lead demographers to temper their predictions on the likelihood of the dominant population becoming a numerical minority in the coming century. Certainly, all things being equal this would likely happen. But all things have never been *equal* in the United States. The history of the use of power by the dominant population would suggest that controls will likely be implemented to forestall racial and ethnic minorities from becoming a numerical majority.

Moreover, it is a misperception to think that the United States could not secure its borders if it truly wanted to. It is clear that illegal immigration serves the interests of the dominant population. The true question that we as demographers might want to ask is, "At what point does increased levels of immigration, legal or illegal, become detrimental to the dominant population's interests?" Alternatively, we might ask, "What is the threshold of the dominant population's tolerance of immigration?"

Demographer Leon Bouvier presents a thoughtful and balanced discussion of the immigration issue in his recent book, *Peaceful Invasions* (Bouvier, 1992). He argues for placing limits on immigration, but *not* on the basis of race and ethnicity. Instead, he presents reasoned arguments on the impact of continued immigration at current or higher levels on the underclass, economic development, the polity, cultural adaptation, and the environment.

Bouvier correctly argues that the United States is long overdue for the establishment of a comprehensive, *population policy*. He also predicts that his arguments on immigration limits will be misconstrued as racist. It is maintained here that to avoid the discussion will leave the debate to those who are likely to exacerbate racial tensions.

Because of the magnitude and implications of this policy, its development cannot be left to the politicians. Once again, the historical demography of this nation lays the blame of America's legacy of racism at their feet (DuBois, 1935; Anderson, 1988; Blackwell, 1991). In this instance, it is the responsibility of demographers to lead. This leadership must take the form of sounding the alarm, initiating and developing a conceptual and theoretical framework that explicitly brings racism to the fore of demographic analysis.

The Challenge to Demography

> "Obviously the kind of knowledge that counts is not simply descriptive. The fleeting moment, the current event, possesses no significance except as related to past and future occurrences through systematic interpretation. For social knowledge to have value, it must comprehend the basic principles of society as opposed to the mere surface phenomena. Decisions made on the basis of superficial information are likely to yield results opposite to those expected." Kingsley Davis, *Human Society* 1948, p.16.

The above passage was written by a famous social demographer, Kingsley Davis, over 50 years ago. It is no less valid today than when written. In fact, given the dramatic population and structural changes that America is currently undergoing, one might argue that those words are more relevant than ever before. As demographers, the next decade promises to rewrite much of what we purport to know about racial and ethnic demography. And, as correctly noted in an earlier chapter in this volume, our demographic techniques do not provide us with the means of knowing what shape the new population reality is likely to take. Perhaps that is as it should be. As with any science, it is the development of *theory* that will be the litmus test of its relevance and viability. Thus, the greatest challenge that we demographers face is the development of the theories and concepts that will serve us well in the Twenty-first century. We must be able to explain these phenomena. And yes, like any good science, we must be able to *predict* demographic trends and phenomena. Of course, mathematical models alone *cannot* provide us with the knowledge and insight that we seek. But logically, why should they? To understand the complexity of *social* phenomena, it follows that we should employ *social* rather than mathematical models. To answer the major questions that are likely to arise in the next century, *we as demographers must set about the task of developing new demographic theories.*

In the case of racial and ethnic demography, it is maintained here that one of the concepts that facilitates theoretical development is *racism*. Unlike the demographic transition, the baby boom and bust, the met–nonmetropolitan turnaround, or any of the other major trends that we demographers have written about and debated, racism has consistently been an intrinsic element in the historical demography of the United States and the Western world. Moreover, there is ample evidence that it will play a major, if not pivotal, role in America's demographic future. Hence, this chapter considers the implications of the incorporation of racism as a concept of explanation in future studies of racial and ethnic demography.

Racism and the Demographic Significance of Culture

In earlier chapters in this volume, the issue of culture arose as an explanation of differentials by race, particularly between blacks and whites, in various demographic processes. In fact social scientists in general, and demographers in particular, are beginning to voice concerns and write about the need to include cultural explanations to account for the persistent (and generally highly significant) net effects of race in their various multivariate models[10].

Without question, culture should be part of the overall explanatory scheme in the demography of race and ethnicity. However, the question that we should ask is, "*Whose* culture are we making reference to?" Whereas it is a simple task to employ cultural explanations when all else fails, it does relatively little to advance the understanding of racial and ethnic demography. For instance, in the case of Black male mortality, demographers can cite the impact of an inner-city underclass culture that condones violent behavior. Yet, that explanation is only partially true. Missing from that explanation is the *culture of indifference* of the dominant population that relegates the Black, urban poor to high population density areas that are all but abandoned by the nonpoor (Wilson, 1996). These areas of high poverty concentration are devoid of jobs, quality schools, and hope. The primary form of "public safety" that this population receives is in the form of "controls" by the dominant population in an effort to contain it. In short, the dominant culture supports the existing, racist social order (Massey and Denton, 1993; Yinger, 1995). The dominant culture places an exceedingly low value on Black life (Hacker, 1992). Thus, any demographic analysis of this population that attempts to include culture as an explanation *must* include a discussion of racism in order to be complete.

Racism and the Demography of Racial Inequality

The incorporation of racism as a concept of explanation is likely to be highly fruitful for demographic studies of racial and ethnic inequality. In the context of diversity in the Twenty-first century, racism is expected to continue to be relevant to the allocation of wealth, status, and power. Of course, of these three, the most important is power. With power a population can obtain, or maintain, wealth and status.

As the respective minorities increase in number, *theoretically* so should their political influence. However, it is important to note that influence is not power. Thus, the true question is whether the dominant population will be willing to share power. An appreciation of the role that racism plays in the determination of the allocation of power will allow us to *"predict"* three likely scenarios for the future.

SCENARIO ONE: STABLE, BUT PERSISTENT, RACISM AT CURRENT LEVELS. In this scenario, the dominant population does not perceive the increase in the subordinate populations as a threat to its position in the social order. This would likely be the case if the rate of growth of the subordinate populations did not increase dramatically. Assuming that the rates of natural increase and immigration remained relatively stable, and general economic conditions do not deteriorate, racism should not substantially increase in magnitude. The only exception here would be if new immigrants began to deviate from their established migration streams.

SCENARIO TWO: DECREASING LEVELS OF RACISM. In this case, subordinate populations could increase gradually or dramatically, but not at a faster rate than the economy. Thus, despite their greater numbers, subordinate population members would not be perceived to be competing with dominant group members for employment opportunities. Again, this would assume that subordinate populations did not deviate from their established migration streams. It also assumes that subordinate populations did not dramatically increase in their overall levels of human capital so as to compete with dominant population members for relatively high status positions.

SCENARIO THREE: INCREASING LEVELS OF RACISM. This circumstance is likely to occur should the subordinate populations increase while there is a general downturn in the overall economy. Moreover, racism is expected to increase should subordinate populations establish new population streams; and/or if there is a dramatic improvement in their levels of human capital via selective migration or sustained social mobility. Manifestations of increased levels of racism would be: (1) the establishment of restrictive and/or punitive anti-immigration legislation; (2) the retrenchment in Civil Rights laws and practices; (3) explicit support of anti-subordinate population action by the major institutions in society, particularly government (federal, state, or local) and the media; and (4) the use of military force to restrict or eliminate immigration, or to generally contain subordinate populations.

It is important to note that the full potential of the use of racism as a concept of demographic analysis is not exhausted by the above. However, these ideas and examples underscore the fact that racism lends itself to such consideration because it is inherent to the social structure and thus has long been a part of the "population policy" of this society since its inception. The likelihood that the dominant population in the United States will lose or willingly relinquish its power is infinitesimal. Hence, racism as a concept greatly increases the ability of demographers to *predict* the consequences of increased racial and ethnic diversity in the context of population and structural change. Moreover, it is clear that demographers in general must take the lead in calling for a national debate on U.S. population policy.

Implications for the Future of Population Policy

Addressing the challenges presented by America's increasing racial and ethnic diversity will be one of the defining issues of the Twenty-first century. It also will probably be one of the most difficult. Why? Primarily because of the legacy of racism in this country's history. It is understandable that any discussion of population policy raises the suspicions of the various minorities. It is for this reason that an explicit discussion of racism in the historical demography of the country is necessary.

The first step toward the development of a population policy for the United States is to acknowledge that this country has had an implicit population policy all along: *the maintenance of White domination at the expense of the subordinate groups* (Franklin and Moss, Jr., 1994; Omi and Winant, 1994). In contemporary times the policy has become more subtle, but it is nevertheless consistent with that goal. Yet, using the old policy as a point of departure, a discussion can ensue that facilitates the development of a new population policy for the United States that is based upon fairness and respect for human dignity. This would entail bringing to the table representatives from the various minority populations—including the Native Americans. There have to be discussions on the optimal population size for this society given its resources. And yes, on the table has to be the issue of limitations to immigration—both legal and illegal. However, when discussing this issue, equal time must be given to immigration from Europe and Canada (*invisible* immigrants) as well as from Latin America and Asia (*visible* immigrants). There also have to be discussions on birthrates and family planning. Education and *educational quality* likewise must be addressed. Most importantly, whatever policy that is put forward must not only have the *input* of the minority populations, but also reflect the *interests* of all segments of American society. This would entail a willingness of the dominant population to share the resources of this society in a more equitable fashion. In short, it would require that the dominant population do that which heretofore it has been unwilling to do: *to be fair with those that it has the power to control.*

Conclusion

The purpose of this chapter was to discuss the implications of increasing racial and ethnic diversity for the nature and magnitude of American racism in the Twenty-first century. The goal of this chapter was three-fold. First, the relationship between the increasing population diversity and racism was addressed. Second, the conceptual and theoretical implications of the incorporation of racism as a concept of analysis for future studies of racial and ethnic demography was examined. Finally, the chapter addressed the policy implications of increasing population diversity in the context of American racism.

It was maintained that racism in the context of demographic analysis must be accompanied by discussions of population control and population power. A dominant population in any society exercises population control and power when there is a threat to its position in the social structure. The *population and structural change thesis* was introduced as a means of explaining the social and demographic context within which racism functions and the consequences thereof.

The application of racism as a concept for future demographic studies has potential for rethinking how culture can be employed to explain racial differentials on a number of social and demographic indicators. It also has the potential for allowing demographers to make some predictions relative to the consequences of increased racial and ethnic diversity in the Twenty-first century.

Finally, the policy implications presented revolved around the idea of an equitable use of power by the dominant population. This entails bringing representatives of the various populations together to develop a population policy that represents the interests of all groups. Moreover, the history and nature of American racism make it necessary that demographers take the lead in the framing of a population policy for the nation.

Racism is a concept that is rarely used in demography. Perhaps because it is often misused in society in general or applied inconsistently in different contexts explains its absence in our field. Nevertheless, it is maintained that racism has considerable potential for advancing the demography of race and ethnicity. For instance, given that racism is distinct from race and racial inequality, theoretically demographic models could be developed that measure all three simultaneously. Thus, arguments advanced either by demographers or others on the declining impact of racism on racial inequality could be tested empirically.

More importantly, racism as a concept both facilitates and underscores the need for the development of *critical demography*. In this new paradigm, questions can be raised and issues can be addressed that don't appear to "fit" *conventional* demography. Critical demography allows for the development of theories and concepts that articulate the relationship between the social structure and the existence of dominant and subordinate populations. While not limited to the issue of racism, critical demography is the paradigm that is best suited for addressing the complex social and political issues related thereto. In short, while being mutually exclusive concepts, critical demography and racism can be mutually reinforcing. It is argued here that the study of racial and ethnic demography would be advanced as a consequence.

In conclusion, it is hoped that this chapter inspires other demographers to take up the challenge in applying this powerful concept, racism, in new and innovative ways. Given the dramatic population and structural changes that America is experiencing, it is clear that many of the existing concepts relative to racial and ethnic demography are limited at best. As we continue marching into the Twenty-first century, perhaps we will be better able to understand, explain and predict the consequences of racial and ethnic diversity by embracing the *"rword."*

Notes

1. It should be noted that there are many bases of power for the dominant population of any society. However, the ultimate expression of power is the use of force. Thus, in modern societies, it is military power that truly maintains the existing social order. Once the order has been firmly established, other forms of power (e.g., political) determine the manner in which scarce resources are distributed within the entire population. Nevertheless, it is the monopoly over military power that ensures the position of the dominant group in any society. This is less obvious in the United States because the prevailing social order has been in place for a relatively long period of time. The only serious internal threat to it occurred over 100 years ago in the form of the Civil War. Consequently, no minority population in the United States has true power. Instead, depending upon a myriad of factors, not the least of which being happenstance, minority populations have varying degrees of influence. Finally, it should be noted that this definition of population power builds upon the classic work of Max Weber. Interested readers should consult, *The Theory of Social and Economic Organization* (Weber, 1947) for further reference.

2. Examples of racism in the historical demography of American society are plentiful. The genocide practiced upon the Native American population, the enslavement of Africans, the repatriation of Mexicans, and immigration restrictions placed upon Asians are but a few. Unfortunately, there is no one study that brings all of these and other examples together from a demographic perspective. Interested readers should consult Snipp (1989), Daniels (1990), Franklin and Moss, Jr. (1994), and Horton (1995).

3. By "good" job I mean a relatively stable and well-paying position in the labor force with benefits (e.g., medical, dental, insurance, etc.).

4. This was evident as early as 1899 in DuBois' classic, *The Philadelphia Negro*. DuBois reported that Blacks, irrespective of educational attainment, skills, or experiences were systematically excluded from all but the most undesirable jobs. Blau and Duncan's, *The American Occupational Structure* (1967), demonstrated that Blacks from middle-class origins were more likely to experience *downward*, rather than upward, mobility. Feagin and Sikes', *Living with Racism: The Black Middle Class Experience* (1994) document a renewed effort on the part of the dominant group to exclude Blacks from opportunities in contemporary times.

5. Ironically, in the 1970 Census, Latinos were inadvertently categorized as Whites and thereby were unidentifiable. However, the change in the "Hispanic" category from a race to an ethnicity has practically resulted in a similar, though purposeful, procedure.

6. Only the relatively small size of the population of North African and Middle Eastern Americans has spared them of the type of discrimination historically reserved for Blacks.

7. In the final analysis, the true suspect was a "real" American with ties to the anti-government White militia movement.

8. For an alternative perspective on the meaning of Whiteness, readers should consult Alba (1990) and Waters (1990).

9. Tiger Woods, a professional golf superstar of Black and Asian parentage, has similarly created a designation for himself that essentially says "anything but Black": *cablinasian*. Ironically enough, his new racial category did not allow him to escape the racist slur that was made by one of his fellow golfers. It should be noted that the reference was to his Black rather than his Asian heritage.

10. Wilson (1991), a nondemographer, was perhaps the most prominent scholar to call for a return to culture as a causal factor of the plight of the disadvantaged. He argued that the attack on Moynihan (1967) during the 1960s, primarily led by Ryan's classic, *Blaming the Victim* (1971), caused sociologists to refrain from discussions of culture for fear of being labeled as racists. Wilson goes on to contend that in the interim, conservative scholars, journalists, and politicians have filled the vacuum and have dominated the culture debate. On the other hand, the unwillingness of sociologists (at least those in the center and on the left politically) to acknowledge the

cultural component leaves them with relatively obtuse, structural arguments. Structural arguments appear weak and perhaps nonsensical to an American public that has grown accustomed to three decades of simplistic, conservative and mean-spirited propaganda about the poor (Katz, 1989; Wilson, 1996).

References

Alba, Richard D. 1990. *Ethnic Identity: The Transformation of White America*. New Haven: Yale University Press.

Anderson, Margo J. 1988. *The American Census: A Social History*. New Haven: Yale University Press.

Bennett, Lerone. 1987. *Before the Mayflower: A History of Black America*. Chicago: Johnson Publishing Co.

Billingsley, Andrew. 1992. *Climbing Jacob's Ladder: The Enduring Legacy of African-Amerian Families*. New York: Simon and Shuster

Blackwell, James E. 1991. *The Black Community: Diversity and Unity*. New York: HarperCollins Publishers.

Blassingame, John W. 1979. *The Slave Community: Plantation Life in the Antebellum South*. New York: Oxford University Press.

Blau, Peter M. and Otis Dudley Duncan. 1967. *The American Occupational Structure*. New York: The Free Press.

Blauner, Robert. 1972. *Racial Oppression in America*. New York: Harper & Row, Publishers.

Bluestone, Barry and Bennett Harrison. 1982. *The Deindustrialization of America*. New York: Basic Books.

Bonilla-Silva, Eduardo. 1997. "Rethinking Racism: Toward a Structural Interpretation." *American Sociological Review* 62:465–480.

Bouvier, Leon F. 1992. *Peaceful Invasions: Immigration and Changing America*. New York: University Press of America.

Butler, John Sibley. 1991. *Entrepreneurship and Self-Help Among Black Americans*. Albany: State University of New York Press.

Cohen, Joel. 1995. *How Many People Can the Earth Support?* New York: W.W. North & Co.

Daniels, Roger. 1990. *Coming to America: A History of Immigration and Ethnicity in American Life*. New York: Harper Collins Publishers.

Davis, Kingsley. 1948. *Human Society*. New York: The MacMillan Company.

Dubois, W.E.B. 1899. *The Philadelphia Negro*. Philadelphia: University of Pennsylvania Press.

————1935. *Black Reconstruction in America:1860–1880*. New York: Harcourt, Brace.

Feagin, Joe R. and Hernan Vera. 1995. *White Racism: The Basics*. New York: Routledge.

Feagin, Joe R., Hernan Vera, and Nikitah Imani. 1996. *The Agony of Education*. New York: Routledge.

Feagin, Joe R. and Melvin Sikes. 1994. *Living with Racism: The Black Middle Class Experience*. Boston: Beacon Press.

Franklin, John Hope and Franklin Moss, Jr. 1994. *From Slavery to Freedom: A History of African Americans*. 7th edition, New York: McGraw-Hill, Inc.

Frazier, E. Franklin. 1957. *Black Bourgeoise*. Glencoe, IL: Free Press.

Hacker, Andrew. 1992. *Two Nations: Black and White, Separate, Hostile, Unequal*. New York: Charles Scribner's Sons.

Horton, Hayward Derrick. 1992a. "A Sociological Approach to Black Community Development: Presentation of the Black Organizational Autonomy Model." *Journal of the Community Development Society*, 23:1–19.

————.1992b. "Race and Wealth: A Demographic Analysis of Black Homeownership." *Sociological Inquiry*, 62:480–489.

————.1995. "Population Change and the Employment Status of College Educated Blacks." *Research in Race and Ethnic Relations*, 8:99–114.

Horton, Hayward Derrick and Norma J. Burgess. 1992. "Where are the Black Men: Regional Differences in the Pool of Marriageable Black Males." *National Journal of Sociology*, 6:1–19.

Katz, Michael. 1989. *The Underserving Poor: From The War on Poverty to the War on Welfare*. New York: Pantheon Books.

Lieberson, Stanley. 1980. *A Piece of the Pie: Blacks and White Immigrants Since 1880*. Berkeley: University of California Press.

Massey Douglas S. and Nancy A. Denton. 1993. *American Apartheid: Segregation and the Making of the Underclass*. Cambridge, MA: Harvard University Press.

Omi, Michael and Howard Winant. 1994. *Racial Formation in the United States*. New York: Routledge.

Ryan, William. 1971. *Blaming the Victim*. New York: Vintage Books.

Snipp, C. Matthew. 1989. *American Indians: The First of This Land*. New York: Russell Sage Foundation.

Sowell, Thomas. 1980. *Ethnic America: A History*. New York: Basic Books.

Spickard, Paul R. 1989. *Mixed Blood: Intermarriage and Ethnic Identity in Twentieth-Century America*.

Thomas, Melvin E. and Hayward Derrick Horton. 1992. "Race, Class, and Family Structure: The Case of Family Income." *Sociological Perspective*, 35:433-450.

Ture, Kwame and Charles V. Hamilton. 1992. *Black Power: The Politics of Liberation*. New York: Vintage Books.

U.S. Bureau of the Census, 1992. *1990 Census of Population and Housing: Public Use Microdata Samples*. Washington, DC: U.S. Department of Commerce.

van den Berghe, Pierre L. 1967. *Race and Racism*. New York: John Wiley & Sons, Inc.

Waters, Mary. 1990. *Ethnic Options: Choosing Identities in America*. Berkeley: University of California Press.

Weber, Max. 1947. *The Theory of Social and Economic Organization*. Translated by A.M. Henderson and Talcott Parsons. Edited with an Introduction by Talcott Parsons. New York: Oxford University Press.

Willie, Charles Vert. 1979. *Caste and Class Controversy*. New York: General Hall, Inc.

Wilson, William J. 1973. *Power, Racism and Privilege: Race Relations in Theoretical and Sociohistorical Perspectives*. New York: The Macmillan Company.

———. 1980. *The Declining Significance of Race: Blacks and Changing American Institutions*. Chicago: University of Chicago Press.

———. 1987. *The Truly Disadvantaged: The Inner City, The Underclass and Public Policy*. Chicago: The University of Chicago Press.

———. 1991. "Studying Inner City Dislocations." *American Sociological Review* 56:1–15.

———1996. *When Work Disappears: The World of the New Urban Poor*. New York: Knopf.

Yinger, John. 1995. *Closed Doors, Opportunities Lost: The Continuing Costs of Housing Discrimination*. New York: Russell Sage Foundation.

Contributors

Nancy A. Denton is Associate Professor of Sociology at University at Albany, State University of New York, and Research Affiliate in the Center for Social and Demographic Analysis.

Stewart E. Tolnay is Professor of Sociology at the University of Washington and Faculty Associate in the Center for Studies in Demography and Ecology.

৵

Charles Hirschman is Boeing International Professor of Sociology at the Uni-versity of Washington and Faculty Associate in the Center for Studies in Demo-graphy and Ecology.

Hayward Derrick Horton is Associate Professor of Sociology at University of Albany, State University of New York, and Research Associate in the Center for Social and Demographic Analysis.

V. Joseph Hotz is Professor of Economics and Department Chair at the Uni-versity of California Los Angeles.

Douglas S. Massey is Dorothy Swaine Thomas Professor of Sociology and Department Chair at the University of Pennsylvania as well as Research Assoc-iate in the Population Studies Center.

S. Philip Morgan is Professor of Sociology at Duke University.

Richard G. Rogers is Professor of Sociology at the University of Colorado at Boulder.

Eileen Shy will receive her MBA from Harvard University in 2002.

Gillian Stevens is Associate Professor of Sociology at the University of Illinois at Urbana-Champaign.

Gray Swicegood is Associate Professor of Sociology at the University of Illinois at Urbana-Champaign.

Cynthia M. Taeuber is Senior Policy Advisor at the Jacob France Center at the University of Baltimore and the U.S. Census Bureau.

Marta Tienda is Maurice P. During '22 Professor in Demographic Studies, Professor of Sociology and Public Affairs at Princeton University, and Director of the Office of Population Research.

Michael K. Tyler is an analyst at HNC Software in Irvine, CA.

Mary C. Waters is Harvard College Professor and Professor of Sociology and Department Chair at Harvard University.

Michael J. White is Professor of Sociology at Brown University and a Research Investigator at the Population Studies and Training Center.

Name Index

Subject Index

1924 National Origins Act, 77
1965 Amendments to the Immigration and Nationality Act, 77, 82; effects of, 83; overestimation of effect of, 82; removal of ban on Asian entry, 83; undocumented immigration and, 84
1968 Fair Housing Act, and "Dirksen compromise", 171; compared to 1988 amendments to, 171
1975 Home Mortgage Disclosure Act, 171
1986 Immigration Reform and Control Act, 10
1988 Amendments to Fair Housing Act, 171, 176-178; compared to 1968 Fair Housing Act, 171
1989 Housing Discrimination Study, 169
1990 Civil Rights Act, 178
1990 Immigration Law, 10

A
Abortion ratio, 116
Abortion, Black vs. White differential in, 116
Accidents, 139, 144
Activities of Daily Living (ADL), 250, 257n4
Administrative classification, of race and ethnicity, 26
Administrative Law Judge (ALJ), 172, 176
Adolescent fertility, of Blacks, 115
Affirmative action, attacks on, 264
AFQT, 193; effect of scores on labor force entry, 212-213; race/ethnic differences in, 204-205; need for research on, 215
Africa: immigrants from, 10; immigration from, 93

African American or Black, terminology, 266
Age structure: effect of fertility on, 103; effect on population diversity, 9
Age-specific fertility rates, 102
Age-specific mortality, 139-140; by ethnicity, 139-140; by race, 139-140
Alaska Native: life expectancy of 138; multiple race choices of, 43, 64; single race, 30
Alcohol use: by Cubans, 142; by ethnicity, 142; by Hispanics, 142; by Mexicans, 142; by Puerto Ricans, 142; by race, 142
ALJ. *See* Administrative Law Judge
Allocation, of non-response in census, 61-62
"American Dream," 16
American Indians: Age-specific mortality of, 139-140; births to, 31, 109-110; changing identification of, 32; change in group size in multiracial simulation, 41; decimation of, 101; differential fertility of, 103-104; government programs and, 64; growth rate of, 29-30, 56, 103-104; identification of, 62, 232; intermarriage of, 58, 232, 237; lack of desire to maximize population size, 64; life expectancy of, 138; mortality by tribe, 131; multiple race choices of, 43, 64; postneonatal mortality, 136; relative size of in population projections, 53; SES and racial/ethnic identity, 32; segregation of, 161; single race identification, 30; Spanish culture and, 133; Spanish surnames among, 132; Total Fertility Rate, 107; tribes 29, 144
Americas, immigrants from, 79
Amnesty Program, 84

287